LESSONS
of the
Heart

Four Novellas in Which

Modern Teachers Learn about Love

Kristin Billerbeck
Linda Goodnight
Yvonne Lehman
Pamela Kaye Tracy

BARBOUR
PUBLISHING, INC.
Uhrichsville, Ohio

W9-BOB-991

Love Lessons ©2000 by Kristin Billerbeck
Beauty for Ashes ©2000 by Linda Goodnight
Scrambled Eggs ©2000 by Yvonne Lehman
Test of Time ©2000 by Pamela Kaye Tracy

Illustrations by Gary Maria.

ISBN 1-57748-792-3

Scripture taken from the Holy Bible: New International Version®. NIV®. Copyright © 1973, 1978, 1984 by International Bible Society. Used by permission of Zondervan Publishing House.

Published by Barbour Publishing, Inc., P.O. Box 719, Uhrichsville, Ohio 44683 http://www.barbourbooks.com

Member of the
Evangelical Christian
Publishers Association

Printed in the United States of America.

LESSONS
of the
Heart

Love Lessons

by Kristin Billerbeck

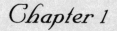

Chapter 1

"*Buenos dias, Senorita Knight,*" the class called in unison.

"*Buenos dias, clase.* How nice to see you all sound so ready for your first test in Spanish Two."

"Awww," the class groaned.

"Now you've had plenty of time to prepare for this test, and I have full confidence in you. If you'll take out your test booklets, we'll get started immediately. For those of you who forgot to purchase a test booklet in the office, you may pick one up on my desk. Please leave a dime and deduct question number one from your test. That was your first test question."

"That is *so* wrong!" a student whined.

Beth Knight just rolled her eyes and checked off student names as they filed up to her desk. Kids today never took responsibility for themselves. She tried to force it upon them with little chores like getting their own test sheets, but it rarely worked. All she succeeded in doing was gaining a reputation for being the strictest teacher in Spanish. Still, she took pride in the fact that an "A" in her class was earned, not given.

Just as she explained the exam, a loud roar emanated from the adjoining classroom, followed by a big thump against the wall. Beth jumped, then seethed. *That man has no respect for the teaching process. He thinks it's all a big game. Well, it's time he learned a little respect.*

"Excuse me, class. Please get started on your tests." Beth crossed her arms and strode to the next room with vengeance. *Why on earth I have to share a wall with this ridiculous JNROTC instructor, I'll never know.* His macho ways and lack of leadership in the classroom only proved he was an unfit teacher. The shortage of classrooms in California was becoming epidemic, yet they made space for folly like this. She had grown up in the military; she knew Ken Barrett's actions were nothing like military decorum.

Beth slammed opened his door. A running, jumping classroom of young students stopped in their tracks. Like the proverbial deer in the headlights, they all gazed in her direction. From out of nowhere, marched Lieutenant Commander Ken Barrett, and they waited patiently for his command. Ken approached with his trademark charismatic grin, hoping to charm her, but she'd have no part in it. Not this time.

Ken Barrett knew he was handsome, which only exasperated Beth. In his dress whites, he was devastatingly gorgeous, but it hardly excused his behavior. Beth dismissed her entire army-brat childhood and the cold memories it brought with it. With one tiny exception: She loved the sight of men in uniform. It was a terrible chink in her armor, but was there a woman who could resist such a sight? A man cleaned and pressed for duty was an inspiring sight. She sighed, remembering her mission.

"Miss Knight," Ken smiled. His voice was low with a mock innocence. "Is there something I can help you with?"

Beth woke from her state, her anger flooding back. "May I see you outside, Lt. Commander?"

"Of course. Class, continue as before," Ken said authoritatively, as though he had any influence with those hoodlums at all. "It's nice to see you, Beth. You look beautiful in that green. It matches your eyes perfectly."

The grin again. Beth sighed aloud again, this time for his benefit. "I've never met a military man with less propriety or structure, Ken. How can you just let those students run wild? I have testing going on today, and my students can't hear themselves think, much less think in Spanish!"

"I'm sorry," he drawled, taking her hand with southern charm. "I allowed myself to get a little carried away with their leadership lesson today. They're learning to be responsible for others, to work together as a team to gain respect of their peers. It's been quite effective, and I think quite a few of them would make valuable officers someday."

Beth yanked her hand away. "Well, could you teach *leadership* in a quieter tone?" Her heels clicked along the laminate flooring as she made her getaway, but he followed closely behind. She could feel his presence, and she turned on her heel. "Is there something else?"

"Beth, my classes are marching in the California Admission Day parade in Sacramento. You should come see us. If you saw the results, maybe the noise wouldn't bother you as much. I'd be happy to drive you up, if you're interested."

She softened at the question. Ken really did make an effort with her, but she'd seen an enlisted man's charms far too often to be swayed by him. "Ken, I appreciate what you're doing with your students, but you have to admit, it's not standard protocol. I'm just trying to teach my Spanish class. I would like to just peacefully coexist. Thanks for the offer, but I don't think so."

"We're neighbors, Beth. Can't we at least act like it?"

"I certainly hope so, Lt. Commander." Beth walked into her room and closed the door behind her. Her class looked up at her, and she focused on her desktop, embarrassed by their stares. *Can they see me blush?* She wished her stomach didn't flutter every time Ken Barrett focused those deep blue eyes upon her, but it did—and she despised it. She knew better than to be attracted to military men. Hadn't she lived that mobile life enough?

Why couldn't she be attracted to men in business suits or the engineers that dominated Silicon Valley? Men that had a reason to stay put. Why did she keep that penchant for a man in uniform? With all the base closings around her, military men were all but a dinosaur in her area, yet God managed to put one right next door to her. One temptation she faced every day. It wasn't fair.

Then, it hit her. If she wasn't next door to Ken Barrett, his daily drills couldn't exasperate her. Nor could his constant use of "Atten-tion!" *And I wouldn't have to feel that feeling in my stomach on dress whites day,* she admitted to herself. She'd speak to the principal that afternoon. There had to be a quieter place on campus. Perhaps she could trade with the art teacher or something equally benign when it came to noise.

With her Spanish tests collected, Beth strode determinedly into the principal's office, anxious to remedy her situation. The secretary, Kay, peered over bifocals, her lips pursed at the sight of Beth. "Yes, Beth, what is it you need this time?"

Beth ignored the apparent reprimand. "Is John in?"

"Is he expecting you?" Kay inquired impatiently.

"No, but it's important I see him."

"It's always important." Kay clicked her tongue.

Just then, John, the school principal, peered out his door. "Beth? Did you need something?" A generous smile crossed his lined face.

"Would you mind sparing me just a few minutes? It's important," Beth explained.

"Come on in." He opened his door wider and headed behind his desk.

Beth felt Kay's scowl and, despite herself, smiled. Rules were necessary, and if Beth needed to insure they were upheld, she'd do so—even at the risk of being unpopular.

"John, I have a situation that really needs attending," Beth said.

"If this is about the noise from Lt. Commander's room, you've come to the wrong place."

"But—"

"Beth, you have such a nice reputation at church. You're kindhearted; you teach Sunday school; you volunteer for the choir—why must you be so difficult here at work?" John asked gently.

Beth's mouth dangled. "John, I hardly think I'm being difficult. I teach, and for that I must have quiet. I don't think it's too much to expect for students to be in a learning environment here in school. Being next to the Junior Naval Reserve Officer Training Corps is cruel and unusual punishment. Especially when taught by the eccentric Ken Barrett. It would be difficult for any teacher, not just me."

"But it is *just* you, Beth. Look, I'm going to be straight with you because I think you need to hear it. This is Ken's second year here at Valley High School. I admit when he first came here I was more than a little concerned by his outlandish ways, but in one year he managed to send 90 percent of his seniors to college. Ninety percent, Beth! I can't argue with statistics like that. Can you?"

Undaunted, she continued, "Well, my ways are more traditional. I like a structured environment for my students. I feel it's the most secure learning atmosphere." Beth squared her shoulders, feeling extraordinarily confident. "I appreciate that he's motivating students, but at what cost to my class?"

"Beth, Ken's classroom is the most structured environment on this campus. He has taken troubled students, who took his class simply to get out of geography, and turned them into college candidates by raising their self-esteem and their grades. His methods are a little boisterous, I admit that."

"So he's allowed to disrupt my class because he's effective—is that what you're saying?"

"I'm saying, he has a classroom on the other side of him, too. And across the hall, and below him. Yet, you are the only one I'm hearing from, Beth." The principal tapped his glasses on his desk. "Which brings to mind a thought. If you understood Ken, perhaps you might understand his teaching style. Then, you'd be less upset with him for disrupting your class. You might even get used to it. Tomorrow, I will be teaching your Spanish Two classes. You, Beth, will be attending the Junior Naval ROTC classes for the entire day."

"Wh–what? You can't be serious!"

"Beth, I'm absolutely serious. You are getting a reputation for being difficult. Your students are in here complaining you don't cut them an ounce of slack, and you're giving B-plus grades to students who have never had less than an A. I've had valedictorian candidates in here pleading to get out of your class before their grade point average drops. I think Ken Barrett's class and a healthy dose of reality are just what you need."

"I give students what they deserve, John. I don't give courtesy grades."

"Neither does Ken Barrett and, tomorrow, you're going to see how he does it with some of the worst students on this campus. I'll let him know you'll be observing the class tomorrow."

"But—"

"Does the word tenure mean anything to you, Beth?"

"Are you threatening me, John?" Beth's voice came out as a mere whisper. John Palmer was a gentleman, a respected elder in her church. How on earth could he reprimand her so harshly for wanting what was best for her students? It just didn't fit his personality at all.

"I'm not threatening you. I'm giving you an assignment for your own good. If Ken Barrett wanted to conduct a naval weapons show on campus, I daresay I'd find a place for him to do it. He's a responsible, wonderful teacher who is very effective."

"It's because I'm a woman, isn't it?"

"Beth, don't start that feminist stuff with me. You know me better than that." Suddenly, John stood behind his desk, abruptly halting their conversation. "Ken, we were just discussing your classroom."

Beth turned and, to her horror, Ken filled the doorway. His six-foot-plus frame caused her heart to pound like a high school student's stereo. She tried to tell herself it was out of guilt for tattling, but she knew why her heart beat rapidly around Ken Barrett. It was the real reason she was in John Palmer's office.

Ken smiled at both of them. "Oh, Beth, I'm glad I found you. I came to apologize for my class today; your students told me you headed this way. I hope your test went well."

Beth opened her mouth to speak, but John cut her off. "Beth is fascinated by the way you operate your class, Ken. I'm going to sit in her classes tomorrow so she can witness firsthand the ROTC classes in action."

Ken's smile broadened, making his perfect white teeth appear. "How nice. A room with a view."

Beth looked to John, her eyes pleading with him, but he simply avoided eye contact. "John?" she asked weakly.

"Did you have lunch yet, Beth? I'd love to discuss your teaching," Ken said. "I understand you're classically trained, unlike me. It's always fascinated me how people decide they want to do this for their life's work. I'm just glad I finally fell into it for a second career, but I'd love to hear your experiences."

Beth felt tears forming. She frantically tried to blink them away. *This man, this irritatingly annoying man has gone too far.* Not only did he make her look ridiculous in front of their boss, but now he placated her by mocking sincerity.

Outside John's office, Ken looked down at her. "So what do you say about lunch?" He raked his fingers through jet-black hair, obviously understanding his masculinity.

Knowing he made knees weak with his actions, Beth forced her tears back again. "Ken, please just leave me alone," she whimpered. "I'm glad you've managed to win the whole school over with your unusual style, but some of us worked hard for the privilege of being a teacher. We scrimp and we save on our meager salaries, so we can see these students succeed because we can't get it out of our system. Unlike you, we don't have naval pensions to help make up the difference! We do it for the sheer love of the students."

She started to walk away when he grasped her arm. His blue eyes, the color of the deep, dark sea, gazed into hers. "Do you think I don't do it for the same reason? I would never mock what you do. I'm in awe of it, and I mean that sincerely." He looked down at his shoes. His brows lowered in what appeared to be confusion. "I'm sorry if I offended you with the lunch offer or anything I said. I'm looking forward to tomorrow." He walked away, leaving her like an empty shell. She wouldn't have thought it possible, but she had really stung him.

"I can't imagine why you're still single," Kay mumbled under her breath as she watched the whole scene.

Beth turned and ran for the comfort of her classroom. She cried her entire lunch hour away.

Chapter 2

I can't believe I have to do this!" Beth shouted to her roommate. "Ken Barrett thinks I'm a complete shrew, and John Palmer did nothing to change his opinion. John, who's always been so good to me. Ken commits all these teaching travesties, and I get the punishment. It's a man's world."

Heather simply sighed. "Wasn't it you who said you didn't care what Ken thought of you?"

"I am a Christian, Heather. I should care to a point."

"Well, he's a Christian too. I don't know what you're complaining about. You can either spend today with 120 ungrateful, disrespectful teenagers or staring at a hand-some man in uniform while he does all the work. What a harsh penance! We should all be so lucky."

"Heather, you're laughing! You think this is funny, don't you? I would just as soon stare at my feet as stare at a navy man in uniform! I know better. I've seen it happen to so many women. The uniform gets to you, and you start to forget. . .forget that falling in love with a man in uniform means falling in love with every empty,

19

white-walled military installation house in the world. Just when you get that empty box-house the way you want it: transfer! It's time to move. And you pray this won't be the time they break a significant piece of furniture. Or that you sell everything you don't need at the base sale before you go."

Heather laughed. "Honestly, aren't we dramatic today? You'd think you grew up abused, instead of the privileged princess you were on base! You might as well realize we, as women, cannot fight the lure of the uniform. It's genetic. Like a moth to the flame, we go unwillingly. . .focusing only on the beautiful, bright light, except in this case, it's the impressive dress uniform—until, BAM! We crash and burn." She shrugged. "Face it; it's like firemen. No one can explain it rationally, but all women find firemen attractive. CEO or bathroom attendant, as a woman, you're still attracted to a fireman." Heather shrugged. "Trust me, the only way to fight a charming man in uniform is to run the other way. And you don't appear to be running."

"I don't have a choice; our boss set this up! I either go, or I can kiss tenure and my coveted stability good-bye. Besides, Ken won't be in uniform today. So I'm immune. Even if I were attracted to him, which I'm not—"

"Oh, right, because he's not attractive in the classical sense." Heather cleared her throat. "Spare me. I don't care what you *think* of the guy—you cannot possibly deny his good looks. He is stunningly gorgeous, the kind who makes your tongue go in knots so he thinks you're stupid. Say what you want about his teaching credentials, but he makes the eyes dance."

"Now, who's being dramatic? I told you what he's like. He thinks teaching is a joke. Now I ask you, Heather. As a twenty-eight-year-old teacher who can't afford your own apartment, how can you laugh at this situation? If teachers lose respect, we lose everything."

"I just don't think Ken Barrett is going to single-handedly bring down the teaching profession in Silicon Valley. Face it, Beth. He's charming, he's gorgeous, and he looks good in that uniform. The single female teachers are practically tripping over themselves to get near him, and you think he's society's blight. If it were me, I'd risk ruining the teaching profession just to see what he's like on a date!" Heather winked.

"Oh, you. You're incorrigible. I'm going to be late if I wait for you. I'll see you at lunch!"

"Sure thing," Heather called just before Beth shut the door.

Beth's drive to work was quick and uneventful. Once at the school, however, her heart began to thump with a steady pounding she could hear in her head. The idea of walking into Ken's classroom sent shivers up her spine. If her principal wanted Beth to have a taste of humility, he got his wish. Without even stepping into the classroom, she felt humbled.

Ken's expression changed to an immediate smile at the sight of her. He stopped reading some type of manual and came toward her. Instead of his uniform, he was still dashing in a creased pair of khakis and a light blue oxford-cloth shirt. She suddenly wished he was in uniform. He didn't look any less attractive on casual day, and the uniform would serve as a constant reminder of base life.

"Beth, I'm glad you made it. I stopped at Starbuck's on the way to school. Do you drink coffee? I picked you up a latte."

A chill raced through her when she felt his hand on the small of her back, chivalrously guiding her into the classroom. Fear gripped her as though the threshold of the classroom would somehow erase her memories. Fear that she might forget how many times her life has been packed and moved elsewhere. Of course she was being ridiculous; Ken hadn't shown anything but friendly interest in her, but still, she'd watched how many women fell victim just that easily. Feeling his touch, she knew she wasn't immune.

"Actually, I don't drink coffee. I feel badly. For the price of that cup of coffee, you could probably have bought your lunch." Beth smiled shyly.

"Don't feel badly. I'll make the kids do sit-ups for it. All the kids are drinking coffee these days. I got a decaf, so they won't be too hyper." He grinned again. "I'm not stupid." His blue eyes disappeared into tiny slivers, and she felt her knees buckle just for a second.

"I think I should probably check on my classes first. Just to make sure John has everything under control." She pointed behind her, desperate for the safety and sanctity of her classroom.

"I just came from your class. John has everything under control. Come and enjoy your day. How often does a hardworking teacher get to enjoy the view from the other side of life? Come on; I promise I won't call on you or make you spell anything. Partly because I can't spell myself," he mused.

Beth swallowed hard. Ken wouldn't get to her with his southern charms or his uncharacteristic teaching. "Listen, I hope there's no hard feelings about yesterday in John's office."

He held up a palm. "I completely understand. A simple miscommunication; let's just put it in the past. No sense dwelling on the negative." Opening the door, he surveyed his class and allowed them to file in.

"Certainly," she agreed faintly. She was more than willing to put the humiliation behind her.

"Attention!" he yelled, nearly scaring her to death.

The class stopped all activity. Their eyes and ears focused on their leader. Beth took a seat in the back and admitted, *Ken has a commanding presence. It must be easier to gain a class's respect when you stand six foot two, instead of a mere five foot six inches.* It probably didn't hurt that he could bellow like that, scaring everyone out of their wits.

"Today, we have a special guest visiting us—Miss Knight. For those of you who don't recognize her, Miss Knight teaches Spanish Two here at Valley in the room next door. I understand Miss Knight has an extensive military background, and I expect her to be treated as a fellow cadet. Is that clear?"

"Yes, sir!" the call came back.

"Very well, our assignment for last night was—"

"World events, sir!" Again, Beth jumped at the loud answer in unison. There was the crackling of newsprint and soon, everyone in the class was sitting behind an open newspaper.

Scanning the room, Beth couldn't help but notice several of his students who had been her very worst. They were the type she thought certain to become dropouts, but here they were, relishing this man barking command at them. They actually listened to him. It was incredible. If Beth hadn't known Ken Barrett was a Christian, she might have wondered if he possessed some kind of supernatural powers. However, the first time she'd complained to John, he'd explained Ken's Christian beliefs were as strong as his own.

After the class discussed world politics and wars, the students marched out at the bell all in line. Ken strode toward her and sat on the edge of the table. "Well, what did you think? Are you ready to turn in your Spanish cap for JNROTC?"

Beth suppressed a laugh. She certainly was impressed with the way Ken managed his classroom, but she also knew it wasn't typical, or she wouldn't hear what sounded like a war three days a week in his classroom.

"I don't think I'll give up Spanish just yet. Why?"

"Isn't that why you're here? John's looking for my replacement, right?"

"Your replacement? What are you talking about?"

"I explained to John I'd be leaving at the end of this school year. I just assumed you were considering the position. What's your military background?"

"My military background?" Beth giggled. "I'm an army brat. That's the extent of my military background."

"So what are you doing here then?" Ken crossed his brawny arms in front of him. Beth wasn't easily intimidated, but something about Ken's stance demanded a sound answer. Something she didn't have. How on earth did she explain John Palmer simply thought she needed to be humbled? Or that she'd actually been in the office to tattle on Ken and been quickly put in her place?

"I–I, um, I needed to know what goes on in here. Why it's so loud all the time." His harsh gaze told her he wasn't satisfied. "I think I'll just get back to my classroom." Beth stood, and he surprisingly took her trembling hand into his own. Did he have to touch her that way? This was not the South, and she was not comfortable with his chivalrous ways.

The door opened with students and he shouted at them. "Line up, outside!" The door immediately closed and once again, Ken and Beth were alone.

"How can you have so much authority in this room and have it sound like wild banshees from the next room? Something just isn't right here. What are you doing differently today?"

He hadn't relinquished her hand, and she felt his touch to her toes. So many times in the last year she'd avoided him. Now she knew why. With his imposing proximity, she tried to push aside his gentleness, his intensity. She tried to avoid what his large, warm hand made her feel. Then, he spoke intimately. "You were hearing war games, Beth. Sometimes, I allow the kids to take turns being the general. They are in charge of the choreography of a battle. More importantly, they are in charge of getting their troops out alive. It's my own pro-life battle. I show these kids what life is like without a part of the group. I want them to understand that the tapestry of God's design is important. Leadership has its privileges, but more importantly, it has its responsibilities."

Speechless, she simply blinked. She opened her mouth, hoping the words caught in her throat would magically appear, but they didn't.

"Are you an only child, Beth?"

"Yes," she answered. "How did you know that?" She was still a bit daunted by his comprehension of things.

"Only children seem to struggle with volume level. I've noticed that in my short time teaching. It really bothers you when it's loud, doesn't it?"

"Yes, as a matter of fact, it really does bother me, Lt. Commander. I work hard to maintain order in my classroom. It's not as easy for me as barking a bunch of commands. I can't make my students shave their heads or dress properly like you can. My voice doesn't resonate down the hallway. I'm just trying to teach them Spanish in the best possible way I know how."

"Now that I know how much it bothers you, I'll try to keep it down. I wouldn't want to get on your bad side." He grinned.

"I beg your pardon. What do you mean by that?"

"I may be the new kid on the block, Miss Knight, but your reputation is no secret. I'll be sure and keep it down before I really do something to upset you. I wouldn't want you to have to go to John again." He laughed, letting go of her hand.

The allegation sent her temper flaring. "Just be certain to let me know about your firm departure date, Lt. Commander. I'll want to throw you a going-away party. I have the perfect red dress for the occasion."

He threw his head back in laughter. "It sounds delightful, Miss Knight. I'll wait with breathless anticipation." Crossing his arms, he watched her leave.

Beth clambered to get away from Ken Barrett. Once in the hallway, she peered at the door to his classroom. His students had lined up single file along the wall and waited for his word to move. Beth just shook her head at the sight. How could a man so undisciplined make it look like he had everything within his control?

He thought her spoiled? Men didn't understand her. Her father never had. Every time her family had packed up and moved, she was just supposed to go on as before. Even though her friends were somewhere else, her teachers abandoned, her tennis teams dismantled. The right man would understand her need for stability. Beth kept her life organized and everything just so because it was the only thing she could control. She wasn't ready to relinquish it to a lighthearted sailor. . .no matter how he made her heart sing.

Chapter 3

W hat are you doing back here, Beth? It's only second period." John passed a worksheet to her students. The familiarity of her classroom brought peace. A small groan emanated from the class, indicating she wasn't exactly a welcome sight.

"It's okay, John. I've seen all I need to see of Ken Barrett's style. He's not being his unusually loud self anyway. I'll take over from here. I'm sure you have other duties to attend to. May we just speak outside a moment?"

"Sure. I'll be right back, kids. Get working on this verb sheet, and we'll go over it when I get back," John announced.

Beth crossed her arms, not enjoying the hint of mirth she saw in her boss's eyes. "John, if you knew Ken was leaving at the end of the year, why didn't you just tell me it would all be over in June?" Beth flipped her blond hair with indignation. "I wouldn't have bothered you with this had I known there was an end in sight." Beth fidgeted, anxious to get back to teaching.

John smiled, shaking his head back and forth. "If I had told you that, you'd just assume your troubles were over. I don't think Ken Barrett is your issue, Beth. And according to my watch," he checked his wrist, "it's only second period. That gives you another three classes to go before Ken's teaching day is over. I want you to take it easy." He patted her back. "Enjoy your day off and let me know what you've learned at the end of it."

"Oh, no, John. I'm not going back. You can't make me. I was hired to teach, not observe. You just want me to look ridiculous," Beth accused. She knew it was unjust, but it seemed like everyone was picking on her. Just like when she was the new kid, she was being subjected to the taunts of others. She felt it to her soul.

John spoke gently. "Beth, Helena and I have known you for quite some time now. Nearly six years, I believe. In all that time, I've never seen you contented in anything. Not your teaching, not your ministry, and especially not your social life. There's always something that takes the joy from you. I want you to watch how Ken handles strife. I think it will be good for you. And so does Helena. I think you would enjoy teaching a great deal more if you only focused a little less on the bad and more on the good. You are a delightful woman, but life isn't perfect, Beth, and it never will be, not in this lifetime anyway."

"You talked to your wife about this?" Beth asked, incredulous.

"We're praying for you, Beth," John answered gently.

"You're praying for me? You think I need to be

prayed for about this?" Beth was mortified. Never before had she suffered such humiliation at the hands of an elder in the church, and especially from her boss. She took pride in being the best possible teacher; yet this principal, a man she respected, was asking her to watch an amateur and learn.

"Just get back to class, Beth. I have students to teach, and you still have a few hours with Ken. I'm only asking you to put up with it for one day. Certainly that won't do any major harm."

"But—"

John closed the door on her. Breathing deeply, she started toward Ken's room. The class was void of Ken and his students, except for one lone teen who sat with an open newspaper.

"Hey," he nodded coolly, "I was waiting for you. Lt. Commander Barrett said to tell you they'd be outside for drills. You can meet them at the field."

"Hi," Beth said. "Okay, are you coming with me?"

The student, a tall boy with clean-shaven head responded in single syllables, (even though his answers seemed to require more effort than necessary). "Yeah." He made no movement to get up.

"Well, let's go."

Before he answered, the student suddenly lurched to the ground, writhing on the floor as if in terrible pain. Beth was dumbfounded, unsure of the proper steps to take. Before she had time to think, Ken arrived, shouting at her. "Get the tables out of the way! Move those chairs!"

Beth acted without further questions. She recklessly tossed chairs aside and pushed the laminate tables away from the eerie sight of the boy on the hard flooring. Ken rushed to his side. Beth swallowed hard, wanting to take further action to help him, but Ken pushed her away. He pulled a tiny cell phone from his shirt pocket and dialed 9-1-1, requesting immediate help at the school.

Soon the boy's restless body began to slow. Still frightened to death, Beth watched helplessly as Ken made sure the boy's air passages were clear and stood over the student, speaking softly to him while they awaited the ambulance. Beth could only watch in awe. The arrogant, self-assured naval lieutenant commander had disappeared. Mysteriously, in his place was a kind, considerate, loving teacher who knew how to react in an emergency. Beth couldn't help but be spellbound by this new side of him.

"It's all over, Cole. It's all over," Ken said soothingly. "That wasn't too long. You'll be fine now. Did you time that for the kids being outside?" Ken joked. Cole simply smiled listlessly.

Firemen were the first to arrive on the scene. They checked the boy's pulse and confirmed that he was indeed fine. The emergency crew thanked Beth and Ken for quick action and went about further testing. They explained since the seizure was longer than normal, they'd take Cole in for observation.

Ken took Beth aside and explained, "Cole has epilepsy. It's been some time since he's had a seizure in my class—not since last year, in fact, but I got quite used to it. His doctor prefers he wear a helmet, but he refuses because of the coolness factor. I suppose I can't blame him. You know how kids can be."

Beth's heart softened immediately, but she still trembled with fear of what might have happened had Ken not appeared. "Praise God you came in when you did. I wouldn't have known what to do. I probably would have tried to give him mouth-to-mouth or stop his shaking."

"God's timing is perfect. Cole will be fine. Are you okay? It's traumatic to watch a seizure, especially when you don't know what it is."

Beth nodded. "I'm fine. I'm just so glad you were here," she said honestly.

"I'm glad you're here, too, Beth. You and I keep getting off on the wrong foot. I really hope we can change that."

His deep blue eyes were sincere, and Beth no longer questioned Ken's motives. Perhaps his room was noisy and seemed like a zoo, but she couldn't argue with the results. His kids listened to his authority. They all seemed interested, and participated in class and showed up—which was more than she could say for many of her students.

When she didn't respond, he continued. "I forgot my students! They've been running around the track forever. They're getting a taste of boot camp today."

"Of course. You go ahead. I'll wait here until the authorities have left."

Ken bent down over Cole who was stretched on a gurney. "You go easy on the nurses, you hear? You give 'em a hard time and I'll make you drop and give me ten."

"You got it, Lt. Commander." Cole held up his thumb.

Beth stood by helplessly as the EMS workers finished their work. Never had she felt so useless as this day. She wasn't teaching, she wasn't able to help a student in need, and her own class *enjoyed* her absence. *What a day.*

❧

Ken jogged to the school's track. His students, breathing hard, rejoiced at the sight of him. To their credit, they were still running, albeit a bit slower. He gave them the signal to stop. Nearly all of them bent at the waist, hands at their knees to catch their breath. He stifled a laugh. *Just wait for those of you going into the service. This day will feel like a cakewalk.*

"Great run, crew! Rest for ten and we'll get started on world events. Class is outside today!"

A whoop went up among the students. He knew just how they felt. Late September in California was more pleasant than most summers elsewhere. Although the temperatures were in the high seventies, a cool breeze blew off the bay and made the weather absolutely perfect. It reminded him of the moist sea spray filling his senses on deck of an aircraft carrier. . .only without the deafening roar of jets landing and taking off. Today was perfect. It was too beautiful to be locked up inside.

Beth Knight appeared like a vision, standing on the steps by the doorway. Her blond hair blew easily in the gentle wind, like something out of a romantic movie. In

33

her perfectly tailored pantsuit, she looked like a catalog model, but without the ready smile or calculated wave. He waited to see if she'd join them, but she didn't. She just tarried, a picture-perfect illusion.

What was it about her that is so fascinating? Beauty had little to do with it, although that was undisputed. As clear as emeralds, her eyes sparkled with an unmentioned delight. Her high cheekbones and her full, red lips somehow hid a smile that he knew she needed to let shine. There was a childlike innocence about her —a sweet spot that lay protected behind her severe, serious teaching style. He wished she'd join them. Every time he saw her, he wanted to start fresh and be a gentlemen instead of the thorn in her side.

Maybe he'd just been in the navy too long, but he'd watched so many gruff exteriors fall by the wayside in times of turmoil. He longed for that familiar distinctness in people. He longed to know what made Beth want to hide in her carefully orchestrated surroundings. He knew his offbeat way offended her. Against his better judgment, he just needed to know why. Perhaps he could change it.

While his students rested, he meandered back to the stairway towards her. Beth started to turn, but with nowhere to go, stopped, looking firmly at him. "Don't your students need you?"

"They're learning leadership, remember? I find the more leeway you give students, the more responsibly they often act. There are exceptions to the rule, of course, but they usually don't make it through my course."

"Ken, is there something I can do to help you? I feel ridiculous standing around watching you work. I'm the proverbial third wheel."

"Can't you just enjoy being outside? Look at this weather. Those small clouds up in the sky—" he pointed to the horizon— "they just make the blue that much more blue. Have a seat with the kids and just enjoy the creation of today." Ken shrugged. "We all yearn for a day like that. I wish these high schoolers could appreciate the freedom they have now, before the world requires so much of them."

To his chagrin, her cold response shot him down. "I grew up an army brat. I was taught that you worked for your dinner. It's just something that doesn't leave you, this work ethic. Relaxing just induces guilt." She suppressed a smile behind her long, slender hand.

"Where did you grow up?" Ken inquired, looking into the prettiest green he'd ever seen: Beth's eyes.

"I think an easier question would be where didn't I grow up. I've been to Virginia, North Carolina, California, Germany, Hawaii, and a few places here and there in between."

"Sounds wonderful!" Some days he really missed that life. Not the one being stuck on an aircraft carrier, but the one where a new port came into view. A new adventure waiting to be had.

"Wonderful! That's what my father always said, but it's not all that wonderful leaving your friends and your school every couple of years. Worse yet, to be the new kid at the school. You military men never do think of that when you start families."

"A typical complaint." He nodded. "But you forget I haven't started a family, so you can hardly blame me." He looked into her tormented eyes. Clearly, she did blame him and probably every other military person.

"It's over now. I'm old enough to make my own decisions and live where I want to live. They'll have to drag me kicking and screaming before I'd move again." Beth stated emphatically.

"What if God calls you out of here?" It was a realistic question. He knew she sang in a local church choir and taught Sunday school, so she obviously had some concern for the ways of God. Was she willing to change her plans for Him? He waited anxiously for her answer.

"God won't call me out."

"How do you know?"

"Because He knows I need to stay," she said simply. "God wants what's best for His children."

"I hope you're right, Beth." And he did, but her views on life and God seemed strangely innocent. God didn't always want what His children wanted. That had been made more than clear to him on several occasions. "I'd better get back to my students and get them started on their newspapers. Care to join us?"

"I'll watch from here, thanks."

Ken hiked to his students, but couldn't help looking back. He couldn't shake the feeling there was more she wanted to tell him. For two people who had such a difficult time communicating with one another, they certainly didn't lack a silent interaction. Neither one of them really felt the conversation was over. It was in her eyes and probably his, as well.

"I'll find out what you're trying to say, Beth. If it's the last thing I do here in California, I'll find out," he mumbled to himself. "You're far too young to have your whole life planned out. I think life is bound to give you a few surprises. I hope I'm one of them."

Chapter 4

"Well, how was your day with Captain Dreamboat?" Heather grinned as she tossed a salad. "Did you want dinner? It's just salad tonight. We're getting towards the end of the month, you know. School loans and rent due soon, but luckily so is our paycheck." Heather and Beth's shared apartment was modest by any standards. The kitchen was so cramped it didn't allow for two people at once. Consequently, Beth and Heather usually took turns cooking.

"I'd love a salad; thanks. Actually, today wasn't as bad as I thought it would be. Ken assisted a student with a seizure, his kids listened to his every word, and I found out for being handsome, he can still read a newspaper. For all his faults, the students love him. I have to admit he was better than I gave him credit for." Beth laughed.

"You're terrible."

"Besides, the best news of my day is he's leaving in June." A triumphant grin developed, but in her heart guilt reigned. How would she really feel when Ken left?

"Oh, so that's the reason for your giddiness. You think you won."

Beth shrugged. "I guess I did win."

"I don't see how we win losing a good teacher. Ken's departure will break the heart of many a teacher at Valley High."

"Well, it won't break mine," Beth claimed. "Maybe Ken isn't the arrogant, self-absorbed sailor I thought he was, but I'm still happy I won't have to teach next to him."

"You know, this brings up an important point. Where are we as teachers supposed to meet men?" Heather complained. "I mean, we don't do the club scene, we're too shy to go to the singles' group at church, and with our meager salaries, we can hardly afford to do much else, except pay back our school loans. Where does that leave us?"

"Single," Beth quipped.

"Worse. Single and broke."

"I know. I was a little miffed when I saw Ken's cell phone. Now there's a luxury we could never afford. We're lucky we have a phone in the apartment."

"Maybe if we moved to a small town, we could afford a condominium or something," Heather suggested. "I understand there are lots of teaching opportunities up by the state capital. Our loans will be paid off soon."

"Yes, but then we'd have to move. They'll have to pry me out of this apartment before I'll move again."

The phone rang, startling them both. Heather answered and passed the phone to Beth with a big smile. "It's Captain Dreamboat."

"Hello?" Beth fully expected her mother or someone of the like, thinking Heather was pulling a fast one, but the rich, deep baritone was indeed Ken Barrett's.

"Hi Beth, it's Ken. Listen, I was heading over to your church for the concert tonight and wanted to know if you and Heather wanted a ride."

"A ride where?" Beth asked innocently.

"To the concert."

"Can you hang on a second?" Beth covered the phone with her hand, whispering at Heather. "Do you know anything about a concert at church tonight?"

"Yeah, the singles' group is doing a praise and worship concert with a popular Christian band. They're also having an espresso bar out front. Don't you read the bulletin?"

Beth just shrugged. "You want to go, Heather? It's Ken. He's going."

Heather grabbed the phone. "Hi, Ken. We'd love to go. What time should we be ready? Half an hour?" She shot Beth a grin. "Perfect." Heather gave their address and soon they had plans for the evening. She hung up the phone casually. "Well, perhaps you weren't the only one impressed today, Beth."

"I never said I was impressed and don't start, Miss Matchmaker. For one thing, maybe he was calling me to get to you, Heather. Did you ever think of that?"

Heather sighed aloud. "Many times, but he asked twice if you were going tonight, so I was set straight. Now we just have to figure out where we're going to get an extra ten dollars for the concert."

"Ten dollars?" Beth exclaimed. "It's not free?"

"It's just a donation, Beth. We'll find it somewhere. We're not at the point where we need to rely on charity yet. Weren't we just whining about how there are no men in our lives? Well, there will be a couple hundred of them at church tonight."

"Yes, you're right," Beth admitted. It had been far too long since she'd had a date. Today, the attention from a strong, successful man just felt good. Besides, nothing could ever come of it. Ken Barrett was leaving in June, so a little harmless friendship wouldn't hurt anyone.

❧

After splashing aftershave on himself, Ken knew he was more intrigued with Beth Knight than was probably wise. With reckless anticipation, he drove quickly to her apartment. He hoped he didn't appear too eager and had to wait in the car for about ten minutes to make sure he wasn't too early.

Ken checked the address twice on his scrap of paper. *This is it.* It certainly wasn't the best neighborhood. Ken was nervous for Beth and Heather when he noticed the black iron bars across the windows of their apartment building. He knew what rents were in the Bay Area. But certainly two teachers could afford a decent neighborhood. *Couldn't they?* Thinking about his salary without his naval pension, he suddenly wondered.

He knocked quietly, waiting patiently. After a short sensation of being watched through the peephole, the door opened. To his delight, Beth stood in the doorway with a warm smile. As usual, she was exquisite. Her blond hair was pinned back in a large barrette and her lips wore a gentle touch of pink. He never saw her wear a hint of lipstick at school. Although she tried to appear casual, her jeans and cotton shirt were perfectly pressed. He smiled. Her acute attention to detail intrigued him to no end, probably because it was so foreign to him, and yet so close to what he knew in the navy.

He definitely had a new appreciation for Miss Beth Knight. She was actually very loving with the students, asking them all sorts of questions about their future and really taking the time to listen to each of the answers. She never seemed put off when the kids tried to play cool or didn't answer. She just kept asking more questions, sharing small details about herself to get them to open up. He hadn't had the impression of her warmth before today. Seeing a glimpse of it made him crave more.

"I'm so glad you two decided to come. Apparently, there are plenty of tickets still available at the door," Ken said. "We'll get there early enough to get good seats."

"Tickets. Yes, Heather just told me." Beth's face contorted into a worried frown. "I didn't realize when you called. . .oh, never mind. I'm being silly."

What on earth could Beth spend her money on that would make her sparse lifestyle necessary? Ken eyed her, then her apartment suspiciously. Besides being in the poor part of town, her apartment was filled with blocky, functional furniture from another era. Her style was apparent, however, with handmade quilts thrown over each sofa and home-style curtains on the barred windows. She'd done what was necessary to make the living quarters very homey, although the sunny yellow curtains lost something with the black bars behind them.

Ken cleared his throat. "The tickets will be waiting for us at the door." He smiled. Of course he didn't mention he'd be paying for them. He watched Beth smile broadly.

Beth went to get her sweater, and Heather came out smiling. "Tickets are waiting for us, huh?"

"You're not going to tell her, are you?"

"She's going out tonight, which is something of a highlight, so, no, I'm not going to tell her. I think it's sweet what you're doing, Ken, and we certainly appreciate it. Even if Beth is too proud to say so. She's so careful with her money; I think she might only see this as frivolity."

"Do you mind if I ask—"

"Why we live in this dump? You'd never believe me if I told you, Ken. Suffice it to say Beth's money—"

"Ready?" Beth, breathtaking in a baby pink sweater, cut off further conversation. Ken drew in air at the sight of her. She had such impeccable taste and always appeared ready for the runway, instead of her mundane day at school. *Perhaps that's where her money goes. No, no woman would pursue vanity and compromise safety in this apartment, would she?*

Once at the concert, Ken quietly rounded up two more tickets. Together, Ken and the girls entered the great sanctuary. The congregation was milling about, talking and laughing while they waited for the show to start. A grand piano nearly filled the altar area, along with a few guitars and a drum set. All the instruments were behind a Lucite protector to keep the noise from being overwhelming.

Ken couldn't take his eyes from Beth. With childlike wonder, she watched every detail happening around her. When the music began, she enjoyed the concert with wide, bright eyes, clapping along to the music and dancing in place. She seemed to forget anyone was with her, raising her hands in praise and singing along with the musicians.

Ken wished he could focus on anything besides her.

She frowned when it was over. "That's it? They just started."

"Beth, they played for two hours!" Heather said. "Give the guys a break. It's not their fault you never get out!"

Beth shot Heather a dirty look. Before Ken knew it, he heard his own voice. He was so enamored by his guest, he hated the idea of waiting until Monday to see her again. "Beth, some of my students gave me a gift certificate to a fancy seafood restaurant last year. Would you care to join me in spending it tomorrow night? I don't want to take one of my navy buddies to a dining establishment. They're just as happy with pizza."

"Really?" Beth's eyes lit. She batted those long, luxurious lashes, and Ken wondered how anyone could ever tell her no. "I just love seafood. When we were stationed in Hawaii, I quickly got spoiled. Are you sure you want to spend your certificate?"

"I know it's short notice, but it's getting ready to expire. The year's almost up, and God just brought you to mind. What do you think? We'd have fun."

"I'd love to! Did I mention lobster was my favorite?" She bit her lip to contain her grin. Ken was definitely smitten. He'd buy her two lobsters if that's what her heart desired.

"Lobster it is," he agreed.

"She's teasing, Ken. She'll probably make you stop at McDonald's along to way to spare you further expense." Heather shook her head. Beth elbowed her friend gently, while Ken just delighted in their familiar banter.

"Remember, I don't have to pay for this, so if you want lobster, Miss Knight, we'll pick him out of the tank ourselves. I'll even find him a companion steak if your heart so desires."

Beth clasped her hands. "This is too good to be true, Lt. Commander. I think I'll fast all day tomorrow to get ready for it."

"You better watch out, Ken. She doesn't splurge too often. She may eat you out of that cell phone you carry."

Beth threw her hands to her hips. "Isn't that your friend over there, Heather—You know, the one you haven't alienated yet?"

"I can take a hint," Heather laughed and went on her way.

"I hate to admit it, but Heather's right. I love a good restaurant meal. It's been awhile and I know I sound really pathetic, but I'm so thankful you asked me. I don't even have to feel guilty about you struggling to pay for it. What a delight!"

"Beth, I can afford to take you out as well. I would gladly pay for the opportunity."

"I didn't mean to imply—"

"Never mind, Beth. You and I have gone that route before. No more misunderstandings. I'm thrilled to spend tomorrow with you. Let's leave it at that. Did you want something to drink before we go? I know you're not a coffee drinker, but they have sodas."

"No, I'm fine. Thanks."

They both looked up at a familiar voice. "Well, it's nice to see Valley High's best and brightest teachers out on the town tonight." John Palmer, their principal stood with crossed arms. "I'm glad you two are getting to know each other a little better since you're both chaperoning the Marine World trip."

Beth and Ken looked at one another in stunned silence.

It was Beth who finally found her tongue. "You're going on the trip?" A slender, accusatory forefinger pointed at Ken.

"Well, yes. A lot of my students earned the right to go on this trip. I wouldn't miss it. Some of my kids have never been rewarded for anything. I thought the trip was the best reward planned, and it just takes a weekend from me for them to get it."

Beth's finger still pointed, unknown to her. "My students have earned this right every year! And I always take them." There was an edge of competition in her voice, and Ken was disappointed. Why she didn't want him or his students coming was apparent. Beth thought he was incompetent and his less-than-perfect students were unworthy of the annual field trip for honor students.

Suddenly, he wished with all his heart he hadn't given in to his feelings for her. Regardless of Beth's innocent features, she felt only honor students were worthy of rewards. The exact reason he'd decided to teach instead of reenlist. Those many years ago, if Stuart Greene had never come along, Ken's potential might never have been recognized. He would have been as burned-out as any high school dropout. Ken believed in second chances. Clearly, Beth didn't. Instead of anger, he only felt disappointment.

Chapter 5

Beth picked up the phone several times but dropped it back into the cradle. "I should just cancel!" She chastised herself. "Pick up the phone!"

"If I told him how you talked to yourself all the time, I'm sure *he'd* do the canceling." Heather entered the living room, dressed in tired gray sweats and a bright red sweatshirt. "It's only dinner. When's the last time you went out? Ken will be the perfect gentleman. I have no doubt. You just have to learn to get along with people you disagree with, and this is the perfect opportunity to practice."

"Heather, my students have worked hard for three years to earn the right to go away on Junior weekend. It's just not fair that Ken's students get rewarded the first year they're off probation."

"Beth, they weren't all troubled students. He's probably selected only the best and, besides, it's not your place to decide who's worthy. That's Principal Palmer's job. It's just your job to chaperone those going on the weekend."

"But of all the teachers to have to chaperone with me, why him? Didn't any of the other teachers offer to take their students? As sweet as Ken is, his students are wild. How do you think they'll be on a trip to Marine World? I guarantee you it will be me bailing them out of jail."

"You said yourself the students really respected him, and I'm sure only his best are going. Look at the bright side: Only you and he were willing to give up a weekend to do this for the students. That says something about your love for the students."

"Yeah, it says we both have no social life!"

"That's not true. I have no social life either, and I didn't volunteer to take twelve teenagers to Marine World. Go get dressed. Ken will be here soon. A lobster has your name on it, remember?"

Beth sulked to her room, still upset over last night's concert fiasco. She should have known better than to tempt fate and accept a date with handsome Ken Barrett. Their differences would only haunt them.

⁂

Beth's stomach fluttered at the sound of the doorbell. She drew in a deep breath, bracing herself for a long evening. Knowing Ken dreaded it as well didn't make it any easier on her. She vowed to make the best of the situation and had prayed for an hour beside her bed beforehand.

Beth had dressed in a deep navy silk dress with a matching scarf that wrapped elegantly around her neck. It was a designer gown she'd picked up on her last visit to Goodwill. She hadn't known where she'd ever have occasion to wear it, but when she saw the size and the price, she couldn't resist. Now, she was glad she'd purchased it. She wouldn't have to feel self-conscious in the fancy restaurant.

Opening the door, she felt her apprehension melt away. Ken's warm smile and striking appearance suddenly made their differences minute. He wore a dark gray suit with a rich, crimson tie. A wealthy banker would not have dressed as well. Standing beside his six-foot two-inch frame, she could only marvel at the opportunity to be on this man's arm.

After an uneasy silence, Ken spoke. "Beth, you look beautiful. That dress—" He shook his head, but actually was speechless. Beth smiled shyly at his approval.

"You look wonderful too, Ken."

"I made reservations for six-thirty. Are we all set?"

"Absolutely." Beth let Ken take her arm and lead her to his car. She was awed by the luxuriousness of it. She drank in the scent of leather seats mingled with his light spicy cologne. Envy bubbled up for just a moment when she looked toward her embattled Honda Civic. Its ripped, cloth seats and chipped paint job glimmered under the orange, evening sun, reminding her of her money woes.

Immediately, she shook the thought from her head, trying to focus on Ken's good fortune. God ordained what a person had financially, and she knew a car would not make any difference in the long-term scheme of things. He had far more important plans for Beth.

"You are sure quiet," Ken commented. "Is everything okay? You're not still upset about us taking the kids to Marine World together, are you? You know all the kids going really deserve it, and we'll just have to focus on them."

To avoid conflict, Beth just nodded. Ken would never see her side of it. He had a soft spot for reckless, wild hoodlums and wanted to reward that type for their small strides. Beth, on the other hand, chose to reward students who were in it for the long haul, who acted with responsibility throughout their high school years. Since they'd both unknowingly been on the nominating committee for the big trip, there were bound to be upsets. She'd cross that bridge when she came to it, not dwell on it during this elegant evening.

"How did you decide to select your students for the trip, Beth?"

"I picked the kids I thought put in the most effort at school. Not necessarily the perfect students, but the ones who tried the hardest to accomplish the most with what they had been given."

"Amazing, so did I," Ken replied.

Beth turned away and rolled her eyes. As Ken neared the restaurant, he approached the valet parking. "Ken, don't park there! Right across the street is free parking! We can walk, and we won't have to tip anyone," she said excitedly as she pointed to an empty lot across the street.

"Well, I thought since we didn't have to pay for dinner, we might afford the luxury—"

"No, no. It's not a luxury, Ken. It's a waste of money. We can walk and you can save your money for something more important, like those expensive coffees you drink."

Ken laughed. "That's fine, Beth. I didn't realize it would bother you so much to be pampered."

"You're pampering me with dinner, remember?" She patted his knee, but felt slightly guilty with his returned look. He really was trying to be chivalrous and her frugality just got the best of her.

"Beth, I have to ask—"

"Ken, I'm sorry. Old habits die hard. You park wherever you want to."

"No, no. If you're willing to hike across the street in your heels, we'll go with the free parking. I am a teacher, remember?"

Beth brightened. "If Heather were here she'd let you know, I'd walk a mile in these shoes to avoid paying for parking." She giggled at herself and he watched her curiously. "It's become a bit of a game, I suppose. If I was Mrs. Bill Gates, I'd still shop at Goodwill."

"Goodwill? Beth, you can't expect me to believe with your fashion sense, you shop at Goodwill." Ken laughed hysterically, but stopped when he saw her straight face. "You're kidding!"

She smoothed her elegant, designer gown. "$14.95!"

"Beth Knight, I cannot, for the life of me, figure you out. I thought your money went to feed your clothes habit."

"You can't believe the things people get rid of, Ken.

Dresses go out of style, and women get bigger or make more room for new clothes in their closets, and I reap the rewards. Of course, it takes a little time to shop. You just can't easily go to the rack or find what you're looking for, but the hunt is kind of fun."

"You're serious. You really got that dress at Goodwill."

"I did," she said triumphantly.

He parked the car and came around to help her out. She trembled at his touch when his masculine hand grasped her own and assisted her from the car. She closed her eyes and allowed his fresh scent to cling to her senses until it overwhelmed her, reminding her what his presence did to her. As though time stopped, she stood before him, floundering in her own emotions —knowing what she *should* feel and marveling at what she *did* feel.

Ken touched her heart in a way she couldn't explain. She knew better than to be attracted to a military man, and yet, there she stood, allowing his cologne to mingle subtlety with her senses. She opened her eyes and saw him bow. She braced herself for his soft kiss and felt it to the core of her stomach. His lips met her own with a kiss she experienced with her whole self. Passionate and chaste all at once, she returned it with something unknown willing her toward him.

He pulled away, still grasping her hand. "How can we disagree on so many things and still feel the way we do?"

"It's not just me," she whispered, as much for herself as him. She'd always imagined her first kiss in a romantic park with rose petals strewn about her. Yet, here she was in a dirty parking lot, and nothing could convince her such a setting wasn't perfect.

"Beth, I know we have our differences, but I also know there's something else underneath those petty arguments. I just pray you'll allow us to find that out before our good sense kicks in. Let me indulge you tonight. Forget about money and things that will pass away and allow us to see where this is headed."

Beth nodded, wishing he'd kiss her again. When he spoke, she nearly lost all the words and she willed him to come closer. He placed a brotherly arm about her, and they walked across the street to the candlelit restaurant. The rough Bay waters, a tortured green hue, rocked before them. Their window view over the waters made it look like they were actually on a boat. Planes landed at the San Francisco airport, and she took in the view to capture this moment in her mind.

The waiter, dressed in a tuxedo, came and offered them a wine list, which Ken politely refused. "How's the vintage on your Coca-Cola?" Ken asked with a smile.

"Make it two," Beth added. They shared a small laugh and again Ken took her hand.

"So does anything look good on the menu? I was thinking of the lobster, but when I walked past that tank, my conscience got the best of me. Call me funny, but I don't like to see my food alive before I eat it. Or looking at me."

"I was thinking the same thing!" Beth exclaimed. "Have you ever been to Chinatown in the city? Is there anything more unappetizing than watching the catfish writhe on those tables and flop off onto the sidewalk? Eww, there is nothing uglier than a catfish. I don't think I wanted to eat for a week after seeing that and worse yet, hearing that slimy plop when it hit the ground." Beth shivered at the memory.

"What about the chickens hanging in the windows?" Ken laughed.

"Here we are at this fabulous restaurant and suddenly my stomach isn't feeling all that great. Let's talk about something else."

"Beth, you're the one that brought up the squirming catfish."

Beth raised a palm. "I admit it. I started it. Now I'm thinking steak sounds awfully good."

"I love Chinatown, though, don't you?"

"The excitement and the bustle of it are exciting," Beth admitted.

"Why don't we go after dinner?"

"Really?"

"Why not? It's not that far, and we'll be done early enough."

Beth simply shrugged. "Why not, indeed? It's late enough in the day. All the catfish will be long gone. The tourist shops will all be open. It will be fun; let's do it! They still barter in Chinatown!"

Beth and Ken ordered their elegant meal and toasted one another with their sodas. They laughed, sharing memories from their military histories. They had a lot more in common than she thought, and her past hadn't been nearly as scarred as she remembered it. It couldn't have been, or she wouldn't have had so many happy memories to share.

Beth couldn't remember when she'd had a better meal. She stared at Ken's blue eyes for an eternity and it seemed only a flash. His animation in sharing his past brought her sheer joy. Beth no longer cared how Ken taught; she only knew he was different from her. And God made him that way.

They shared a crème brûlée for dessert. Ken took his spoon and fed her a tiny bite. She relished the flavor, but more so the look in Ken's eyes when he forgot about the dessert altogether and came closer. He placed a light kiss on her lips, and she'd never tasted anything sweeter.

He cleared his throat, pulling away from her. "Chinatown. We'd better get going or it will be too late for me."

"Uh-huh," she agreed absently, "Chinatown."

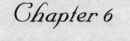

Chapter 6

A wash with dazzling red and yellow hues, Chinatown bustled with activity. Brightly lit signs in both English and Chinese beckoned visitors within, to taste a foreign feast or to purchase a new, exotic gift. The aura of excitement sent Beth's breath racing. This was like being on an international adventure without leaving the comfort of her backyard.

"What should we do first?" Ken asked. "Eat?" he joked.

"Oh, Ken, look at these jade figurines. Aren't they beautiful?" Beth stared in a window. An array of tiny trinkets was set up in a beautiful display. Jade, gold, and opal artwork glistened under the shop lights. It wasn't that she cared for fanciful gifts, but she loved to look at beautiful things. When she lived in Hawaii, her mother had often taken her to the Hawaiian shops and pointed out the intricacies of Asian craftsmanship.

"Not as beautiful as my date, but I suppose they're nice enough. Still, I'd rather look at you." He placed an arm around her, and they walked enthusiastically up the crowded street, anxious to see more of the famous tourist spot. She tried to ignore what the compliment did to her already thundering heart.

Kite shops, herbalists, acupuncture shops, and traditional restaurants lined the busy walk. Colorful, painted balconies with signs in Chinese hung from above while the financial district's huge buildings loomed in the background, reminding them they were still in their own country.

"I wonder what these are." Beth pointed into a window when the shopkeeper came outside.

"Netsukes, animal figurines of zodiac. This Cancer, this Virgo," the shopkeeper said in broken English.

"Oh," Beth answered despondently, "thanks. They're lovely, but I don't believe in the zodiac. Jesus Christ told us to have nothing to do with mediums and seers." She smiled kindly at the shopkeeper. "Thank you for sharing, though; the artistry is beautiful!" Beth grasped Ken's hand roughly and pulled him away. "Do you think I offended him?" she whispered loudly.

"No, Beth, I don't think he understood you well enough to be offended." Ken laughed. "But it was a good bit of preaching."

Beth playfully slapped him. "You're teasing me."

"I'm not teasing you. I was just waiting for you to lay out the Gospel for the man. I think he pretended to be less American to spare himself more preaching."

"Do you think I should try again?"

"I think he got your message."

"Dim sum!" Beth licked her top lip. "Oh, I haven't

had dim sum since I was a little girl. I wonder if it's as good as I remember it." Beth pressed her nose against another window with innocent wonder. "We used to have it all the time in Hawaii."

"For someone who hated living everywhere, it sounds like you made the most of your culinary experiences."

"Just in Hawaii. We had a good life there. At first it was really hard because there was nothing to do and nowhere to go but this. . .island. I wasn't much into nature then, so I didn't appreciate the beauty; but after I made friends, it got easier. I learned how to snorkel and body-surf and do what the locals did. Pretty soon I fit in and then, it was time to move again." Beth shrugged. "To Mississippi. Let me tell you, there's not much use for bodysurfing or snorkeling in Mississippi." The joy of dim sum was now overshadowed by dark visions of leaving Hawaii.

"But Mississippi has good food too! Did you enjoy the southern cuisine while you were stationed there?" Ken asked brightly. "That's where I'm going when this year is over. To teach in Mississippi."

"Mississippi? You *want* to move to Mississippi?"

"I was stationed in Pascagoula. It's on Singing River Island. One of the most gorgeous places I've ever been. It was a sailor's dream. I played tennis, ran track, and hiked the nature trail. I sure have fond memories of those days."

"You can't always go back, you know. What makes you think you can recapture that time by moving to Mississippi?" She asked bluntly. She'd move back to

Hawaii in a minute if she thought she could recapture those days of her youth. But they were gone, long gone. It was futile to chase a memory.

"Nearby, there are some really troubled youth areas in some of the poorer parts. I'd like to work with them and see how many recruits I can get into the University of Mississippi. I guess I left my heart there."

"That's an odd thing to say in San Francisco. You left your heart in Pascagoula?" Beth joked, but inside her heart ached. She'd allowed Ken a little closer because he was leaving. Now the thought terrified her. *He's leaving.* She'd kissed the man! The first man she'd ever kissed, and he was leaving town in a few months. *How smart was that?*

After a lengthy silence, Ken spoke. "Beth, you're so quiet. I take it you didn't care for Mississippi when you were there."

"It's just another place, Ken. Honestly, I couldn't tell you what it looks like or if I liked it at all. They all run together in my mind anymore. A different accent, different scenery; it all just jumbles my brain. I just don't care to remember it anymore."

"When you enjoy the different cultures as much as you do? Everything about Chinatown has just fascinated you, and yet you want everything in your life to stay the same. Are you sure you really feel that way?"

"Positive. The plainer my life, the better. All this flash is nice for an evening, but then I'm ready to settle into my nice living room with a customary cup of peppermint tea." Beth tried to avoid looking at him. His

eyes pierced her somehow. The intensity and his familiarity made it seem like they'd known each other for an
eternity. It had really only been little more than a year.
Why had she waited so long to get to know him? *No, the
question is, why did I let him into my life at all?*

Ken stepped closer, hovering far too intimately for
her present comfort level. "And what if life gets too
complicated, Beth? What happens to your common
cup of tea? Do you drink it in India?" he growled.

Somehow their relationship had changed already.
Maybe it was the proximity they'd shared teaching next
to one another. Or maybe the exchanged looks in the
hallway. The silent communication she'd always fought.
She faced it now. She and Ken had been seeing one
another affectionately for far longer than two nights.
It was only now she admitted it to herself: the glances
in the hallway, the excuses to quiet his class, even the
avoidance of him. They'd felt this way for a long time;
displaying it was the only difference.

Beth stepped backwards and he pulled her close,
away from the masses on the street. She wanted to
avoid the consciousness. "Look at this herb shop!" She
exclaimed, walking toward another shop. Ken didn't
follow. He stood with his hands clutched behind him
at the edge of the sidewalk. "Ken? Did you want to see
the jars full of different Chinese herbs?"

She pointed behind her, but noticed he didn't care
one iota about the herbs. He wanted an answer to his
question. *How can I answer it?* She didn't know what
she'd do if things got complicated. She just did what

she needed to insure it didn't get too complicated—such as avoiding intimate questions from Ken.

"You seem to have an agenda for everything, Beth. What happens if you start to care about someone who lives halfway around the world?" He approached her, and she twisted toward the window.

"I do care about people that live around the world. I just miss them, instead of see them. My parents are in Honduras now. They're missionaries there." She fought back her tears at the thought, trying to focus on the beautiful, inanimate objects in the window. Her mother had never had the opportunity to make a real home. The little cabin in Honduras was the closest she'd ever get. Did her father ever appreciate all the sacrifices her mother made?

"Do you ever see your parents?"

"Only when they come back to the States on missionary visits," she said plainly. "Maybe once every two years or so. If they need medical attention, they'll come back for doctor visits. They have their own life now. I can't fault them for that. They come back when it suits them."

"But not to see you?" He asked, as though reaching into her soul.

"They see me on all their trips," she answered defensively. He drew her nearer, sensing her need for comfort. She didn't want to admit her need for it, but she relished the caress as his arms came around her. She couldn't afford to fall in love. Everyone she loved left. Just as Ken would do.

Ken didn't say more for awhile. He just held her hand tightly as they continued to take in the scenery —a tightness that defied simple hand-holding. She sensed his concern and it was sincere. "You haven't been to Honduras?"

"Ken, I've traveled enough in my short lifetime. This is my home now. Maybe I'll be poor here forever, and I'll never make enough to live the way I'd prefer, but I'm staying."

"What about me, Beth? Will you stop seeing me since I'm moving?" They found a bright red bench, and Ken sat beside her.

She swallowed hard at the question. How did she answer when her mind said one thing and her whole being another? "Why are you leaving, Ken?"

"I told you. I want to help those children in the poor sections of Mississippi. Without guidance, their chances for college are nil. I want to show them they have the opportunity within them. Just like someone showed me once. If it weren't for a man in Mississippi, I'd probably be in jail today."

"That's very noble, but you sound just like my father. Why can't you help the people in your backyard first? Why do you think your work has to take you to another state? Or another country? I don't understand that. I was always taught if you weren't serving in your present situation, nothing would change that."

"But I am serving in my present situation, Beth. I just feel called to serve in Mississippi."

"And what about your students in San Jose? Don't

you think they need you, too?"

"I think the need for college is more obvious here. With the Silicon Valley in your backyard, it's hard to avoid the necessity of education. This area has one of the highest populations of educated people in the world. I know the kids see that. They see the wealth, and, with it, the possibilities. These kids in this part of Mississippi don't see the light at the end of the tunnel. Do you see it from my side?"

No! She wanted to shout. *I only see that I'm starting to care deeply for you and you're leaving. I don't want you to leave.*

"This night has been perfect. Let's not dwell on our differences, Beth. For once, just let your heart feel something without thinking about the consequences."

She stood, shaking her head negatively. "I can't do that."

His warm hand captured her chin. "Just once," he whispered, stopping her brisk getaway. He bent and kissed her. The clamor and lights disappeared from her world. Only Ken's warm lips existed and she returned his kiss. Again and again, until she couldn't remember why she'd resisted in the first place.

"Just a minute!" Ken held up a finger and walked into a small shop. First, he handed her a Chinese almond cake. Then, he disappeared again. She sat on the bench, relishing the small cake until he returned a few minutes later.

He held a tiny green velvet box in his hand. "What is this?" she asked, as he handed it to her.

"It's a token of our night together. I don't want you to go home and remember all the reasons you can't see me anymore. I want you to remember the reasons you should."

She opened the box to reveal a beautiful jade ring. A simple design, it was a smooth circle with bright patches of apple-green color and some whiter areas. The translucence of the ring amazed her. It was nearly lucid, and she remembered her mother telling her in Hawaii about quality jade.

"But—" Beth tried to protest. Although she knew jade wasn't expensive in comparison to other jewelry, she knew it was more than she could afford. And more than she should accept from Ken. He sensed her trepidation.

"Wear it, Beth. Remember our international night as I will remember it. Fondly and often."

She slipped the ring onto her finger and it fit snugly. Maybe this was the closest she'd ever get to true love. Tonight, it was enough. If she lived on this forever, it would still be better than never feeling it once.

Chapter 7

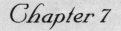

Beth didn't feel that love once. She felt it more strongly every day she saw and spent time with Ken. When he'd call and she'd wanted to say no to a date, she'd only have to look at her jade ring and her resolve would be broken.

The Indian summer gave way to winter. Ken and Beth, nearly inseparable for months now, cherished their evenings and weekends together—sometimes with Heather, sometimes with only each other. They spent their time grading papers, attending church, and doing all the mundane chores of life. Beth grew to depend on his presence, remembering less and less he wouldn't always be there. She'd even grown accustomed to the racket his class made each day, sometimes even laughing at the disruptions.

Just before the Christmas vacation, the field trip to Marine World was arranged. Although the amusement park was only two hours away, the event was huge for students and required an overnight hotel stay.

In general assembly, the winners of the trip were

announced. Beth took a quiet pleasure in the fact that Ken would see the excellent students she'd selected. She hoped his former delinquents wouldn't cause her too much trouble while they were away. Maybe he'd see the advantage to teaching the ambitious students and put away thoughts of going to Mississippi's slums.

Early Friday morning, the school van was packed to the gills with student duffel bags and backpacks for the occasion. Beth prepared a study quiz for the amusement park, just to insure her students had paid attention to some of the educational aspects of the park. Marine World had a fine collection of animals, from killer whales and dolphins to camels and mountain lions. Beth hoped her kids wouldn't just stay on the roller coasters and whittle their entire day away playing.

"I think that's everything," Ken said as he slammed the tailgate shut.

"Let's just take roll and we'll be on our way." Beth stood at the door and called out names as students filed onto the supersized van. "Six girls, seven boys all accounted for."

Ken told dumb jokes while he drove and laughed at the kids' versions of humor. Some of them were in questionable taste, but Ken didn't say anything to reprimand the students, just casually mentioned the jokes weren't funny. "You're trying too hard with that one," he'd say and the group would simply laugh at Ken's replies, instead of the rude jokes.

As they approached the park, the murmurs in the van blared louder and louder with excitement. Filing off the van, Ken laid out the rules. "Okay. You all know the rules. You have ten dollars for lunch and sodas for the day, so use it wisely. I think a Coke here is two dollars. If you get lost or in trouble, and running out of money doesn't count, just go to the nearest phone booth and call my cell phone number. We're meeting right here in front of the whale fountain at six o'clock. Is that clear?"

Antsy to get moving, the kids all moaned, "Yeah, yeah."

"Can we go now?" one of them asked.

"What time are we meeting?" Ken bellowed.

"Six!" They screamed, clearly annoyed at the baby treatment.

Beth gave them one last instruction. "I've written Ken's phone number on top of your quizzes as well, in case you lose his card."

Ken burst out laughing. Despite Beth's glaring looks, he couldn't contain his uproarious giggle. He tried to cover his mouth, but couldn't stifle his laugh in front of the students. "Go ahead, kids!" he managed before bending over in hilarity. When they were all out of sight, which took about twenty seconds, Ken looked at her, still caught up in his mirth.

"I fail to see what's so funny." She threw her hand to her hip.

"Do you honestly expect those poor kids to fill out a quiz while they're here?"

She ignored his obnoxious laugh. "This is a very educational place. I called the zoo director here this week and asked about the displays to write down questions for the kids. I even supplied the answers in Spanish for my students. I went through a lot of trouble to—"

"I'll bet you I find at least five quizzes in that trash can right there." Ken pointed to a dolphin-shaped garbage can.

Beth crossed her arms. "All right, smartie. I bet you I find *your* students' quizzes, but mine know better." They strode towards the can, with Beth confident they'd find Ken's six students' quizzes, but her seven still missing. Ken willingly stuck his hand into the trash and pulled out several white sheets. "It doesn't mean a thing, only that your students don't appreciate what an education can do for them. That's what happens when you bring delinquents."

He counted them aloud, "One, two, three, four, five, six, seven, eight." On and on he counted until he reached thirteen. "All thirteen tests present and accounted for, sir." He clicked his heels and saluted.

"Fine. I'll say no more about the tests. Happy?" She tossed them into the trash where he'd first rescued them.

"Come on; let's go ride that new roller coaster!" Ken encouraged.

"Ken! We should head to the oceanarium first. The kids shouldn't see us acting like children." She unfolded the park map and studied it seriously.

Ken laced his hand through her slender fingers. "You're right. We should definitely act our age." He kissed her, and she blushed brightly. "Come on, Miss

Knight. What's it going to be? Kong? Boomerang? Or Roar, the old wooden model? Are you into modern thrills or the classics?"

She straightened the map. "I've never ridden a roller coaster, and I see no reason to start now. Let's go see the elephant seals. Did you know they're born weighing upwards of sixty pounds?"

"A former bodysurfer, and you've never ridden a roller coaster? Oh, I have the perfect ride for you. Come on." He gripped her hand and pulled her behind him. Clearly, they weren't headed to the elephant seals.

She folded the map away, certain it was going to do her little good. They headed to a ride called Boomerang. She scanned the line for their students. None of them were present, and Beth secretly hoped they were at the oceanarium or tiger pen learning something instead of wasting time on rides. The line stretched, twisted, and turned. "Look at this line. People stand in line for that!" She pointed to the small ride in front of them.

"No, Beth. They stand in line for that!" He pointed upwards and Beth's jaw dangled. A towering steel track loomed high into the sky. The screams of riders tore through her eardrums. The track corkscrewed into the air into a vertical loop, then just as riders were thrust into the air, the track ended and they did it all again backwards.

Beth should have been afraid, but the adventurer in her shone through. She missed the thrills from getting tossed by a rogue wave. The thought of a safe drop from a roller coaster didn't appear too frightening compared to the pounding Hawaiian surf. Beth clambered to get into the line, hoping her students wouldn't spy her, yet longing to taste a bit of the quest before her. "This is going to be fun!"

After a forty-five-minute wait, they finally climbed into the middle of the train. Beth felt her throat in her stomach but couldn't wipe the anticipation or the smile from her face. Like a shot, they were off. Her adrenaline soared with the force of being hurled through space. Before she knew what happened, she was upside down, then right-side up again. The most frightening part was seeing the track end and only blue sky in front of them. Just as she closed her eyes, the ride launched them backwards at the same rapid force. Upside down again then to an abrupt stop.

Beth cracked up wildly. "Let's do it again! Let's do it again!"

Ken stood and helped her from the train. "Don't you think we should be getting the answers to that quiz of yours?"

"Oh, be quiet!" Beth ran to the next line for Kong. Kong allowed the riders feet to dangle loose in the air while it flipped, corkscrewed, and turned through a mind-boggling, engineering feat of a track.

After they'd ridden all six roller coasters, one of them twice, Ken commented he was certain he'd created a monster. "Can we stop for lunch?" Ken queried.

"Lunch? But the lines will get longer," she whined.

"I thought you wanted to check on your students in the zoo section." He grinned.

"Oh, get real. None of the kids are anywhere near the animals," she admitted. "All right. I give in; let's get lunch."

"Hey, Lt. Commander!" a few of the kids called from the lunch table.

"How's your quiz coming along?" Beth asked as she approached the table.

"Uh, um—" the kids stammered.

"Never mind. What did you all have for lunch?"

"Pizza," Ted answered.

"A burger," Kelly said.

"Nachos," Amber sheepishly admitted.

"Sounds like a nice, healthy lunch," Ken teased. "Come on, Miss Knight, let's go see if there's anything decent on that menu."

Back at the table, the kids continued to discuss their teachers. "I think she likes him," Kelly suggested.

"No way. She's too proper for Lt. Commander. She'd be with some Clark Kent kinda guy. Big, dorky glasses and a book in his hand all the time. And Lt. Commander would never go for her type. She's too stuffy," Ted said.

"I think you're both wrong. I think they're in love and secretly they hide their feelings to fight what they feel inside. It's an unrequited love thing, like in *Wuthering Heights*." Amber said dreamily, only to be slapped on the arm by Kelly.

"Cut it out! Gross. You read too many books, Kelly."

They were still laughing guiltily when Ken and Beth returned. "What's so funny?" Ken asked.

"Nothing. We better get in line for the rides," Ted said, clearing away his plastic tray and pizza crust. Without a glance backwards, the kids darted toward the roller coasters.

The couple sat at the empty table. "Was it something we said?" Beth asked.

"They were probably worried you'd give them a pop quiz on their lunch's nutritional values. You know, Beth, I just have to tell you I've never seen anyone enjoy life more than you when you allow yourself to have fun. That day in San Francisco when you studied each little trinket or that day at the beach when you made the sand mansion. Even today, riding the roller coasters like a kid. I just don't understand how you want to stay in the same place your whole life and do the same things. You seem so much more adventurous than that. Like you come alive when you're living something new."

"I just try to live in the moment, Ken. I want to relish the time we have left together."

"You know our time together doesn't have to end," he said softly.

"What kind of choice is that, Ken? You won't stay in Mississippi. You're restless, just like my father was. You think your dream is in the backwoods of another state, but then you'll be there awhile and discover it really lies somewhere else. I've been there, Ken. I've done that. It's time for me to settle down."

"That's what I'm talking about, Beth. Settling down —but doing it in Mississippi, instead of California. Not another country, not another base, but a real suburb with a white picket fence, if that's what you want."

"It *is* what I want, but I have it now."

"Not with me, you don't have it. Do you want to have it alone? With your white, picket fence as black iron bars instead? Poor Heather wants out of that disastrous neighborhood and she stays there for you. Can't you see how your will is determining other people's lives already? It's what you always complained about with your father, but now it's you doing the same things. You're fighting me. You won't talk about marriage and you're just playing with my heart. I don't even understand why you live like a pauper. I watch you scrimp and scrape to make enough to get by and I have no idea why. This relationship is just one-sided," he accused.

Beth stared at her turkey sandwich, unable to swallow the bite in her mouth. "I can't eat." She shoved her tray away and stood.

"Beth, where are you going?"

Unable to answer, she walked away. She sauntered slowly along the perimeter path that lined the park. She halted when she came to a huge, two-humped camel. His enormous, brown eyes looked back at her, willing her closer to the fence. The animal appeared as sad as she felt. The camel came toward her, nestling his head near her. She patted the wide nose. "Look at your sad, brown eyes. You understand what it's like to live in a place that's not your home, don't you?"

"Did you have a question about the camel?" A safari-clad keeper came up beside her.

Beth smiled at him cryptically. "No, we just have a

lot in common." Beth sighed and moved away. She wandered toward the tigers. They playfully jumped in and out of the blue stream in their man-made jungle, making the best of their new, fake home.

Beth wistfully thought of Ken's offer. He hadn't really made one. Granted, she never gave him the opportunity. She always changed the subject when he talked about marriage. She didn't want to follow Ken all over the world, but she didn't want to live without him either. *Is this what Ken had meant about God's plans for my life changing?*

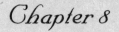

Chapter 8

A t five minutes to six, Beth waited at the whale fountain for the students. . .and for Ken. She wished she could avoid him, but that obviously wasn't possible. Many times, she'd thought of calling him on the cell phone in the park. Each time she passed a pay phone, in fact. But she kept walking past them, missing the opportunity and Ken.

"Miss Knight! Miss Knight!" A breathless Kelly ran toward Beth. Before continuing, Kelly bent over, frantically gulping for more air.

"What is it, Kelly? What's the matter? Are you sick?"

She shook her head in the negative. "I can't find Amber, Miss Knight. I think she left the park. Trevor and Ted went looking for her, but I don't think she's here."

"What do you mean, you don't think she's here? Where is she? Did she go to the hotel?"

Amber Ross was one of Beth's best students. A candidate for the honor roll every semester of her high school career. Beth had little doubt Amber would show up shortly, just as scheduled. So, although Kelly was shaken up, Beth felt confident.

Kelly shook her head violently. "You don't understand, Miss Knight. After lunch, we met these guys from Sacramento. One of them drove a Boxster. It's Amber's favorite kind of car. The guy promised to take her for a spin, and we haven't seen her since, Miss Knight. She was supposed to meet us at the Boomerang at three. She never showed up."

Beth's heart started to pound fiercely. "Why didn't you call us? Are you sure she left the park, Kelly?"

"No, but—"

"Can you describe the boys she went with?" Beth tried to remain calm. *Everything will be fine*, she told herself. *Oh, Lord, let everything be okay. Please be with Amber. Bring her back to us, Lord.*

"They weren't boys, Miss Knight. They were in their twenties, at least."

Beth raked her hair roughly, trying to comprehend her choices. "Think. Think," she told herself. She breathed a sigh of relief at the sight of Ken. "Ken, Amber's missing. Kelly thinks she may have left the park with guys in a Porsche Boxster."

Ken immediately took control, relieving Beth to no end. The consequences were too frightening and it halted Beth from taking appropriate action. She was terrible in an emergency.

Ken remained completely at ease. "Kelly, are you sure these boys even had a Porsche? Did you see her get in it?"

"No, no!" Kelly cried, as she covered her face. "They were men; they said they went to Sacramento State.

Oh, Miss Knight, I'm so sorry. We should have called you right away. Ted and Trevor wanted to call, but I didn't want Amber in trouble. It's all my fault." The girl's tears turned to racking sobs and Beth started to feel the gravity of the situation.

What if I lost a student? I need to breathe. I need to breathe, she reminded herself. Beth, so fastidious in everything, was not the teacher to lose a student. Had she paid too much attention to Ken? Her focus was not where it should have been. *Oh, it is all my fault!* She felt her eyes flutter shut. Ken, in the meantime, called 9–1–1 and had the park page Amber over the intercom system.

Within minutes, the police were there. First, they said they'd search the grounds for Amber. Through an employee radio system, all employees of the park were informed to be looking for Amber. Police asked for a complete description: her clothes, her hair color, her eyes.

Six forty-five came and went with no sign of Amber. All the kids were now getting anxious for their friend. Ken scanned the nervous group. "Beth, I think you and the kids should go back to the hotel. The dinner buffet will be waiting and there's no sense in all of us being here. Go back, and I'll take care of things."

Beth wanted nothing more than to leave the situation in Ken's capable hands. But how could she? Amber's parents were expecting Beth to be responsible for their daughter. "Ken, what about Amber's parents?"

The police officer intervened. "Ma'am, we don't consider kids missing for twenty-four hours normally, but since she was on a school field trip, we look at these situations differently. It's very helpful if you know what time she disappeared. We may have to widen our search area. Especially considering she may be in an unidentified vehicle."

"Oh, Ken." Beth began to tremble, her limbs shaking violently. *What if? Oh, it is too unbearable to consider.*

"Beth." Ken pulled her aside, his voice low and stern. "The students are frightened. You need to be their rock. Call on the Lord and stay calm. We'll find her."

Ken was right. Beth took a deep breath and silently called out to God for strength. Her students were depending upon her. Their stricken faces told her that much. "Okay, kids, Lt. Commander Barrett is going to handle things here. Let's get back to the hotel and wait."

"Kelly, would you be willing to stay in case we need help identifying the men?" Ken asked.

Kelly only nodded. Ted spoke up. "Trevor and I will stay, Miss Knight. We know what the guys look like. Kelly's scared; she needs to go back with you."

Beth came out of her world to see the concern on Ted's and Trevor's faces. The hoodlums, she'd called them. Delinquents, and yet they were the voice of reason with her star student—the two who tried to pull her back from her stupid choice. As if the day wasn't devastating enough, Beth had to learn how wrong she was about Ken's students.

"I'll call Mrs. Ross from the hotel," Beth murmured, silenced by her own humility.

"No," Ken ordered. Again he took control, taking her aside with the officer. "I'll call her. Leave me her number. Think only of the other students. You'll have your hands full with them. I don't want you getting emotional on Mrs. Ross. It will be a hard enough phone call to make. I want to do it. I'll be able to stay calm."

"We'll do it," the police officer said. "Often, parents don't believe their darlings are capable of action like this and tend to blame the teachers. Nothing much gets accomplished after that but a lot of finger-pointing. Usually, we can let them know we're doing all we can, but we'll also tell her Amber left of her own accord."

Ken and Beth agreed to let the police make the phone call. Beth left for the hotel across the street. The students were stunned silent, their fun for the day overshadowed by the darkness of the night without their friend. The eerie quiet of what should have been boisterous teenagers was numbing for Beth. It meant something was truly wrong.

She tried to appear calm, but anxiety gripped her. After the kids ate, they quickly excused themselves to their rooms. At nine o'clock, there was still no word from Ken. Beth prayed and prayed, kneeling in vigil beside her bed. At nine-thirty, there was a knock on the door. It was Amber's parents, red in the face and looking for someone to blame.

"Our daughter has never been in trouble before! Before you took her with these juvenile delinquents. I knew we should have said no when we heard who was coming! I knew it!" the father raged. "Every year this has been the cream of the crop, but this year you decide to let these motorcycle animals come!"

Beth understood his anger. She had felt the same way until she'd known the truth. Ted and Trevor, the animals he referred to, had attempted to stop Amber. They'd been the responsible kids, while Amber, her star student, acted like a complete idiot, leaving the park for the lure of a car, which probably didn't exist. Beth wouldn't have believed it herself if Kelly hadn't confirmed the story.

"This is all irrelevant, Mr. and Mrs. Ross. What's important is that we find Amber. Lt. Commander Barrett is working closely with the police, they'll find her."

"They'd better!" Mrs. Ross threatened.

"Why don't you come in and sit down?" Beth offered.

"We're going to the police station. We just wanted to let you know, Miss Knight, we know who's responsible for this. You and your lieutenant commander bringing along kids from the hood. You'll pay for this!"

"Mr. and Mrs. Ross, I realize you're upset. I'm upset too, but Lt. Commander's students had nothing to do with your daughter's disappearance. As a matter of fact, they tried to stop her. They provided the information to help the police with the search. I think you're pointing fingers in the wrong direction." Normally, Beth wouldn't have questioned upset parents, but she'd had enough. She was worried too!

Just then, the door opened. Ken stood with Amber at his side, a policeman behind them. Beth let out a long, cleansing breath, unable to believe her impossible prayer was answered. A tearful Amber ran into her parents' arms.

Unable to restrain herself, Beth ran to Ken, nuzzling herself into his chest. "Oh, Ken," she sobbed. "Thank you, thank you, thank you. I don't know what I would have done without you here."

The policeman coughed. "Excuse me. I'm really glad this all turned out well, but Mr. and Mrs. Ross, we'll need a few statements from you. Would you excuse us?"

Beth and Ken left the room, anxious for the serenity of the hallway. "Oh, Ken, I was so wrong about your students."

"I know," he said calmly. "But, unfortunately, they're used to it. I'm hoping they'll use that prejudice to overcome more obstacles in the future."

"I'm ashamed I felt the same way about them coming. It was quite an eye-opener to have my student find the trouble. A little humbling, you might say."

"Once, that was my goal, Beth. To see you humbled, but I take no pleasure in being right. Amber could have been killed."

"What happened to her for so long?"

"When she got to the Porsche Boxster, it was a 1980 Camero with no rear license plate or paint. She tried to bolt back into the park but was shoved inside the car. For the next three hours, she used her debating skills to negotiate her release. Finally, they ran out of gas and had to stop. She screamed at the station, and luckily, an off-duty policeman was filling up. He managed to get her out of the car while the men skidded off with the pump still attached to the car. They have an excellent description of the car and the men, but they still haven't found either."

"She wasn't hurt?"

"No, thank God, no. She wasn't hurt, but she had a

good scare and was pretty shaky. I don't imagine you'll have to worry about Amber acting out again." Ken gripped Beth just a little tighter. "You've had a scare, too. I'm sorry our big outing was ruined. The kids really lost out this time. We'll have to plan something else for their hard work." She felt his warm breath on her ear. Being in his embrace, nothing was lost for her this weekend. Beth only felt at home reaching for the strength he offered her. "I love you, Beth."

She sought solace in his whispered words of love. She always pretended she hadn't heard them, knowing if she shared her feelings, she'd never be able to deal with his leaving. At this moment, in his arms, she realized saying them made no difference at all. She still felt it to her very soul. If he left, she'd be devastated.

It all came tumbling out. "I love you, too, Ken. Oh, I love you so much; I can't bear to think of life without you."

He pulled away. "Then don't think of life without me. Come to Mississippi with me. Marry me, Beth." He knelt down to one knee in the crimson-carpeted hallway of the tacky motor lodge. "I can't promise you we'll live in one place forever, but I can promise you we won't go anywhere God doesn't lead."

Beth nervously fingered her jade ring. "I can't move again, Ken."

"Why?"

"For one thing, it would be so impractical financially."

"Tell me why, Beth. I know your childhood was traumatic, moving so much, but I'm not leading that kind of lifestyle. I'm not enlisted anymore, but I feel

God's leading to Mississippi, and I feel God's leading to marry you. I want both."

Beth shook her head. "I can't give you both. I need to stay here."

Ken stood abruptly. "Beth, no offense, but you live in a dump. You have no money, for reasons I still don't understand, and yet you cling to living in one of the most expensive real estate markets in America."

"Moving costs money. Money I don't have."

"But *I* have it, Beth. Never let money stop you from doing what God wants. If you want to marry me, if you feel God leading it, give the money aspect up to God. I can take care of you, but more importantly, God can take care of you." He leaned in closely, whispering gently into her ear. "Tell me where your money goes."

"It goes to student loans," she said flatly, leaving off a significant aspect of the truth.

Ken wasn't fooled. "And?"

Beth finally relented, her strength zapped by the emotion of the day. She didn't have the will to keep her secret any longer. "It goes to my parents in Honduras. The board of deacons declined to support my dad's missionary work. They didn't think he'd done enough short-term mission work to warrant support for a full-time ministry. Mom and I forged a letter of acceptance, and I send him one of my checks every month through the church. Since he has nonprofit status, they simply send him the money. He's none the wiser."

"Your dad doesn't know this?"

"No. Forgive me if I'm leery of letting God work, but He didn't work in my dad's case financially. If

I hadn't supported them, he would have dragged my mother all over the earth again. This way she has a home."

"Beth, you never gave God the opportunity to work there. Maybe He didn't want your father in Honduras."

Beth ripped herself away. "He didn't want my mother to spend her last days without a home either, Ken."

"Do me a favor. Pray about this. Ask God if He wants you here or in Mississippi with me. Ask Him— not your history, not your ideals—what He wants from you. And while you're at it, ask Him to forgive you for trying to manipulate your parents' future."

"How can you say that to me? I watched my mother whip out her throw rugs and try to make everywhere a home. Honduras may be rustic, but it's a home they won't have to leave for a long, long time."

"Ask God, Beth. I just want to love you for the rest of your life. I want to have children with you and pamper you the way I think you deserve to be. Marry me." Ken kissed her forehead and left for his room. Beth leaned against the door, her mind a veritable whirlwind of thought.

Chapter 9

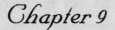

B eth, are you okay? You're as pale as whitewash."
Heather met her at the door and took her overnight bag. "What happened?"

"I think tenure is a lost cause. I lost a student on the trip."

"Oh, Beth, no! Did you find him?"

"It was Amber Ross, Heather. My best student. I just don't understand how this could happen. Ken's kids tried to talk her out of it, but she went off alone with some boys she didn't even know."

"I knew you weren't giving Ken enough credit. He's been where those kids have been. He knows what it's like to get a second chance."

"God's been trying to tell me that all along, I think. I can't be perfect. I'm not perfect, and I need to stop judging others as if I am perfect."

"Don't be so hard on yourself. We all have to learn that sometime."

"I'm going to get to learn it firsthand when I have to start over at a different school."

"John won't fire you over this, Beth. You've got a solid reputation."

"He may not have a choice if Heather's parents decide to sue. I was responsible for her. Ken's leaving for Mississippi, so I'll be left to take the fall."

"This probably isn't the time to tell you, but I've been praying for a long time about this. I have to move out of this apartment. It's time. When you weren't here this weekend, I had someone try to break in while I was home. He pressed the doorbell with his knuckle. I saw him do it twice while looking around suspiciously, so I called 9–1–1 really quickly and bolted out the back window onto the terrace."

"You weren't hurt?" Beth froze at the thought of Heather in peril. No one who could afford otherwise deserved to live this kind of life. Beth was selfish to keep her there anyway. "Did they catch him?"

"They caught him. He had a long record, so they didn't even need me to make a statement or anything. Apparently, since they caught him on the premises, it's as good as sewn up."

"I'm so sorry, Heather."

"Beth, I don't want you living here, either. It's not safe for a woman alone. You have to move. Maybe this trouble at work was meant to happen so you'd take some kind of action. Your parents wouldn't want you living here for their sake."

"Maybe," Beth answered despondently. Looking around the apartment, she could scarcely come up with a reason to stay. After Amber's disappearance, money seemed a moot point compared to her own safety. As much as she dreaded it, she would move. Not to Mississippi, but to a decent apartment. "All right, Heather. I think we should move."

"No, Beth, not us. I'm going to get my own place. My loans are paid off, and I just think it's best for now."

Beth's head snapped up. "But I can't afford my own place!"

"I'm not moving until the end of the school year. You'll have plenty of time to find another roommate. I'm telling you, though—you need to take the roommate who comes with a lifetime commitment, not waste your life working so your parents don't have to move. That's stupid. You're smarter than this. Beth, your dad wouldn't want to be in Honduras if he knew *how* he was in Honduras. I know your father. He's a proud man."

"And look how far pride has gotten him. They've spent their entire life like desert wanderers."

"You think you're any different, Beth? You're just like your father! If you weren't, you would have let the church's decision stand!"

"The church was wrong not to support my father in his ministry. It's a legitimate ministry!"

"That may be, Beth; but if it were God's will, the money would have come from more places than you." Heather's words felt like a slap across the face. The loving truth was harsh. Deep within, Beth recognized the truth for what it was, but she didn't want to hear it. Not yet.

Beth sulked into her room, justifying her actions.

Heather and Ken were obviously working together. Possibly even John. Everyone was plotting against her, trying to make her leave the life she was comfortable in. Why didn't anyone care about what she wanted?

She pictured Ken's wavy dark hair in her mind. His deep, dark blue eyes melted her heart. Then, she saw the uniform, and the ideal picture evaporated in her mind. She had promised herself—no military men. No men who put their careers above their wives. Ken was just an easy opportunity, a way to get herself out of this mess—but she wasn't going to take the easy way out. She'd find another roommate, and she'd stand up for herself with her principal. She was a good teacher, and her parents depended on her, even if her father didn't know it.

Ken was only the short-term easy route; in the long run, she'd live a mobile life just like her mother. If she followed once, she'd do it for the rest of her life. A throw rug would become home—the only semblance of familiarity in another lifetime of change. She couldn't do it, no matter what her heart said.

The phone rang, and Beth, still caught up in the sadness of her uprooted life, answered solemnly. "Hello."

"Beth, it's Mom."

"Mom! Where are you? You sound so close."

"I'm at the San Francisco airport, darling. We're taking a cab to your apartment."

"Let me come get you!"

"No, we're still not through customs yet. Your father tried to bring some crafts back for the church, and they're searching his bag thoroughly. I don't know when we'll be out of here. Just let us come to you."

"What are you doing here?"

"We're back home for good, Beth. I'll explain when we get there. Love you." *Click.*

Is it possible my parents are in on it too?

⁂

Ken carelessly tossed his gym bag on the bed. Why did he have to go and fall in love with such an exasperating woman? It served him right for trying to humble her. The only one humbled was him. He was the fool offering marriage to a woman unwilling to leave her ghetto apartment to get married. If it weren't for his students, he'd leave for Mississippi tomorrow. There was no sense hanging around the Bay Area for six months. Beth's nonanswer was probably the only answer he'd receive.

He let out his breath, which to his surprise, he'd been holding. He wasn't going anywhere, and he knew it. As much as he wanted to help the youth of Mississippi, he wanted Beth more. But was that God's will? Or just his own stubborn, selfish desires? And were they any match for Beth's own determination?

At least he knew now where Beth's money went. She wasn't a clotheshorse or secret gambler. She sent her money to her parents' ministry in Honduras. A noble enough cause, but proof that Beth didn't allow for God to control things. She took care of them herself. As he knelt in prayer over the matter, the doorbell rang.

He opened the door wide to his principal. "Hi, Ken. Do you have a few minutes?"

Ken nodded, shaking hands with John Palmer. "Sure,

come on in. Can I get you anything? Something to drink?"

"No, thanks."

"Amber's parents have decided to sue the school?" Ken asked fearfully. "I didn't think they'd work this fast."

"Oh, no, nothing like that. The police informed the Ross family their daughter's bad choice is what caused the problem. I think the police scared them enough to be thankful their daughter is alive and to stop worrying about blaming someone else for the disappearance."

"Whew! I know Beth will be relieved to hear that. She was really upset."

"Actually, Ken, it's Beth I've come to speak to you about. I notice you two have been spending more time together."

"Is there some kind of rule against that sort of thing?" As a Christian, John had to know Ken would never intentionally break a school rule, but he was also in deeper with Beth than John knew.

"No. No rules, unless it becomes something which affects your teaching. I'm here on a personal note, not in an official capacity as your principal. My wife and I think of Beth as a second daughter, and we don't want to see her hurt."

"The last thing I want to see is Beth hurt, John. I can guarantee you that."

John stood, pacing the room. "I know you wouldn't mean any harm, Ken, but Beth is a fragile case. She's lived all over the world with her father on very short missions for the military. Sometimes, her family moved every six months. In confidence, she's shared with us how difficult that was for her."

"She explained that to me."

"I know Beth's parents personally. I don't begrudge them anything. They have a huge heart for the unsaved all over the world, but I'm afraid sometimes their own daughter has been the victim of their ministry. It's one of the reasons his ministry support was turned down by the church when they came to us. We allowed people to give to their ministry through the church, but the church itself never supported it."

"John, I understand why Beth clings to one place so vigorously, but I'm at a loss as to why you're here. Why are you telling me all this?"

"I struggled with coming here. I don't want to let out classified information or have it become gossip, but I think I understand you care about Beth. She's spread herself too thin to make her father's ministry work, and the man is too proud to have ever figured it out."

"So stop routing the money," Ken suggested.

"We can't do that, Ken. We have a legitimate commitment to missions. Beth's father runs a tight organization. He's not cheating anyone. He's just doesn't meet our particular qualifications for a missionary."

"So what do you want from me?"

John looked him in the eye and said nervously, "Let us take care of Beth, Ken. You're leaving at the end of the year. Beth has been left enough in her young lifetime. Please, just leave her alone. I know I don't officially have any right to say such a thing, but

I'm asking you as a friend."

Ken was stunned. Couldn't John see how much Ken cared for Beth? He wasn't playing games. "John, I've asked her to marry me. I don't want to leave her. I want her to come with me."

John stared at Ken pointedly. "You asked her to marry you? What did she say?"

"She said nothing."

John stood quickly.

"Where are you going?"

John's jaw flinched. "She's lived for other people long enough. It's time she thought about her future. I've had it with Beth's choices. Get your jacket! We're going to confront her."

"I'm coming with you?"

"You're going with me to talk some sense into that woman of yours, Ken!"

⁊℮

Beth opened the door, her face lit with excitement. "Mom, Dad! It's so good to see you." Beth stepped into their outstretched arms and hugged them vigorously. "Why are you here?"

"We're here to stay, honey. Your father decided to accept a job with a contract pilot company. Our ministry in Honduras is over, I'm afraid." Carol Knight dropped her head, obviously disappointed with the outcome. "Your father thinks it's best if we stay here in the States for awhile."

"Well, that's okay, Mom. You're going to live here with me? Maybe this was God's design all the time."

Beth chastised herself for feeling elated. She was thrilled she'd have her parents, and her salary, back. Looking around her apartment, she realized she wanted to move. She'd find a decent place, maybe even move in with her parents. She'd have a real home once again, and she wouldn't have to move to Mississippi to do it. Beth opened the door wide to welcome her parents.

"I have to get the bags from the cab. I'll be right back," Roy Knight said evenly. Her father had never had much in the way of a personality, but something seemed worse. It was clear he felt like a failure. Hopefully, he still didn't know how his ministry had been supported.

"Mom, is Dad okay?" Beth asked.

"He's fine. He's just not sure he wants to work again after working in the ministry. But you know your father—he had difficulty with the Hondurans and their culture. He wanted them to adapt to his lifestyle and it just didn't work out. I'm sure you'll be happy to have your money back again, huh, sweetie?"

"Not if it means you and Dad won't be happy, Mom. Money is not worth that to me. I want you to be able to find a home. Maybe we can even get a condominium together? Or rent a house with a lawn?"

"Beth, Heather wrote us in Honduras. She told us about your beau. Lieutenant Commander Barrett, is it?"

Beth looked to the floor, unwilling to discuss the matter. "Mom, are you hungry?"

Her mother wasn't deterred. "Beth, your responsibility to us financially is over. It never should have happened to us in the first place."

Beth knew she'd sinned, keeping the money a secret from her father. She knew she'd done wrong, but the ends always seemed to justify the means. Her mother's solemn expression said something entirely different now. Conscience swept over her like a dust storm. "Does Dad know what we did?"

"Not yet, but I plan to tell him now that we're back. It was wrong to deceive him. I didn't set the right example for you." Carol looked around with distaste. "Beth, I didn't know you were living this way. Forgive me. Forgive us. But don't turn away from the man who loves you because you feel you owe us something. It is we who owed you the ability to make a life for yourself."

"It's not you, Mother. Ken is a former navy man. You know how I feel about men in uniform. What if he reenlists? Or what if he keeps searching for the place God wants him? I don't want to spend my adulthood moving around. No offense, but I did enough of that in my childhood. Would you wish your transitory life for me, Mother?"

"Beth, I'm so sorry. Clearly, I did not live the life of a proper wife who respects her husband's decisions, or you wouldn't feel this way."

"No, don't blame yourself, Mother. I'll be fine now that you're moving back."

"No. No, you won't, not if you love this Ken. The Bible says we are to leave our mother and father and cleave to our spouses."

"He's not my spouse." Beth shrugged.

"I've taught you wrong, Beth. A stationary house is a nice thing, but it's not the home. Your home is your family, your love for your husband. That follows you everywhere. Get a Bible, Beth." Beth reluctantly pulled a Bible down from the living room bookshelf. She wasn't in the mood for the sermon she knew was forthcoming.

"Here." Beth rolled her eyes.

Her mother opened the Bible to the book of Ruth and read, "Where you go I will go, and where you stay I will stay. Your people will be my people and your God my god. Where you die I will die, and there I will be buried. May the LORD deal with me, be it ever so severely, if anything but death separates you and me." Her mother sat back on the couch. "That is what makes a home."

"I'm not getting married, Mom. I'm too set in my ways." Beth stood abruptly.

The door opened and her father stood with John Palmer and Ken Barrett alongside him. All three of the men stared directly at Beth. She felt herself swallow. "Dad? You remember John. This is another teacher at my school, Lieutenant Commander Ken Barrett."

"We've met," her father answered harshly. He pushed his way into the house with Ken and John following behind. "John has just shared with me that I've been supported in Honduras by my daughter, and only by my daughter. Is that true?" Roy looked at his wife and Beth. Both women stuttered but didn't answer.

"John!" Carol finally said, betrayed by his announcement. "How could you?"

"Don't blame John. You two are fully responsible for this fiasco." The pain was evident in Roy's eyes.

Carol ran to her husband's side. "I'm so sorry, Roy. We were wrong."

Beth felt the stinging tears trace her cheeks. Seeing the pain in her father's eyes, she suddenly understood the ramifications of what she'd done. She'd tried to take the place of God. "Oh, Daddy!" She threw her arms around her father. "I'm so sorry! I thought I was doing God's will, but I know now I was only serving my own purposes."

"Ken, is this the kind of woman you want to marry?"

Ken stood up straight, in military fashion. "Yes, sir!"

"You're borrowing a lifetime of trouble." Roy shook his head.

"Yes, I know, sir!"

Beth put her hands to her hips. "I beg your pardon. I am not a lifetime of trouble! I would only enhance and enrich your life, Lieutenant Commander!"

"Prove it!" Ken bellowed.

"We'll just make ourselves scarce." Her parents and John Palmer exited the apartment, leaving the couple alone.

"I guess you understand what I did," Beth said sheepishly.

"I do," he answered evenly. "Are you sorry for it?"

"I don't think I've fully realized the depth of what I did yet. I know I will be. I had no right."

"No, you didn't. You've got nothing to keep you here now."

"No," she agreed. "nothing. My parents won't stay for long."

"You'll need to make yourself a new home."

Beth smiled at the man she loved. Ken Barrett was her home. Nothing else would ever come close. Overwhelmed by her new reality, she ran into his arms and smothered his face with kisses. She snuggled into his warm, lightly scented neck. "This is my new home. Wherever you go."

"Don't you forget it!" Ken commanded. "But I'll do my best to stay in one place."

Beth began a rousing version of "Ol' Man River," determined to work with the young in Mississippi and give them the second chance she'd been given.

"I love you, Beth Knight."

"I love you, Ken. Wherever you go, I will go."

They kissed each other with relish. Home, sweet home. Finally.

KRISTIN BILLERBECK

Kristin lives in the Silicon Valley with her engineering director husband Bryed, and their three sons, Trey, Jonah, and Seth. When not writing, Kristin also enjoys reading, painting, and conversing with her on-line writing groups. She has four published novels with the **Heartsong Presents** line and two novellas in anthologies from Barbour Publishing. Visit Kristin on the web at http://*www.getset.com/kristinbillerbeck.*

Beauty for Ashes

by Linda Goodnight

Dedication

To every child who cries for a mother,
and to every mother with aching,
empty arms—may you find one another.
And to my family,
especially Gene, Sundy, Cody, and Travis—
for believing.

. . .to bestow on them beauty instead ashes,
the oil of gladness instead of mourning. . .
ISAIAH 61:3

Chapter 1

Amy Rogers pulled into the parking lot alongside Hazelwood Elementary School, killed the motor, and gripped the steering wheel hard enough to turn her knuckles white. She sucked in a chest full of September air and held it, tension building in the muscles of her neck and shoulders. She had to do this. The surgery had been a success. The doctors had given her a clean bill of health. Her body had healed. The time had come to refocus her life.

With a determined jut of her chin, she slowly released the breath and surveyed her image in the rearview mirror. Not once in the last six months had she looked at herself without giving thanks for the long, brown hair curving around her shoulders. That, at least, had been spared.

Though she wasn't model gorgeous, she had big green eyes, a nice smile, and kept her petite shape by riding horses on her brother's farm. She'd always been considered fun company, and at twenty-seven she'd had her share of interested men. But that was all in the past.

"Help me, Lord," she prayed. "I can't do this alone."

Though she'd been to the school every day for the last week, making preparations for the new year, today the students would arrive for the first time. She loved teaching, but now she worried. Would she be able to give herself wholly to these gap-toothed, eager little people, or would she hold herself emotionally apart, unwilling to chance the pain of caring too much?

Someone knocked on the car window.

"Hey, girl, you gonna teach school this year or sit there and admire yourself?"

Amy turned toward the smiling face and her anxiety eased. Thank the good Lord for Trish, fellow teacher and best friend. With a relieved sigh, Amy opened the car door and stepped out.

"Boy, am I glad to see you."

"Of course you are. I'm bringing the doughnuts." Trish laughed, her dangly southwestern earrings glittering in the rapidly warming morning. "But you won't have time to eat any because I've already been inside, and there's a parent waiting to see you."

"A new student?"

Though school wouldn't officially begin for another hour, eager students and parents often arrived early on the first day—especially the new enrollees.

"Just wait until you see him, Amy." Trish winked. "And I'm not talking about the cute little second grader. I'm referring to his hunky-looking dad."

"Shame on you. You're an old married lady."

"But you're not."

The painful reminder brought Amy to a halt in the hallway next to a brightly colored "Back to School" bulletin board. Other teachers had already arrived, and the scent of fresh coffee wafted through the hallways, mixing with the smell of new books and freshly waxed floors.

"Quit stalling," Trish said, nudging her chin in the direction of second grade. "You just might enjoy the view."

"Trish," Amy warned.

Trish held out the doughnut box in defense, her pixie face serious. "Don't start with me, Amy. God gave you a life, and He expects you to live it."

"Yes. Alone."

Trish smiled, a tight little smile that said, "We'll see about that." Then, she shook her head and disappeared into the teacher's workroom.

Amy heard the chorus of greetings from other teachers as her friend arrived bearing breakfast. Sorry that she'd have no time to join the camaraderie, Amy rounded the corner and headed to her classroom, unwillingly curious about the parent Trish found so appealing.

In a small town like Hazelwood, Amy knew just about everyone, and though the man waiting in the second grade classroom looked vaguely familiar, she couldn't place him.

"Miss Rogers?" He came toward her, looking large and out of place amid the little wooden desks and dinosaur decorations. He was nice-looking, all right, but more than that, he looked like the kind of man that other people leaned on—trustworthy and solid. The small blond boy clinging to his hand added to the impression of strength.

Amy's heart did strange acrobatics. Nothing was quite as appealing as a big ol' cowboy with a small child. Suddenly, she knew why he looked familiar.

"Garrett Collins?" she asked, incredulous. "Don't I remember you from junior high?"

Considering she'd had a mad crush on him from fourth grade on, and they'd "gone steady" for about two weeks in seventh grade, how could she forget? He still had the same dark good looks—slightly curly hair that might have gotten out of control had he not kept it closely cropped, and eyes the color of Hershey Kisses —or so the girls in seventh grade had all agreed. Neatly dressed in black boots and starched jeans with his white shirt open at the neck, he looked trim and fit and very handsome. A flurry of interest came, but Amy squelched it immediately. Number one: He was obviously married with children. Number two: She'd accepted the fact that no man would ever want her once he knew the truth.

"Amy Rogers." Hand extended, Garrett smiled, displaying a bright gleam of even teeth in a sun-baked face. "I knew that name sounded familiar. So, how have you been?"

"Fine." Not that it was entirely true, but how could she blurt out her horrible medical history to a man she hadn't seen in fifteen years? Amy took the proffered hand and found herself captured by a pair of intent brown eyes. "And you? You disappeared after seventh grade, and no one ever heard from you again."

A flicker of emotion—was it pain?—came and went across his face. He drew his hand away, but the gentle, interested smile remained. "Long story. But now I'm back. Bought the old Tucker Ranch."

Amy returned his smile, though hers was wistful. "I've always loved that old place." Once upon a time, she'd dreamed of owning it herself and filling the big old farmhouse with lots of children. Now, her students were the only children she'd ever have.

"Well, in that case, you'll have to come out sometime and see the improvements the boys and I are making." Garrett lay a hand on the little boy's shoulder. "We've got a long way to go, but things are shaping up. Right, Cody?"

Amy turned her attention to the boy, who shrugged as he looked up with eyes as blue as periwinkles. The worry in them tugged at her heart. Poor little guy. He'd probably been too busy checking out the unfamiliar schoolroom to hear a word they'd said. Being the new kid wasn't easy on anyone, especially a seven-year-old. She reached out to smooth the top of his neatly combed, pale blond hair, turning her full attention to the new student.

"Hi, Cody. Is that a new backpack you've got there?"

"Yeah." The boy gripped the bag as though she'd threatened to steal it. "I got crayons and stuff, too."

"Well, terrific." Amy felt Garrett watching her as she motioned to the long rows of brown desks. Each one was decorated with an alphabet strip and a colorful dinosaur cutout. "Tell you what. Why don't you pick any desk you want and put your things inside? You're the first one here, so you get first choice."

Cody backed away and huddled close to his father, fighting tears. His lower lip trembled. "I want to go home."

Garrett Collins hunkered down in front of the boy, his blue jeans stretching taut over strong, muscled legs. "Hey, buddy, it's okay."

Tears slipped down the trembling boy's face. "This is not my school. I want to go home."

"I know you do, little man. I know you do." Garrett rubbed the boy's back sympathetically, speaking to him in quiet, reassuring tones. He was incredibly gentle, and watching him set off a fluttery feeling inside Amy. But this time, it wasn't his good looks that moved her, or the memory of a schoolgirl crush. It was the calm, caring way he handled the child.

He must be a good father, Amy thought, but couldn't help wondering why his wife hadn't come to help ease the boy into the new situation. *If* she *had a child as adorable as Cody. . .* Amy stopped short, the pain of her careless thoughts jabbing at her. She didn't have a child. And she never would.

"Miss Rogers."

Garrett Collins's deep voice snapped her back into focus. He had risen and stood with his hands on Cody's shoulders.

"Cody's ready to choose that desk, now."

"Oh, of course." Flustered for reasons she didn't understand, Amy held out a hand to the child. "Would you like my help?"

"Nah." Cody shrugged away from his father and plopped down in the nearest desk, shoulders hunched, lower lip protruding.

"The last couple of months have been pretty rough on him, Amy," Garrett said softly as he studied the forlorn child. "There isn't enough time this morning to discuss all that, but my number's on this card if you should need me." He handed her a light blue business card that read COLLINS RANCH in bold letters. "I carry a mobile phone in my truck in case the boys need me."

He started toward the door, and Amy fell in step beside him, curiosity getting the better of her.

"You keep saying 'boys' so I assume you have more than one?"

He nodded, pausing in the doorway. "Two right now. Caleb's in fourth grade."

Amy pondered his strange choice of words. How did anyone have two boys "right now"? Asking seemed presumptuous, so she said, "Cody will be fine once he gets acquainted."

Other students had begun to drift into the hallways, calling out greetings as they passed her room. Garrett remained at Amy's side as though he had more to say.

"Miss Rogers!" A small, ponytailed girl threw herself against Amy's brown-and-rust broomstick skirt in a joyous hug.

"Desirae, you've grown a foot this summer. Did you

have fun at your grandma's?"

"Uh-huh. I got new shoes." Desirae stuck one sneak-ered foot out for inspection.

"You sure did, and I love them." Amy admired the blue sneakers, then aimed the bubbly little girl toward the classroom, returning Garrett's grin. "Desirae, we have a new student waiting in there. His name is Cody. Will you be my special helper today and show him where things are while I talk to his dad?"

"Okay." The beaming child skipped into the room.

"You're good with kids," Garrett commented.

"So are you."

He tilted his head in thanks. "I'm working on it. Still got a lot to learn."

"Don't we all?" The first bus had arrived, and a flock of children in assorted sizes and shapes filled the hallways with excited chatter. Amy and Garrett stood in the second-grade doorway enjoying the spectacle. "Every time I think I've heard or seen it all, one of them will surprise me."

"They keep life interesting, that's for sure," he said. "Don't know what I'd do without them, though."

"I know exactly what you mean." As they talked, Amy alternately hugged the children and waved at oth-ers as they passed by on their way to new classrooms, but Garrett's words rang in her head. He was crazy about kids and couldn't imagine life without them. "My stu-dents are everything to me."

"You never married, then?"

Garrett's quiet voice drew Amy's surprised attention

back to him. She searched his strong, serene expression, wondering why he had asked such a personal question.

A slight flush crept up her neck, but she held his gaze. Most likely, she'd hear this question a thousand times in the years to come. She might as well learn to handle it now.

"No, I never did."

"Do you still sing specials at church on Wednesday night?" he asked, the corners of his eyes crinkling.

Amy gave him a puzzled smile. He certainly asked some strange questions, and for the life of her she could not imagine what one had to do with the other; but church was a much safer topic than marriage, and she welcomed the shift in conversation. "You remember that?"

To her recollection, Garrett Collins had never attended church.

"I remember a lot of good things about this little town. That's why I moved back." He leaned against the door facing and smiled at her. "So, are you going to invite us to church?"

"Oh." She felt flustered again. He just kept surprising her with these unexpected questions. "I. . .of course." Regaining her equilibrium, she held out the edges of her skirt in a mock curtsy. "You and your wife and sons are hereby cordially invited to church Wednesday night at seven o'clock."

It was his turn to look surprised. "I don't have a wife, Amy. I'm not married." He frowned, shaking his head. "It's just the boys and me. We're as single as they come."

Not married? How could he be single with two sons? Divorced? Widowed? She wanted to ask and might have done so had another parent not arrived, eager to talk with the teacher.

"Well, listen," Garrett continued, glancing around the quickly filling hallway, "you're busy now, but why don't you let me buy you a hamburger after school? We can discuss Cody and catch up on old times."

The unexpected invitation caught her off guard, again, and that strange fluttery sensation returned. Certain that nerves were the cause, and not the man, Amy stammered, "Well, I don't know, Garrett. . ."

She didn't want to hurt his feelings, but he had no idea what he was asking.

The corner of Garrett's mouth quirked upward, brown eyes teasing. "You do eat, don't you?"

That made her smile. "Of course."

"All right, then." Apparently he considered the matter settled. "I'll see you after school."

Still smiling, he gave a quick nod and disappeared down the hall, his black boots making soft clicks against the white tile. Amy stared after him. She hadn't been anywhere with a man, other than male relatives, of course, since Jeffrey Bartlett had made it perfectly clear that, "No man would ever want half a woman."

Amy sucked in a deep breath and ignored her flip-flopping stomach. She would consider this afternoon a parent-teacher conference. That's what she would do. Just like a hundred others she had conducted over the years. Garrett Collins was no different than any other parent, regardless of their history.

Winning the battle against cancer had cost her the ability to bear children, but she'd come away stronger and more thankful for the life God had blessed her with. She was determined to be content with what she had, having resolved after Jeffrey's cruel rejection never to become emotionally involved with another man.

Then why was she so thrilled to see Garrett Collins again? And why did she have this painful surge of hope tugging at her heart?

Chapter 2

G arrett pulled his king-cab pickup truck beneath the front awning of the Hamburger Hangout, killed the motor, and turned to the woman beside him. Amy Rogers didn't appear to have changed much in the years since he and his mother had left town. Oh, she was older, of course, more grown-up. But he felt confident that she was still the same green-eyed girl who fought for underdogs like him. He'd seen it in the way she embraced and complimented even the most bedraggled-looking children in Hazelwood Elementary School and in the genuine affection she had for them. Good people like Amy didn't change.

He draped an arm over the steering wheel and studied her.

She was turned in the seat, talking to the boys as she pointed out a small play area beside the burger place. The subtle scent of her perfume filled the cab as well as his head. Everything about her looked so clean and fresh. . . and soft. He wondered if her hair, gleaming in the afternoon sunlight, was as silky as it looked. His fingers itched to know, but common sense restrained him. They were, after all, practically strangers, though he felt as comfortable with her now as he had in school. He wondered how she'd react if she knew how he'd clung to the memory of her kindness, of her small hand in his, of that one time behind the football bleachers when he'd pressed his lips against her sweet ones and been sure he'd die of puppy love.

"Penny for your thoughts?"

Garrett jerked. "What?"

Amy smiled at him. "You were miles away just now. Where did you go?"

"Oh. Uh, just thinking. Remembering all the hamburgers I ate in this place, I guess." He shifted in the seat and opened the door. "Are they still as good as they were back then?"

"You can judge that for yourself," she answered, coming around the front of the truck.

The boys tumbled out behind them and sniffed appreciatively. The scent of grilled burgers permeated the outside of the small building. Cody inhaled and asked, "Smells better than 'Donalds, don't it, Caleb?"

"Nothing smells better than 'Donalds," his brother countered.

Garrett laughed softly and ruffled Caleb's hair. "Give the place a chance, big guy. Juanita makes the best burgers and chili dogs I ever tasted." He opened the glass door for Amy. "Juanita still owns the place, doesn't she?"

"Yes, but Sherry does most of the work now."

"Sherry?" A furrow creased his brow. "Juanita's daughter?"

"Mmm-hmm. She was a couple of years behind us in school."

They gave their orders to the tall brunette at the register who Amy introduced as Sherry, then made their way to a booth. The booths were the same green vinyl he remembered, though these were patched in numerous spots. Pictures of early Hazelwood covered the walls just as they had when he'd lived here as a child. The daily newspaper lay on the counter next to a tall napkin holder and a ketchup bottle.

"Nothing about this place has changed," he said. "I'll bet they still serve half orders of fries."

Amy smiled and nodded. "They do."

Garrett found the familiarity of the place comforting. Even after all these years, Hazelwood felt like home. Sitting across the table from Amy Rogers felt even better.

"Don't they got no video games?" Cody frowned around at the old-fashioned diner.

"They've got something even better." Garrett pointed at a huge bottle filled with water, the bottom covered with pennies. "See that bottle over there? There's a tiny glass down inside. If you can drop a coin through the narrow opening at the top into that glass, Juanita gives you a free soda."

"Cool."

Both boys clamored for pennies. Garrett emptied his pockets and was pleasantly surprised when Amy dug into her purse and handed the boys all her pennies, too.

"You don't have to do that." He lay a restraining hand over hers. Immediately, he was struck by how soft and delicate her fingers felt beneath his.

"Oh, let me." She carefully extracted her hand and gave each boy several coins. "I don't have children of my own to spoil."

He heard the regret in her voice and wondered at it. She was still plenty young enough to have children. Just because she wasn't married now didn't mean she wouldn't be someday. Truth be known, he was delighted to find her still single, though he couldn't help but wonder why a woman as pretty and smart and kind as Amy Rogers had never found her match. "Children are exactly what I wanted to talk to you about."

Amy drew in a shocked breath, momentarily taken back by Garret's choice of words. Did he know her secret? That she'd never have children of her own? She mentally shook herself. Of course not. How could he? Garrett wanted to talk to her about children, all right— his own, Cody and Caleb.

Garrett didn't seem to notice her odd reaction. He tilted his head toward the two boys standing at the counter, trying their best to win a free Coke.

"Those two guys have been in and out of at least six schools in the past two years. From what I'm told, they've fallen behind; so I'm concerned if they don't get extra help now, they may never catch up."

A twinge of concern pulled at Amy. Stability was so important for children. Why had Garrett chosen to move them around so much? He seemed so concerned for his sons that she couldn't imagine him selfishly dragging them from school to school without a good reason. Had the separation from his wife been the cause? She longed to ask, but couldn't bring herself to be that personal with a man who piqued her interest more than a little.

"I hope you're planning to keep them in Hazelwood for the entire year, then. They'll have a better chance of catching up if one teacher can assess their needs and work toward meeting them over a period of time."

"My thoughts exactly." He leaned back while Sherry set two quart jars of ice tea on the table. As soon as the waitress left, he pushed the tea aside and fixed Amy with an earnest gaze. "That's why I want you to tutor them."

"Oh." Amy reached for the sugar, stirring in two spoonfuls while she considered his suggestion. "So that's what this is all about."

"I'd pay you well." Placing both elbows on the table, he leaned toward her. "You can come home with the boys each day after school, do whatever tutors do, and when I get home, I'll even feed you supper." He lifted a persuasive eyebrow, teasing, "I make great frozen dinners and super slimy macaroni."

Amy laughed in spite of her anxiety. "Oh, these poor little boys."

Garrett chuckled. "I hope you know I'm kidding. Against the kids' better judgment, I can actually rustle up a pretty decent meal."

He leaned closer, bringing with him the faint scent of a woodsy cologne. Gentle brown eyes, full of humor, studied her. The irrational desire to reach out and smooth the tiny scar above his left cheekbone both enthralled and frightened her. She hadn't seen this man in years, yet one day in his company stirred up all the desires she'd worked so hard to lay aside. Touching him was not a good idea. Yet, she wanted to.

"Are you brave enough to find out?" Garrett's soft voice intruded.

Amy drew in a quick breath and sat back in the booth. Brave enough to find out what? How touching him would feel? She looked down at her hands, found them trembling ever so slightly, and forced herself to refocus on the conversation. Garrett was talking about tutoring, not touching. Whatever was wrong with her today?

She took a steadying sip of tea, avoiding his eyes. "You have this all worked out, don't you?"

"Absolutely." While the humor still lurked in his expression, his softened tone said he knew he'd disturbed her some way. "A man's gotta have a plan."

"Yes, I suppose he does." Amy drew rings on the tabletop with her tea glass. She wasn't so certain that seeing Garrett Collins on a regular basis was such a great idea. She'd once had a tremendous crush on him. She'd even had thirteen-year-old fantasies of being Mrs. Garrett Collins some day and giving him a house full of chocolate-eyed children. He'd grown up to be an incredibly attractive man.

What if today's reaction was a harbinger that those feelings would resurface? Worse, what if he returned them? Then, she'd have to tell him the awful truth and watch him pull away because she couldn't be all he wanted.

Garrett lightly touched her hand. "Amy?"

His face was as earnest and kind as any she'd ever seen. His desire to help his sons was so evident, she felt guilty for worrying about all the what-ifs in her life; but after Jeffrey's rejection, she couldn't open herself to that kind of pain again.

She took another swallow of tea, letting the coolness soothe her jangled nerves. "The beginning of the school year is so hectic; I'm not sure I'll have the time. Perhaps I could ask around, see if any of the other teachers are interested."

A flicker of disappointment came and went on Garrett's handsome face, but he persisted. "We're new in town, Amy. I'd feel more comfortable with someone I already know and trust."

"We haven't seen each other in years. How can you be sure I'd do a good job?"

"Some things a man just knows. Look," he reasoned, spreading his hands wide on the tabletop, "why don't we put the idea on hold for awhile, get settled into the routine, and then reconsider?"

She sighed. Garrett was an old friend and new in town. How could she, in good conscience, refuse to at least consider his request? Kids were her joy as well as her job. Hadn't she tutored other children over the years? And didn't she teach a Sunday school class and sponsor a youth group at church just so she could work with kids? Under any other circumstance, she'd have jumped at the chance to help Cody and Caleb.

"Give me a week or two, and we'll see," Amy hedged, but the answer seemed to satisfy Garrett.

"Deal," he said, thumping one fist softly against the table's edge. "This town and the people in it will help those two grow up with the same sense of security and stability that kept me going through some pretty rough times. I knew when I took them and moved them here, I was making the right decision."

"Took them?" Amy frowned, perplexed by the odd statement. "You mean, from your ex-wife?"

Garrett laughed—a warm, masculine sound that stirred the butterflies in Amy's stomach.

"No, Amy. Not from my ex-wife. From the Department of Human Services. Cody and Caleb are my foster sons. Didn't I tell you that?"

"No, as a matter of fact, you didn't. I haven't had a spare minute to look at their school records, either." She laughed, too, though her chuckle was at herself. "What a wonderful thing to do."

He shrugged one broad shoulder. "I'm crazy about kids. Want a dozen. Being a foster dad is a great way to start."

The hamburgers arrived just then and the boys returned, seating themselves one on each side. Cody sat beside his new teacher, and Caleb flopped down by his foster father. After Garrett's quiet prayer of thanks, they attacked their burgers like ravenous wolves. Other than an occasional request for salt, ketchup, or a napkin, they ate in silence for several minutes.

Garrett pointed at his hamburger. "These have haunted my dreams since the day I moved away."

"I always wondered about you after you left Hazelwood," Amy said. "Where you went, why you left without a word to anyone."

Garrett lay the half-eaten sandwich in its plastic basket. "My mom was sick. Did you know that?"

"You never told me."

"Kids are like that, I guess. If I didn't talk about it, it wasn't real." His lips tilted wryly.

"What was wrong?"

His expression grew serious. "Cancer."

Amy's blood froze. *Cancer.* The most frightening word in her vocabulary. Her enemy. And poor Garrett had fought the same enemy as a boy of thirteen and lost.

"I'm sorry," she said lamely, and despite her best intentions, Amy touched his hand. "More sorry than I can say."

The heavy screen door of the burger shop squeaked open, and an older couple came in. They exchanged waves with Amy before settling in a booth near the front. Cody and Caleb continued eating, poking French fries down faster than Amy would have thought possible. They paid little attention to the adults' conversation.

"She knew she was dying," Garrett continued. "So when the school year ended, she took me to the only relative she had—her grandmother in Wyoming."

"What about your father?"

Garrett winced, and Amy wished she hadn't asked. "Never knew him. Never even knew his name. So when Mom died, I was left with a very old lady who loved me, but she didn't have the vaguest idea of how to handle a teenager who was mad at the whole world."

"I had no idea all that was happening to you. I'm so sorry," she said again, silently thanking God for her close-knit family. How could she have survived the past year without her parents, her three older brothers, and the passel of relatives who gathered for every holiday and birthday? Other than her faith, family had been her mainstay.

Garrett reached across the table, pulled a napkin from the tall holder, and swiped at a spot of ketchup on Cody's face.

"A face that good-looking's gotta be clean, boy."

Cody looked up at him with a gap-toothed grin before chomping into another bite of his burger.

"Losing Mom was terrible, but God was there, taking care of me all the time." He smiled at her. "Though I certainly didn't know it then. The social services people would have said I was more demon than angel."

"So you ended up with social services." No wonder he was so dedicated to Cody and Caleb.

"Yeah. I only lasted a month with Grandma before the caseworker yanked me. I spent the next two years in and out of various foster homes."

With a casualness that belied the serious conversation, Garrett propped his elbows on the table, grasped the burger in both hands, and resumed eating. Like her brothers, he dispatched a meal in several bites, devouring with wholehearted energy.

"How confusing for an already confused child."

"Exactly. The more places I was sent, the madder I got. The madder I got, the more trouble I found." He studied the nearly consumed hamburger. "And believe me, a teenage boy has no problem finding trouble."

"But you seem to be so settled, so solid now. What happened?"

"An old rancher named Clarence Whitelow. He and his wife had been foster parents for years before she died. He'd earned a reputation as a man who could straighten out rebellious boys." Garrett's mouth quirked up at the corners. "Did I ever fit that description. The first day on his ranch I tried to pick a fight with him." Garrett wadded up the paper from his sandwich and tossed it into the basket. "You know what he did?"

Amy shook her head, trying to imagine a confused and frightened Garrett exiled to a life of limbo in foster care.

"That wiry little man put his arms around me and just held on. Held me like a baby while I fought and kicked and cursed. He was strong as an ox, I'll tell you that. After awhile I quit struggling. Then Clarence took me in the house and laid down the law. Every action had a consequence. Whether that consequence was good or bad was up to me." Garrett shook his head. "That tough little man worked my tail off, but he never asked me to do anything that he wasn't right beside me, encouraging, guiding. Years later, I figured out he was teaching me all the things I needed to know to be a man—a real man like him."

Amy touched Garrett's sleeve. "You loved him."

"Yeah, I did," he said without embarrassment.

Amy's insides turned to mush. She'd come here as a favor to an old friend, and already he was having the same effect on her that he'd had when they were teenagers. How would she ever remain aloof with Garrett Collins?

"Dad," Caleb interrupted, plopping his pop glass down for emphasis, "can me and Cody go play on that playground out there?" He indicated a swing, slide, and merry-go-round at the side of the cafe.

"Finish your meal first."

Both boys poked the last bite of hamburger into their mouths, then mumbled around it, "We're done."

With a grin and a wave of his hand, Garrett gave his permission. "Go on then, but stay where I can see you."

In a burst of energy, the two boys were out the squeaky door. Once they were safely on the playground, Amy said, "Clarence sounds like a wonderful man."

"Clarence was a true Christian. A man who put his faith in action."

"I had a feeling you were a Christian."

"Thanks to Clarence. He never preached at me, never told me I needed God in my life. He just lived his faith every day in front of me. Before long, I knew I wanted to be just like him. Right down to taking in castaway kids like me."

Amy fought back tears and rising panic. Garrett Collins was an amazing man; exactly the kind of man she'd have been attracted to in the past. Why did he have to come into her life now that it was too late?

Chapter 3

The Hazelwood High School marching band filled the football stadium and half the town with the sound of the Warriors' fight song. Red and white crepe paper streamers, stirred by the late September breeze, flew from the goalposts. Amy draped a sweatshirt over her arm as she and the Collins men crunched across the gravel parking lot toward the ticket box.

She felt more than a little surprised to find herself walking into the stadium beside Garrett and his sons. In the three weeks since school began, she'd seen him nearly every day when he came for the boys, and again at church on Sundays. He seemed to be seeking her out, asking her opinion about the boys and the ranch, sitting beside her at church. Keeping her distance was proving difficult indeed.

This is not a date, she reminded herself. Garrett had convinced her that he needed an old friend to help him get reacquainted, and what better place to start than a Friday night, hometown football game?

"Half the town must be here," Garrett said over his shoulder as he slid several bills beneath the ticket window.

"More than that. No able-bodied citizen of Hazelwood misses the first football game, especially when we play our rival, the Tateville Tigers." Amy followed Cody and Caleb, who'd made a beeline for a table where the cheerleaders were selling pom-poms, Warrior buttons, and T-shirts. "I think these two are about to cost you some serious money."

Garrett groaned in mock dismay as two sets of blue eyes questioned him. "Choose one thing, guys."

"Can we still have popcorn, too?" Cody asked, choosing a T-shirt.

"Popcorn?" Garrett sniffed the air. "Is that what that awful stink is?" Cody giggled and poked him. Garrett hooked an elbow around the boy's neck and gave a gentle shake. "Sure, popcorn and pop later. Right now, we better find a seat before they're all taken."

After he paid for the T-shirts and Amy purchased three pom-poms, they threaded their way across the grass toward the bleachers, stopping frequently when they met an old classmate so that Amy could reintroduce Garrett and his sons.

Amy and the Collins men had barely reached their seats when the public address system asked everyone to stand for the national anthem. Football players in each end zone paused with helmets at their sides, and cheerleaders stood at midfield with hands over their hearts. Amy felt the familiar lump in her throat as the band

and all of Hazelwood saluted the rippling flag.

A loud cheer exploded when the football team took the field. Along with Cody and Caleb, Amy waved her pom-pom, then squeezed into a spot beside Garrett. The place was crowded and his warm side pressed tightly against hers, a pleasant sensation that she tried to ignore.

"Dad, can we have popcorn yet?"

Garrett rolled his eyes and laughed. "Later, boys. At least wait until kickoff."

Cody squirmed and wiggled on the wooden bench. "I gotta go to the bathroom."

Garrett looked at Amy, and they both laughed. "Mr. Collins, you have no choice," Amy said. "You will not get to watch this kickoff. At least not from the bleachers."

With a good-natured attitude, Garrett took both boys and headed for the restrooms. He'd no sooner gotten to the bottom steps than Amy's friend, Trish, scooted in beside her.

"Hey, girl," she elbowed Amy gently, "I'm glad to see you out with that new cowboy. He's so nice." Trish wiggled her eyebrows. "And he looks good, too."

"Trish, this is not a date." She repeated the speech she'd given herself ten times since Garrett had invited her to the game. "Garrett and I go way back to seventh grade. I'm simply helping an old friend get reacquainted."

"Oh, sure. I suppose that's also the reason he's been sitting beside you at church."

"Exactly. Because I'm familiar. After all, I am Cody's teacher. Naturally, the child wants to sit by me."

"Mmm-hmm. So his daddy has to sit there, too?" Trish sounded unconvinced. She paused long enough in her probing to leap up and yell, "Face mask," then she started in again. "He likes you, Amy, and he's a Christian, too. Why not go with it?"

"You know why." Amy tried to focus on the game, but she saw Garrett and the boys returning. Her heart leaped in spite of her resolve. "Hush, now. Here they come." Quickly, she changed the subject. "Where are Paul and Kevin tonight?"

Trish made a face. "Two other officers called in sick. Paul had to work. Kevin's getting the sniffles, so I left him with Mom."

Amy sympathized. An avid Warriors' fan, Paul had played football for Hazelwood in his younger days. Kevin, Trish's three-year-old, was a chip off the old block.

"Miss Rogers, we brung you some popcorn." Cody's eyes were worshipful as he handed the treat to Amy.

"Why, thank you, Cody." Amy took the warm bag and made room for the trio to squeeze in.

"Anything exciting happen while we were gone?"

"Number eighty-eight, the tight end, caught a long pass over the middle for thirty-five yards. They have a good drive going."

"Say, you really know the game." Garrett sipped his Coke.

"My brothers played, and I was a pom-pom girl." She shook her pom-pom for emphasis.

"Bet you looked pretty cute out there." Garrett

turned toward her and his warm breath brushed her cheek. For a moment their eyes held, and sweet electricity flowed between them, too strong to ignore.

To Amy's relief, a roar went up as the Warriors scored a touchdown, distracting them both. She leaped up, heart still thudding with misgivings, and yelled at the top of her lungs.

With all her might, she concentrated on the game, but Garrett's nearness proved a constant distraction. In quiet tones, he explained the game to the boys and teased Amy and Trish about their exuberant cheering.

By the third quarter, the temperature began to drop sharply and Amy shivered.

"Cold?" Garrett turned to her with a concerned frown.

"I should have known to bring more than this sweatshirt."

"Here," Garrett began to remove his coat, "take my jacket."

Amy drew back. "No." The thought of snuggling into Garrett's jacket was too intimate, too intimidating. "You'll need it yourself."

He chuckled softly and went right on removing the jacket. "I spent fourteen years in Wyoming. This is swimsuit weather to me."

Without waiting for her consent, he settled the coat around Amy's shoulders, then casually took her hand, tucked it into the warm hollow between his arm and side, and held it there.

The sensation proved just as potent as she'd feared.

The jacket was warm with Garrett's body heat and redolent with his masculine scent. His hand over hers felt solid and strong and comforting. She didn't know whether to laugh or cry, but the fear inside would not let her give in to the pleasure.

At the game's end, the foursome headed toward the crowded exit. "I gotta go, Dad." Cody hung on to Garrett's hand and hopped up and down.

"Again?" Caleb looked at his sibling with brotherly disgust.

"Too much pop." Garrett raised apologetic eyes to Amy and gave her a crooked grin. "You'll excuse us? Again?"

"Sure." She ruffled Cody's hair. "I see my ornery brother over by the concession anyway. I'll go say hello."

Garrett and the boys moved off as Amy threaded her way through the crowd where the oldest of her three brothers stood.

"Hey, Sis," Trent greeted. "Great game, huh?"

"You only say that when we win." She glanced around. "Where are Liz and the kids?"

Trent shoved his hands into the ancient high school letter jacket he reserved just for home football games. "Had to make one last stop."

"Must be an epidemic."

At his puzzled look she explained, "Garrett Collins and his sons are here. They had to stop, too."

"Yeah, I saw you sitting up there with them. Nice guy. I don't mind one bit that he's taking out my favorite sister."

"I'm your only sister, knucklehead," she said affectionately. "And I am not 'going out' with Garrett."

"Why not?" Trent's terse expression said he knew the answer, but wanted to argue the point as he always had.

Amy swallowed a lump in her throat. "Trent," she warned.

"Are you going to stick with that ridiculous notion forever?"

"I have to, Trent. No healthy, normal man would knowingly date a woman who can't have kids."

"Not every guy is as shallow as Jeffrey."

Amy winced. She hadn't been in love with Jeffrey, but his cruel words still pierced her, still clung to her, a reminder of what she'd lost. A reminder of what she could never bring to a relationship.

"Any man deserves children." *Especially a man like Garrett. He should have a dozen just like himself.*

"Why don't you tell him? Give him a chance to make up his own mind."

"No. Absolutely not." The very notion struck terror in Amy's heart. "I'd rather have him for a friend than. . ."

She broke off as Garrett and Cody and Caleb came toward her, laughing together over something. The sight set her insides to trembling.

"Miss Rogers! Miss Rogers!" The two boys broke away from Garrett and ran to Amy as though they hadn't seen her in years. When they reached her side, Cody threw himself against her in a giant hug, while Caleb held back, shyly watching.

Amy reached out and pulled the older boy against

her side. "My goodness, what was that all about?"

"Dad says you might start coming to our house every day to help us with our schoolwork."

Garrett and Trent exchanged greetings while Amy considered.

The boys' grades were woefully low, and, though Garrett had given her time to inquire, none of the other teachers were inclined to take on a long-term tutoring job. Before the football game, he'd asked her once again to tutor the boys. She couldn't put off her decision any longer. They needed help now.

For the past year she'd floundered, not really knowing where her life was headed now that cancer had stolen her dreams of home and family. She still didn't know, but one thing was certain. The gentle nudging of her spirit to help these boys had never waned. Selfishly drawing away from these needy children, just because she feared being hurt again, was wrong.

Pulse jumping in trepidation, she spoke before she could change her mind. "That's right, boys. Starting Monday, the three of us are going to hit the books." Over the boys' heads, she caught Garrett's grateful expression.

"All right!" Cody pumped his fist in the air and danced in a circle.

Less enthusiastic, Caleb drew back and studied Amy's face. "You gonna make us read?"

"Every day. But don't worry. We'll find some things you like to read and concentrate on those."

"I like horses."

"Then we'll study horses."

Liz returned just then with three youngsters in tow. After a round of greetings, Amy's brother and his family started to leave. Trent pulled Amy into a uncharacteristic hug. When he whispered in her ear, she knew why he had.

"This guy is definitely not Jeffrey Bartlett, Sis. Better grab him before some other smart lady does."

Then he sauntered off, his healthy, happy family at his side, and left her fighting the urge to hope.

Chapter 4

The season cooled, the leaves changed, and with them came a change in Amy's routine. The hour of after-school study soon became an entire evening spent in the company of the Collins trio.

True to his word, Garrett was a good cook, though often his ranch work kept him out until dark. On those days, Amy, reluctant to leave the boys alone, prepared the meal. When Garrett arrived, he made no effort to hide his delight in her company. His interest soothed her wounded sense of self, but her conscience ached because she hadn't told him about her past.

One particularly glorious autumn afternoon as Amy and her students arrived at the old ranch house, Garrett was waiting on the porch. Happy welcome written all over him, he held the reins to a quartet of saddled horses. Beside him, Biscuit, the big, hairy, mongrel, thumped his tail so fast Amy laughed. As much as she fought the feeling, she loved coming here.

Cody and Caleb barreled out of the car at warp speed. They'd changed so much since coming to live with Garrett. The painful reserve was disappearing as they wholeheartedly accepted their foster dad. Amy felt especially proud that they were slowly gaining some of the academic skills they lacked. More than once she worried about what would happen to the brothers if the social system moved them elsewhere.

"Hey, guys." Garrett grinned and hunkered down as two human bullets launched themselves at him. Between the boys and the dog, he was almost flattened. "Ready to study?" He winked over their heads at Amy. "Teacher, did you bring plenty of math for these two? Gotta keep 'em busy."

Cody squeezed Garrett's neck in a death grip, shouting. "What about these horses?"

"Horses? What horses?" Garrett glanced around with mock innocence as the boys leaped and danced in excitement. Biscuit added a couple of happy barks for good measure.

"Those horses right there." Cody pointed emphatically. "Please, please, please. Can we ride first and study later?"

"Hmm." Garrett rubbed his chin. "I don't know. . . What do you think, Miss Rogers? Have these two hombres earned a ride?"

Amy smiled. "We won't get many days like this."

"All right, then. We'll ride. Everything else can wait until we get back."

Caleb's expression went from joy to worry. "Will we have to do chores in the dark?" When he'd first come to the ranch, Caleb had suffered with terrible nightmares.

Gradually, the dreams diminished, but the fear of darkness lingered so much that Garrett left a light on in the bathroom every night.

Garrett hooked an elbow around the boy's neck. "Remember that psalm we've been learning?"

Caleb nodded solemnly. "I don't have to be afraid of the terrors at night because God sends His angels to watch over me," he paraphrased.

"Right. You just keep saying that to yourself."

Caleb still looked worried, so Garrett went on. "But we'll head back before dark, anyway. Okay?"

"All right!" Both boys thundered into the house to change.

"A ride sounds great." With a smile, Amy looked down at her blue straight skirt and white blouse. "But I'd better change, too."

As soon as Amy had realized she would be at the Collins ranch longer than an hour or so each day, she'd started bringing a change of casual clothes. The decision had paid off more than once when Garrett had taken the three of them fishing or walking or had drawn them out to the barn to see a new colt.

In minutes she was changed. The boys each grabbed an apple, and soon they were riding toward open pasture. Amy loved to ride and marveled at how quickly Cody and Caleb had learned the skill. Four abreast, they rode while Cody chattered about his day. When he finally wound down, Caleb had his turn.

"Toby tried to fight me," Caleb said in his solemn voice.

The comment drew a sidelong glance from Garrett. "Toby Matthews again, huh?"

"Yeah. He said I must be no good 'cause my mom didn't want me anymore. I think he got mad 'cause I intercepted his pass."

Compassion rose in Amy's chest like a heat wave. Kids could be so cruel. She waited, praying silently for Garrett to find the right words.

In his quiet way Garrett asked, "What did you do, Son?"

Amy blessed him for intentionally adding "Son" to his question. Garrett sensed how badly Caleb needed to belong.

The little boy sat up straight in the saddle, tension in his posture. "I wanted to knock his lights out, but I remembered what you said about praying before I do something that might cause trouble." Caleb exhaled loudly. "So I prayed not to break his face."

To hide her smile, Amy glanced away, toward the fiery autumn woods. A flock of blackbirds chattered in the treetops.

"Words hurt sometimes, Son. They hurt bad. A man who can control his tongue is a real man, a man after God's own heart."

"Yeah, I remembered that, too. So I tossed him the football and told him I was just lucky to catch such a great pass. He looked kind of funny. Then someone hollered 'throw the ball,' and we all started playing again."

"I'm proud of you, Son." Garrett maneuvered his horse next to Caleb's. "Toby was wrong, and you proved him wrong with your reaction. Do you realize that?" Garrett reached out and clasped the boy's shoulder. "You showed a lot of wisdom. I think that calls for added privileges, don't you?"

"The colt?" Caleb asked hopefully.

Amy knew he longed for the leggy new stallion and spent every spare minute grooming and petting the animal.

Garrett held out a hand, took the boy's, and shook it like a man. "He's yours, providing you take over all his care. We'll even put your name on his registration papers."

"You mean it?" Caleb glowed with happiness, the usually solemn face wreathed in light. The pain of childish taunts was lost in the wonder of this coveted prize.

Tears welled in Amy's eyes. What an incredible father Garrett was.

"Hey, look," Cody shouted, pointing at two rabbits Biscuit had flushed from a pile of brush. "Can we chase 'em?"

The rabbits were far ahead, and though the boys had no chance to actually catch them, Garrett gave his permission to ride as far as the pond. The pair galloped away in a flurry of thudding hooves and happy whoops.

"That was a fine thing you did, Garrett." The saddle creaked as Amy twisted toward him. "He'll never forget this lesson."

Garrett rested the reins on the saddle horn and let the gelding amble lazily along. "These boys have a long row to hoe. There are no easy answers to what they're going through." He gave her his crooked smile. "I pray a lot about saying the right thing."

"Giving him the horse was brilliant."

"Ah, I've been planning to do that for awhile. Just waiting for a time like this so he could feel he'd earned it."

"If they follow your lead, they'll grow up to be good men."

Garrett's eyes twinkled. "I'll take that as a compliment." He drew the gelding alongside Amy's mare. "Teacher, did anybody ever tell you that you have the prettiest green eyes west of the Mississippi? Bet one of these days you'll want a whole passel of little girls with eyes that color."

Amy's emotions, so high only a moment before, plunged to the depths at the painful reminder. What could she say? How could she respond without giving away her secret?

Tell him, her conscience urged. *Now is the perfect opportunity.*

Amy swallowed hard and forced a noncommittal smile. She couldn't. Not now. Not ever. Garrett wanted kids of his own. Wasn't that what he was hinting at?

As soon as Cody and Caleb were on grade level in their studies, she'd stop this nonsense. She wouldn't come here anymore. Her life had been fine before Garrett Collins came along and made her wish for what could never be.

Later, at the house, after Garrett "rustled up some grub" and the boys completed their lessons, Cody and Caleb headed for the barn to check on the colt.

"I'll let you pet him if you're real gentle and quiet like Dad says. Otherwise, an animal won't bond to you," Amy heard Caleb say right before the door banged shut. She looked up and caught the smile on Garrett's face. White shirtsleeves rolled up, he was elbow-deep in dishwater.

"I guess I should be going," she said, gathering up her teacher's manuals and the mountain of storybooks she'd brought.

Garrett rinsed his hands and grabbed a towel. "Why don't you stay awhile? There's a good movie on at eight." He came around the bar from the kitchen into the dining room. "You know I make the finest microwave popcorn in the universe."

At Amy's tentative smile, he tossed the towel on the counter and took her hand. "You've been awful quiet all evening. Something wrong?"

"No." She gently extracted her hand.

"Is it something I said? Something I did?" Both hands went up in surrender. "Hey, tell me, and I'll punish myself by eating yogurt instead of popcorn."

That made her smile. "You don't even own any yogurt."

"I'll get some. An entire gallon."

"Garrett, I'm fine, really." To avoid his concerned gaze, Amy fiddled with the wire spirals on a notebook. "Maybe a little tired."

"Is this getting to be too much to ask of you? The tutoring, I mean?"

"No, of course not. Helping Cody and Caleb succeed

is a thrill for me. I love working with them."

"And we love having you here, Amy." His tone grew soft and he stepped near, lifting her lowered chin.

A mix of fear and happiness skittered through her. Garrett held her gaze, telegraphing some unspoken emotion with his velvet eyes. He moved toward her, slowly, cautiously, in the way he'd approach a skittish horse. His strong, cowboy hands cupped the sides of her face so tenderly, she thought she would melt. She knew he wanted to kiss her, and she also knew she'd let him.

His warm breath brushed her face just before his lips grazed hers in the sweetest kiss imaginable. She'd never allowed herself to wonder what kissing him would be like, but the experience was earth-shattering.

The front door banged open and the two adults sprang apart as a wailing Cody rushed into the room, blood dripping from his nose. Caleb followed, his solemn face wreathed in worry.

Concerned for the child and anxious to hide her blushing cheeks, Amy grabbed for the table napkins and rushed to Cody's aid. She pressed the napkins to his nose with one hand while the other stroked his back. Her quiet murmurs of reassurance calmed him, and he allowed himself to be guided into a kitchen chair. Amy drew a chair directly in front of him and sat down.

"I'll get a washcloth." Garrett disappeared, returning with the promised cloth and a wad of paper towels. Kneeling beside Amy, Garrett did his part to comfort the injured child.

In minutes, the emergency was over, the bleeding stopped, and the story told of Cody's fall onto a rock outside the barn.

"No harm done, little man." Garrett rose and began cleaning up the mess. "But you sure could use a bath."

The teary-eyed child looked down at his shirt, his mouth quivering. He looked from Garrett, now in the kitchen, to Amy still sitting in the chair. In the next instant, he dove into Amy's lap and cuddled against her for comfort. A lump the size of Texas rose in her chest as she cradled the little boy.

"I wish you could be my mama," he whispered. Amy thought she would die.

Garrett whirled from disposing of the bloody napkins. Both adults stared at the small child as the air in the room ached with his poignant request.

Amy brushed her lips against Cody's forehead. "You're a very special boy, Cody. Someday you'll have the best mom in the whole world."

Fighting the urge to cry, Amy gathered him into her arms and stood. "Now, let's get you into that tub before this blood dries on your shirt."

"I'll take him." Garrett's voice was deep with emotion as he transferred Cody into his arms.

"I'm okay now." Cody sniffed loudly and swatted at the tears. "I can walk."

Carrying you up is no problem, Son." Garrett gazed down at the boy's dirty face.

"I'm too big to be carried."

"Sure?" No one reminded him that he hadn't been

too big to cuddle.

"Yeah." Cody wiggled to the floor, then batted damp blue eyes. "Can I have some ice cream after my bath?"

"I guess so." Garrett ran a hand through his hair and let out a soft chuckle. "You sure know how to work the system, don't you, little man?"

Cody gave a puzzled, lopsided grin and headed for the bathroom.

"Well," Amy said, gathering her things again, "now that's over, I really do need to go."

Not yet ready to deal with Garrett's kiss, she hurried out the door. Garrett followed close on her heels.

"Amy." He grasped her arm. "Wait."

"It's late."

The glow of light from the front window dimly lit the porch. A slight breeze stirred, and the chilly air raised goosebumps on Amy's arms. She paused, clutching the books against her chest.

Garrett released her stiff arm. "How did you feel when Cody said that? About wishing you were his mama."

Lord, help me. I don't know what to do anymore.

"I suppose a child naturally wants a mother."

"Yeah." Staring out into the night, Garrett leaned against the porch rail, one boot propped on the lower rung. "I'm doing the best I can, but they need a mama."

Far away, a coyote howled, and the last tree frogs of the season filled the night with their pulsating song. Amy pulsed, too, with the need to share her awful secret, and the fear that doing so would ruin a special friendship.

"Garrett," she half turned, saw his uncertainty as he stared into the darkness, and pushed back her own worries. "You're doing an incredible job. Those two little boys are so blessed to have you in their lives."

"And they bless me in return."

"You're a natural father."

"I hope so, because that's my dream. To fill this ranch with kids and be the kind of father I never had."

Now was her chance to close this subject for good. She took a deep breath. "Not me. Teaching school gives me all the children I need."

Garrett's boot thudded on the wooden porch as he pivoted toward her. "You don't want a family of your own?"

Swallowing the horrible ache that rose every time she visualized her empty future, Amy answered, "Absolutely not. My students are enough."

After the terrible truth of her barrenness had finally sunk in, she'd made that promise to herself. Loving her students, giving them her very best, would have to do. Involvement meant pain and rejection, and she could not survive that again.

"You're so great with the boys, I thought. . ." He lifted a hand, let it drop. "So, you *never* want to have kids?"

"Never." She almost choked on the word. Want them? She'd die for a child of her own. "I have plenty of children vying for my attention. Why would I want more?"

Even in the semidarkness, Amy saw—felt Garrett's

bewilderment. She knew how she sounded. Cold. Self-ish. The knowledge tore at her conscience.

"I see," he said, though he clearly did not. "Uh, well, I'll see you tomorrow, then?"

"Sure. Same time. Same station," she replied with false brightness.

Once in the dark confines of the car, she relived Garrett's tender kiss and Cody's poignant request. Then, she cried for all that could never be.

Chapter 5

Guilt gnawed at Amy every time she visited the Collins ranch. Garrett behaved as though nothing had changed, but she knew very well he must think her cold and heartless. Why wouldn't he? Any normal woman wanted children, didn't she?

By Sunday, she was more than ready for an uninterrupted talk with the Lord. Arriving early, she sat in her usual spot and closed her eyes in prayer, letting the reverent atmosphere settle over her. If ever she needed reassurance from God, now was the time. He'd been with her through her illness, through all the pain and questioning. He'd be with her now.

Amy saw her family members scattered around the building as the sanctuary filled rapidly. With gratitude, she thought of how they had all been together in this church for as long as she could remember. The powerful bond of family—Garrett had never had that. Now family was what he wanted most in the world, and Amy prayed that God would give him his heart's desire.

When the pianist began to play the invocation, Amy was surprised to find the Collins family absent. Garrett and the boys never missed church. A wave of apprehension swept through her. Was something wrong?

"Please stand while we ask the Lord's blessing on our service," the pastor intoned from the pulpit. "Join hands with your neighbor as we lift our hearts in prayer."

Amy rose automatically, still wondering at the empty places beside her. She'd barely closed her eyes, praying that all was well at the Collins ranch, when the three slipped quietly in beside her. Relief so strong, her knees shook, swept over her. They were fine—all polished and clean for Sunday service.

A warm, callused hand closed around hers, squeezing gently. Looking up into serene brown eyes, Amy was lost. Suddenly, with great clarity, she knew what she'd been fighting all along. She was in love with Garrett Collins. In the short time that she'd known them, he and his foster sons had become like family. The ache of love inside her for these three cowboys was almost more than she could bear.

I don't understand, Lord. Why is this happening now?

Throughout the service she grappled with the new revelation. For her own sake and peace of mind, she needed to stop seeing so much of the Collins men— but how could she walk away from tutoring those boys? Such selfish behavior certainly would not be pleasing to God. Would it?

Though the choir sang and the preacher preached, she absorbed very little of the message. By the close of the service, she'd come to a decision. The Lord had put those children in her life for a purpose, and she would continue the tutoring as long as necessary. She didn't need the Lord to tell her to put some distance between herself and Garrett. God wouldn't want her to be hurt again.

Gripping the pew in front of her, she tried to ignore the pleasant scent of soap and starch emanating from the trio beside her. She tried to ignore the rich timber of Garrett's voice lifted in song and the high, sweet sounds of Cody and Caleb. Most of all, she tried to ignore the thudding certainty that keeping Garrett at arm's length would not be an easy task.

Her concerns proved valid when, at the end of the service, Cody and Caleb bombarded her with stories of the new colt that had been born that morning.

"That's why we were late. Dad and us had to help the mare 'cause she's a first-timer." Caleb's eyes glowed with excitement. Nothing transformed his serious demeanor like a new colt.

"Yeah, and I got to rub him down with hay," Cody interrupted. "You should see him, Miss Rogers. He's kinda reddish with four black stockings and a little splat on his forehead. A chestnut stallion, that's what he is." He looked to Garrett for confirmation.

Amy smiled at how much of Garrett had been imprinted on his foster sons.

"Are you coming out to see him today?" Cody went on. "You're gonna love him, I know."

Everything in her wanted to say yes. As she fought

the urge, her former Sunday school teacher, Mildred Pearson, came by and patted Amy's arm with the crook of her cane.

"Mrs. Pearson." Thankful for the reprieve, Amy hugged the octogenarian warmly. "How's that bad knee?"

"Wore plum out." Mildred snorted in disgust. "But so's the rest of me, and I'm still getting around. Corky, though, he's a different story. He's not up to snuff."

Amy frowned in concern. Corky was Mildred's cocker spaniel. The old woman doted on the animal, and in return the dog provided adoring companionship to the lonely widow. If anything happened to that dog, Mildred would grieve terribly.

"He's not sick, is he?"

"I think he's got the ear canker. Digging and whining at his little ears 'til he nearly breaks my heart." She thumped her chest; a lavender handkerchief flapped between her fingers. "And with a ticker as old as mine, I can't have that."

Affectionately squeezing the woman's stooped shoulders, Amy smiled. "Why don't I come by before school tomorrow and take him in to Dr. Kohler?"

The offer was nothing unusual. She'd taxied Mildred and her dog to town a number of times. Now, she strongly suspected that was the reason Mildred had stopped to talk.

"Would you do that, child? Sure would relieve my mind."

"Of course, I will. Then, after school, I'll stop at the vet's and bring him home." She glanced down at the boys who stood at Garrett's side, gazing curiously at the old lady. "Is that okay with you two? Corky's a friendly little fellow. You'll like him."

"I don't see a problem with that," Garrett answered when the boys looked to him for approval.

Mildred pointed her cane at Cody and Caleb. "And just who are these handsome swains following you around?"

Amy made the introductions and felt proud when the pair followed Garrett's lead, politely saying hello.

Mildred nodded sagely. "Saw you sitting over there with our Amy." She shook her hankie in Garrett's direction. "She's quite a prize, young man. Treat her right, or you'll answer to me."

Amy felt the flush of embarrassment rise above the collar of her yellow silk blouse. When she gathered the courage to look at Garrett, his eyes twinkled merrily.

"Yes, ma'am," he told the older woman. "She has too many brothers to do otherwise."

Mildred cackled. "Right smart young fella you got here, Amy." Then she tapped Garrett's shoulder with the crook of her cane. "You'll do," she said. "You'll do fine."

After Mildred shuffled off toward the waiting church van, Garrett said, "You heard the lady. Gotta treat you right, or she'll be after me with that cane. So, for starters, how does Sunday dinner at the steak house sound?"

Amy's heart soared, then plummeted. Dinner with these three sounded heavenly. But hadn't she spent the past hour asking God to take this love away? And wouldn't it be unfair to encourage Garrett's attentions any further?

Finding no easy way to refuse, she simply said, "I don't think that's a good idea."

"Aren't you hungry?" Garrett rubbed his palms together. "After delivering the colt, we didn't have time for much breakfast. We're starved, aren't we, men?"

The boys heartily agreed.

"I'm really not hungry at all." She told the truth. Her appetite had completely disappeared. "Thank you for asking, but I'll just head home and grab a bite later. I have so much to do on Sunday afternoon before the workweek starts."

Frowning, Garrett studied her face. "Well, okay," he said hesitantly, "if you're certain."

"They gots ice cream," Cody coaxed, edging toward her. "With sprinkles."

How could she ever completely distance herself without hurting these precious boys?

Bending low, she hugged Cody. "I really can't this time, sweetheart. But you have an extra bowl of vanilla with gummy bears just for me. Okay?"

"Okay," he answered doubtfully, his blue eyes as puzzled as Garrett's dark ones. He clearly sensed that something was amiss. "You're still coming to see the colt, aren't you?"

"Tomorrow after school. Like always." She knew of no honorable way to stop the tutoring. *Those little boys are more important than my fears,* she thought with a sigh, as the Collins males moved toward the door. She watched them go, the lump in her throat the size of a boulder.

Lost in thought, she didn't hear Trish and her family approach. "It's not every day a man offers you a free meal," Paul joked. "Can't believe you'd turn that down."

At Amy's questioning look, Trish shrugged. "Sorry, honey. We overheard."

"Nosey," she said with more humor than she felt.

"What do you expect? I'm your best friend. Interfering in your business is my job. Now," she crossed her arms over her Bible, "I thought you two were getting pretty close. What happened?"

"I'd rather not talk about it, Trish."

Silver earrings swaying, Trish tilted her head and studied Amy for a long moment. Then she turned to Paul. "Honey, would you please take Kevin on to the car? I need to chew on Amy for a minute."

"No problemo." Paul grinned his understanding, then hefted the three-year-old onto his shoulders and walked away.

Trish gripped Amy's arm and pulled her toward a small alcove in the oversized foyer. "All right, girlfriend," she said when they were out of earshot, "tell me what's going on."

Trish would never stop until she had the entire story. With a weary sigh, Amy admitted, "I love him, Trish."

"Well, hallelujah. It's about time." An ecstatic Trish flung her arms around Amy. "Honey, I'm so happy for you. Garrett's such a great guy, and those adorable kids. . ."

"Wait, Trish. No." Amy pulled away, tears brimming. "I can't let this happen. It wouldn't be fair."

Trish froze. "To whom?"

Exasperated, Amy pressed a finger against each eyelid, willing the tears away. "Garrett, of course. He wants kids."

"He has kids."

"You know what I mean. What I haven't told him about. . ."

Arms wide, palms raised, Trish interrupted, "Then tell him. Now. Today."

"And have him pity me? Have him feel guilty about not wanting to see me anymore?" Amy shook her head. "I won't put him—or me—through that."

"What if he doesn't feel that way?"

Amy closed her eyes and sighed. Would no one ever understand? God had allowed the endometrial cancer that stole her uterus. Wasn't that proof enough that His plans for her did not include marriage and children?

"That incredible man deserves the world. The most important thing in life to him is family, and there is no possibility of my giving him even one child. I don't believe God would cheat him out of that."

"Oh?" Trish's eyes snapped in indignation. "So now you're speaking for God?"

"Trish!" First Trent and now Trish. Even Amy's mother and dad hinted at all the positive stories they'd heard about the new cowboy that bought the old Tucker place. What was wrong with all of them? They were among the few people who knew the devastating results of her battle with cancer.

"Have you prayed about this?" Trish demanded.

"Of course I have." Since the moment Garrett had come back into her life, she'd prayed constantly for God to remove the powerful emotions Garrett stirred in her. "How can you even ask me that?"

"Because I want to see you happy."

"Lots of women remain single and are perfectly happy."

"But you're not." Trish grasped Amy's shoulders and gave a quick shake. "Is that the eleventh commandment now? Amy shall not marry?"

Tears clogged Amy's throat. "I can't believe you're doing this. You're supposed to be my best friend."

"I am your best friend. That's why I can talk to you this way. Ever since high school our dreams have been the same. We'd be teachers. Then, we'd meet our knights in shining armor, get married, and raise our kids in this wonderful little town where everyone else sticks their nose into your business because they care." Pixie face wreathed in compassion, Trish went on, "Don't you see, honey? I'm trying to help."

"Well, you're not." Amy swiped at a tear. "You're making matters worse."

With a resigned sigh, Trish stepped back. "All right. If you truly believe you're doing the right thing, I'll shut my sassy mouth." She poked a finger at Amy's nose. "But you better make sure; you make very, very sure that this is God talking and not your own fears."

Chapter 6

For days, Trish's words haunted Amy. To make matters worse, Garrett continued to behave as though they were a couple. More times than not, Amy found herself accepting his invitations. After each "date" she'd sternly vow to stay away, and her resolve worked fine—until she saw him again.

Part of her believed continuing the relationship was sinfully dishonest. The other part of her, knowing their time couldn't last, grabbed for every precious moment.

In late October, with a damp wind blowing from the north and geese winging across blue-gray skies, the annual fall carnival kept her too busy to worry about much of anything.

On the morning prior to the Saturday night event, the old gymnasium was transformed into a carnival midway. While the women decorated with colored paper and crayon drawings of autumn, the men built temporary wooden booths along the sides of the gym floor. Her brothers were there. So was Garrett.

Across the tarp-covered floor, Amy struggled to keep

her gaze off him. He was on his haunches, blue jeans stretched taut, tapered western shirt pulling tight as his shoulders flexed repeatedly to the rhythm of a hammer. Positioning a two-by-four for nailing, he turned, caught her eye, and waved.

A warm glow suffused her. Garrett had a way of making her feel so special.

He'd gained quick acceptance in the little town, and the reason was clear. He'd thrown himself wholeheartedly into the community, volunteering for the carnival, the homecoming cleanup committee, and had even provided a place on his ranch for the church's hayride and wiener roast.

Amy wagged her fingers in his direction, then returned to her job of setting up the cakewalk in the far corner of the gym. Two sixth graders willingly brought in a long table to hold the cakes. With the help of Cody, Caleb, and two of their friends, Amy carried student chairs from the classroom and arranged them in a circle. Now she taped her students' carefully colored artwork to the block walls.

"Hey, Miss Rogers, can you get us more red butcher paper?"

Amy glanced over her shoulder at the speaker, one of the high school cheerleaders. "School colors, huh?"

"Gotta have that Warrior spirit." The perky blond pursed her lips. "How do you think we'll do with the face painting?"

"Great. Marla is a terrific artist." Amy plastered another picture onto the wall, then led the way toward the storeroom, digging into her jeans pocket for the keys. "And every elementary student wants a cartoon on his cheek."

"I hope so. We're saving money for cheer camp in Dallas next summer."

"Dallas, huh? Pretty cool."

"Yeah, and expensive, but the camp will be worth the price. One of the Cowboys' cheerleaders will be there." They went inside the musty-smelling room where rolls of colored paper and other supplies were stored. "And speaking of cowboys, Miss Rogers," the girl let out a long humming sound, "that Mr. Collins guy you've been seeing is so fine."

"Keri!" Amy hid a smile.

The girl laughed. "Well, he is. Nothing wrong with that. And he's so nice, too. Are ya'll a thing now?"

"A thing?" Amy walked a heavy roll out of the corner and gave her usual answer. "No, Keri, we are not a thing. He's just a good friend that I went to junior high with."

"Yeah? Too bad. He may be older, but he's still got it."

Amy laughed at the teenager. "Take this roll of paper and get busy. You must have too much time on your hands."

By seven o'clock the gym was alive with Hazelwood citizens, the scent of Indian tacos, and the muffled tunes of old-time rock and roll coming from the cakewalk. Youngsters roamed the midway, playing such games as ringtoss and dart throw, while the older crowd sat in the bleachers to observe and visit.

Amy manned the fishpond, a particularly popular game for the little ones. She'd seen Garrett and his boys come in, surreptitiously watched them buy a string of tickets, then became too busy to observe their progress around the midway. Now, they ambled across the floor in her direction.

"Here come some fishermen." She grinned at Cody, who thrust two tickets at her. His head sprouted plastic antenna tipped with wobbly eyes. "Even if this one is from outer space."

He returned her grin. "I made two goals at the basketball shoot, and they let me pick this." He behaved as though he'd won the greatest treasure possible.

She exchanged amused smiles with Garrett. Caleb stood quietly by, though he rolled his eyes at Cody's exuberance.

"How about you, Caleb? Any prizes."

"Yeah, I got a pencil and a kazoo." Sounding less than impressed, he pulled the items from his pocket.

"Here." Amy took the prizes and handed him a fishing pole. "See if you can catch a big one."

She indicated the wooden partition where pictures of fish swam on a blue paper cover. Behind the divider a high school student waited to "hook" a prize number onto the fishing line.

Caleb's pole jerked downward.

"Looks like you got a bite, boy. Reel 'er in."

The line popped over the partition. Amy took the paper, unfolded the square, and proclaimed. "A ten-pounder! The biggest yet." She waved her hand over the array of prizes. "Take your pick of anything on the table."

A laugh, strangely rusty-sounding, bubbled up from the usually serious child. Amy laughed with him, delighted to see him releasing some of his worries.

"May I have the football?" he asked, eyes alight.

Amy handed him the prize.

"I won this, Dad." Caleb radiated with pleasure.

"Sure did." Garrett patted his shoulder. "We'll have some fun with that."

"I want to fish. I want to fish." Cody grappled for a pole and Amy obliged. Though he only brought in a five-pounder, he was thrilled with the blow-up iguana he chose as a prize. He thrust the creature under his arm and said, "Can I get my face painted now? I've still got enough tickets."

Garrett lifted his hands in surrender and tilted his head toward the painting booth. The line of customers in front of Amy's booth prevented any further conversation, so Garrett and the boys waved and disappeared into the crowd.

During a lull in the fishing business, Amy's brother Trent appeared, carrying a soft drink. "Looks like you could use a little refresher."

"I could." Amy fanned her shirt. "Sure is warm in here."

"Yeah. Big crowd." Trent leaned an elbow on the prize table and sipped his own drink while Amy tended to a single customer. When the child skipped away with a furry key chain, Trent cleared his throat.

"You know, Sis, I spent all day working beside Garrett on these booths. He's a great guy."

"Yes, he is."

Her brother leaned close, lowering his voice. "Have you ever told him?"

Trent's blunt question surprised her. "No, of course not."

"Maybe you should reconsider." He studied her thoughtfully. "The guy likes you—a lot. Always bragging on how those boys love you and how much you've helped them. How well you treat the old folks at church. Even said you were a great cook. Once I asked him if we were talking about the same woman."

Amy swatted his arm, hoping an amused reaction would distract him.

"I'm serious, Sis. The guy's a keeper."

"Yes. For some other woman."

"Are you saying you don't have feelings for him?"

"I do, but he deserves more than I can give him."

"He's a good man, Amy. A godly man, for crying out loud. I think you owe him the truth." Someone across the way called Trent's name. He glanced over his shoulder, then back at his sister. "Gotta get back to the duck pond." He pointed a finger at her. "But you think about what I said."

Amy could think of little else. Directly across from the fishpond was the face-painting booth. Cody sat in a chair. Garrett and Caleb stood at his back. Marla Thomas, a nail artist who attended Amy's church, painted Cody's face, though her attention centered more on Garrett than her customer. Frequently, she beamed a hundred-watt smile in his direction. When the tiny image on Cody's cheek was completed, Marla placed her long nailed fingers on Garrett's arm and laughed flirtatiously.

When Garrett laughed, too, lowering his head to say something, Amy drew in a sharp breath and nearly squeezed a stuffed poodle in half. But as she watched them talk, cold reality set in. Marla was exactly the kind of woman Garrett deserved in his life. Keri had been right earlier when she'd said Garrett still "had it." If Amy would stop occupying so much of his time, he could have his choice of the single women in town.

A long hour later, the carnival ended and cleanup began. Amy stood out back, hefting bags of trash into the dumpster when footsteps crunched behind her. She turned to find Garrett coming toward her in the semidarkness.

"Need some help?" Without waiting for an answer, he moved to her side, grabbed a bag, and heaved it into the dumpster. "Terrific carnival. Those boys haven't enjoyed anything more since we moved here."

"You seemed to enjoy yourself pretty thoroughly, too." She hadn't meant the words to come out quite so sharply.

He paused, bewildered at her tone. "I did."

"What do you think of Marla?"

"Who?" He tossed in the last of the bags.

"The woman who painted Cody's cheek. She's

nice. Single, too. Maybe the two of you should go out sometime."

"Why would I want to do that?" Garrett clanged the dumpster lid shut, then turned, his arm brushing hers.

She stepped back. "I occupy too much of your time. You haven't had a chance to date."

"I don't want to date anyone else." In the streetlight, his soft gaze sought hers. Somewhere a car door slammed, and distant laughter drifted through the night, but the air around Amy and Garrett seemed oddly suspended, frozen somehow, with unspoken emotion.

"Amy," Garrett started, then stopped and reached out, pulling her into the circle of his arms. "There. That's better."

He glanced up at the trash dumpster with a wry smile. "This isn't exactly where I'd planned to do this, but. . ." Before she could stop him, his lips descended and he brushed hers once, very gently. "Now," he said, his breath warm against her mouth, "no more talk about me seeing the face-painting lady or the booster club president or Sherry down at the Hamburger Hangout. You've no need to be jealous. It's you I'm interested in." He tilted back so that his face aligned with hers. "I love you, Amy. From the moment I walked in your classroom, I knew you were the one." He paused. "I want you to be my wife."

"No! I can't." Her anguished answer clearly puzzled him.

"I don't understand." Expression searching, he

stroked her cheek with one hand. "I love you. I thought you felt the same."

Amy's head throbbed with the need to scream. The love of her life loved her too, and yet, she could not allow him to make a choice that would cost him his dreams. If she truly loved him, she'd hurt him now and put an end to their impossible relationship.

Hardening her heart, she forced the cruel words that would set him free. "Then you've made a terrible mistake, Garrett. I'm a career woman. I'm never going to marry anyone."

As her words soaked in, he slowly dropped his arms and stepped back. His stricken expression threatened to destroy her resolve. "You're a wonderful man. I'm just not the right woman for you. Please don't hate me."

Every nerve ending cried out to touch him, to explain, to give him the chance to reject or accept her as she was. A war waged within her. She could tell him. He was waiting for an explanation. She drew in a deep breath, the cool air searing her lungs. No, she didn't dare. He'd never understand. He'd be sorry for her, but his love would wither and die right before her eyes. Better to walk away, knowing she'd been loved by the best, than to walk away with only his pity.

"I don't think we should see each other anymore." The words were an icy stab of sorrow from her breaking heart to his.

"I. . .see." Garrett shoved his hands into his pockets and stared out over the empty parking lot. "What about Cody and Caleb? I can understand that you don't want to see me." He looked at her and shook his head. "That's not true. I don't understand anything right now. This will take some time." He sighed heavily. "But regardless of how you feel about me, I can't believe you'd hurt the boys. They've had so much upheaval in their lives already. They're so attached to you. You won't have to see me—I've plenty of ranch work to keep me away from the house."

Amy's stomach knotted. She'd devastated him, thrown his love back in his face, and yet, his concern was for Cody and Caleb.

"I won't abandon them." As hard as it would be, she'd continue the tutoring until the semester's end, and she would always be the boys' advocate at school.

"Good." His voice was quiet, resigned. "Well. Guess I'll get back inside. They're likely through helping Pastor Green take decorations off the walls." He turned to leave, then paused and looked back. "You'll be there Monday? For the boys, I mean?"

"Yes," she managed to choke out, "for the boys."

He stood there another fraction of a second, his hunched shoulders silhouetted by the streetlight. In a husky whisper, he said, "I could never hate you, Amy." Then he stepped into the darkness, taking her broken heart away with his own.

Chapter 7

The sky was as gray as Amy's mood when she and the boys pulled onto the Collins ranch. A sharp November wind cut across the valley and whipped the trees, scattering brown leaves across the front porch. Biscuit lay inside his doghouse, huddled into a tan fur ball.

"Brr." Amy glanced at the sky as she dug in her purse for the key and opened the door. "Looks like a cold front is moving in. I wish I'd brought a heavier coat."

Cody bent to scratch the groveling dog. Caleb tossed his books inside the door, then headed toward the barn. Amy knew where he was going. His first thought every afternoon centered on the colt Garrett had given him.

"Come right in after you check on Scout," she called after him. "You can do the feeding after we study."

She whisked Garrett's coffee cup off the table and into the sink, wiped the sturdy wooden tabletop with a cloth, and laid out the study materials. Cody clomped down the stairs from changing, grabbed a banana off the cabinet, and plunked down at the table. In minutes, a rosy-cheeked Caleb joined them, bringing with him the scent of hay and horses and all outdoors.

"You should see Scout, Miss Rogers," he said, blue eyes dancing, one side of his mouth stuffed with banana. "He's full of vinegar today. Jumping and bucking."

Full of vinegar. Hadn't she heard Garrett use those same words? She tamped back the tide of emotion, opened Caleb's English, book and pushed it toward him.

She'd kept her word by helping the boys with their studies, but that was all. No more races to the barn to pet the colts. No more creative peanut-butter-and-raisin sandwiches. No more video game challenges. She was their teacher, and nothing more.

"Are you mad at us?"

Amy's head snapped up. Two solemn faces peered at her. They'd asked this question several times in the past week, but apparently her negative reply had not been sufficient.

"No, I'm not angry. We just have a lot of work to do."

"Are you mad at Dad?"

"No."

"Why don't y'all talk anymore?" Caleb pushed the English book away and studied her. The awful wariness had returned. "Why don't you stay and watch movies? Why do you run off so fast when Dad comes home? What did we do wrong?"

"Yeah," Cody murmured, dropping the uneaten half of his banana onto the table. "Dad's real sad all the time."

These were the times she felt the worst. She'd let the relationship develop beyond friendship out of selfishness. Her ego had desperately needed the boost Garrett's attentions provided, and now these children had to suffer as a result.

Amy leaned her forehead against her hand and sighed wearily. For days, she'd done little else but pray. No mattered how much she begged for God to resolve the impossible situation, the heavens remained silent.

"Boys, you haven't done anything wrong. Neither has your dad." She pushed the English book back to Caleb. "Now, let's get busy so you'll have time to feed before dark."

The reminder proved enough to redirect Caleb, however reluctantly, to his schoolwork. But the heavy stilted air of anxiety remained, and the session did not go well. Caleb kept drawing horse heads on the margins of his paper, and Cody cried when he misspelled Wednesday.

Finally, when the regular homework was finished, Amy gave up. They were getting nothing out of this torture except frustration. She put the multiplication flash cards back in the box and said, "Why don't you two go ahead and do your chores. Maybe tomorrow will be a better day."

The pair dragged out their coats, slammed the door, and disappeared in a flash. Cold air rushed inside, snaking around Amy's feet and legs. She went to turn up the heater and fought the urge to start something warm and hearty cooking on the stove. Instead, she stuffed her books into a tote and waited for a chance to escape the homey comfort of Garrett's house.

"Miss Rogers, Miss Rogers!" The door burst open and a wide-eyed, breathless Cody flew inside at top speed. "Dancing Lady got out. We can't find her."

Dancing Lady. The prized mare due to foal any day. Amy rushed outside. To the north, a line of dark blue clouds hovered on the horizon. In minutes, night would fall and with it the temperature. Dancing Lady was far too valuable, and too old, to give birth out in the open during a cold snap.

"Where's Caleb?" She'd no more than asked the question than the frightened boy barreled around the barn toward her.

"It's all my fault," he cried, panic contorting his face.

Amy caught him by the shoulders. "Whoa there, bud. What are you talking about?"

"Dancing Lady. I looked in on her after school when I came out to see Scout. I wanted to make sure she was okay." Breath coming in great gasps, he hung his head. "I must have left her stall open."

"We'll find her," Amy said with more confidence than she felt, her gaze scanning the near fields. Animals had an uncanny knack of hiding themselves during the birthing process. "Do you have any idea which part of the ranch your dad is working on today? I'll need his help."

Caleb's voice trembled as he fought tears. "He mentioned a washed-out place. Maybe on the north fence, but I'm not sure."

"I'll start there." She ran to the car. "You two stay put in case Dancing Lady comes home. If your dad gets back before I do, tell him I started searching on the north side."

Garrett was, indeed, working on the north fence. When he saw Amy's car bouncing down the rough access road, he tossed his fencing tools into the truck bed and jogged toward her, brows knit together in worry.

"The boys are fine," she called, knowing they were his foremost concern. He sighed with relief and leaned into her lowered window, his handsome face only inches from hers.

"What's up?" The love in his eyes shone steady and strong, though the pain of rejection was there too.

Amy grieved, knowing she'd caused this fine man so much heartache. How little she'd given in return for his love. Quickly, before she did something to make matters worse, Amy apprised him of the situation with Dancing Lady.

"I have an idea where she may be." Garrett stepped away from the car, self-consciously adjusting the brim of his hat as he squinted into the wind. "I'll need your help, though. Will you drive my truck while I walk the mare home?"

Amy felt even worse. He hadn't wanted to ask for her help. "Of course I will. We can come back for my car later."

She turned off the car and followed him to his truck, questioning the decision as soon as she slammed inside. They hadn't been alone since the carnival, and the memory of that night was like an invisible presence between them.

Garrett cleared his throat and started the truck. "A couple of the other mares tried to hide in a little draw east of the creek. I figure Dancing Lady has the same idea."

With all her might, Amy concentrated on finding the mare. She stared out at the fields and woods, longing to help Garrett in this small way. To her relief, his prediction proved true, and within an hour they had the prized animal back in the barn.

"I appreciate this, Amy." Garrett swung the barn door shut and lowered the latch. "I know you'd rather not be here."

Amy shrugged, uncomfortable. There was no place on earth she'd rather be than with him, but he could never know that now.

"Let's check on the boys before we go for my car." The boys were always a safe subject. They fell in step, crunching softly over the blowing leaves to the house.

Cody met them in the yard, lips quivering, expression worried. "Is Caleb with you?"

"Caleb?" Apprehension shivered up Amy's spine. "Isn't he here?"

Tears filled Cody's eyes. "It was his fault that Dancing Lady got lost." He looked up at Garrett. "He said Dad would get mad and send us back to that group home, so he ran off."

Amy stuffed a fist against her lips to stifle the cry of dismay. She'd left them alone, and now Caleb was gone.

Garrett gripped Cody's shoulder. "Did he say where he was going?"

"No. He took off running that way." He pointed a finger toward the thick woods.

Garrett groaned, a sound echoed deep in Amy's soul. The temperature was dropping and the wind chill miserable. Caleb had already been out there awhile.

"Cody, bundle up. You can't stay here alone. Amy, I hate to impose. . ."

Amy bristled. Was that what he thought of her? That she was too cold and heartless to help find a frightened child? "Don't you dare consider this an imposition, Garrett Collins. I love him, too."

A ghost of a grin lifted Garrett's lips, but he sobered immediately. "Come on. We'll both need warmer clothes."

Shortly, they were bundled in Garrett's heavy outdoor clothing and headed across the pasture with flashlights, calling Caleb's name into the north wind. Thirty minutes passed with no sign of him.

"He must be so scared," Amy said, pausing beneath a stand of post oaks to catch her breath.

"Yeah." Garrett gazed around at the vast, dark landscape. Caleb's fear of the dark hovered between them. "He could be anywhere out here, and we'd never find him by ourselves."

"I think we should pray."

"I think you're right."

They formed a small circle, gloved hands clasped as Garrett sent a desperate plea heavenward. "And please,

Lord," he concluded, "open our eyes and our minds so that we'll know where to look."

The amen still hovered in the air when Cody said, "Caleb mighta gone to our special hideout."

Garrett fell to his knees before the child. "What special hideout?"

"The one we made in case the social worker ever tried to get us again." He frowned, uncertain. "Caleb said never tell."

Amy's heart shattered in her chest. From Garrett's pained expression, she knew he felt the same.

"You have to tell us, little man. Caleb's real scared right now, and he needs us to bring him home."

"He doesn't like the dark." Cody fretted with indecision. "But we don't like the group home either."

"You'll never go back there, Son. I promise."

Amy held her breath, praying. Cody's words came out in a whoosh. He pointed toward the creek. "In that old springhouse."

Garrett broke into a run. Amy and Cody followed close behind. Sure enough, when Garrett shined his flashlight inside the crumbling brick structure, a shivering ten-year-old catapulted into his waiting arms.

"I'm sorry, Dad," Caleb sobbed. "I didn't mean to."

Garrett cradled the boy against his chest. "None of that matters now, Son. Let's get you inside where it's warm."

Once in the house, Amy made cocoa while Garrett sat on the couch talking quietly to the blanket-wrapped children. His voice was strong, calm, but Amy heard the powerful emotions.

"Don't ever be afraid to talk to me, boys," he said. "That's what I'm here for—to help when you have a problem."

Caleb twisted one end of the blanket. "But I messed up. I was scared you wouldn't want me anymore."

"I know, but you were wrong." He handed the teary boy a Kleenex. "You can't ever mess up bad enough to make me stop loving you. That's what God teaches us about real love. That's the way He loves us, and that's how I feel about you boys."

The lump in Amy's throat swelled to monumental proportions. She felt certain she couldn't love Garrett any more than she did at that moment. In the next breath, he proved her wrong.

"Fact is, I don't ever want to lose you two. If you're willing to have me for a dad, I'd like to adopt you—make you my sons forever."

Cody shot straight up from the couch like a rocket and danced in a circle, chanting, "Dad, Dad, Dad." An amazed smile spread across Caleb's tearstained face. "You mean it?"

Garrett chuckled and pulled both boys into a hug. "I've already told the social worker to get the ball rolling."

Amy carried the cups of cocoa to the coffee table, her heart bursting with love. Garrett was so wise, so understanding. Life had been unfair to him in many ways, but he'd taken the lemons in his life and made lemonade.

"Did you hear that, Miss Rogers?" Cody raised his face from Garrett's shoulder. "Dad's gonna be our real dad. Now, all we need is a mom."

Everything inside her tensed. A mom. They needed a mom.

Garrett's gaze captured hers as Cody's words vibrated in the suddenly silent air. She'd hurt this man, added more rejection to his life, and yet the love in his eyes still burned as strongly as it had the night he'd asked her to marry him.

Clearly now, Amy saw the truth she'd been too self-absorbed to see before. This good, good man deserved to know why she'd refused his proposal. Regardless of his reaction to her barrenness, he needed to know that she loved him.

Wiping suddenly perspiring hands down the side of her jeans, she said, "Garrett, could we talk, please? Alone. I have something very important to discuss with you."

He never hesitated. "I need to check on Dancing Lady, anyway." With one last hug, Garrett untangled himself from Cody and Caleb. "You boys drink your cocoa and get a hot bath. I'll fix some supper when I get back."

After grabbing jackets, Amy and Garrett hurried through the chilly darkness to the warm, hay-scented barn.

"Guess no baby tonight," Garrett said as he leaned against the stall door, observing the quietly grazing mare. His casual remark and relaxed air gave Amy the opening she needed.

"That's what I wanted to talk to you about."

He tilted his head, frowning. "Dancing Lady's baby?"

"No. Mine." She held up a hand, saw the fingers tremble, and let them fall to her side. No matter what his reaction, she had to tell him. Eyes closed, she took a deep breath. Her words came out in a whisper. "I can't have any. Ever."

In the ensuing silence, she looked up, fearing what she would see. Garrett stood before her, strong, solid, accepting, with not a drop of pity in him, waiting for her to trust him. Courage came, and she stumbled on, telling him of the cancer surgery that had saved her life but stolen her dreams. Midway through, when her voice trembled and tears threatened, Garrett took her hand and rubbed it gently between both of his.

"So that's why I can't marry you. Not because I don't love you. I do. But I know how much kids mean to you and what a great father you are. I can't let you be saddled with someone who can never give you the family you want and deserve."

"Oh, Amy, Amy. We've both been so confused." He pulled her to him, resting his chin on her head. "I knew something was wrong, something to do with kids, because every time the subject came up, you pulled back. I kept hoping you'd trust me enough to share what was bothering you. When you broke things off after the carnival, I decided you weren't interested in an old cowboy who didn't want to have kids the old-fashioned way."

"What?" Hope flared in Amy's chest. Incredulous, she stepped back, searching his face. "I thought you wanted lots of kids."

"I do, and there are plenty of abused and abandoned kids who won't have a chance unless someone takes them in, loves them, parents them. God gave me a dream, a calling, I suppose, to fill this ranch with as many foster and adopted kids as I can handle. I long ago decided against ever having biological children. I've prayed almost that long for a wife who would feel the same. Remember that first day in your classroom? I knew." He thumped his chest. "I knew way down in my spirit that you were that person."

"And I was too afraid. . ." Amy's heart pounded hard enough to explode. She'd been so afraid to trust, she hadn't even prayed for God's guidance. She'd hounded the Lord to take away her feelings, when all the while He had a better plan—a plan that perfectly fit her and the man she loved.

"Garrett." She recaptured his hand, drawing his warmth against her thudding heart. "A few days ago, you asked me to marry you. Does that proposal still stand?"

The corners of his mouth tilted. "On one condition."

"Which is?"

"You promise to say 'yes' this time. I can't take another refusal."

Amy laughed and walked into his arms. "I love you. And if you'll still have me, I'd very much like to marry you and be the mother to any and all children God sends our way."

"Oh, yes, Teacher, I'll still have you," he whispered right before his lips touched hers.

When they broke apart, smiling tenderly into one another's eyes, Amy asked, "Shall we go tell the boys they're going to get that mom they wanted?"

The joy on Garrett's face was beautiful. "Can't think of any better way to end this day."

As Garrett's strong, firm hand closed around hers, and they started to the ranch house that would soon be her home, Amy considered the awesome workings of her Lord. Just as He'd promised in Isaiah, God had taken the ashes of her life and given her beauty in return.

LINDA GOODNIGHT

Linda and her husband, Gene, live on a farm in their native Oklahoma. They have a blended family of six grown children. An elementary school teacher for the past sixteen years, Linda is also a licensed nurse. Her first novella, "The Barefoot Bride," is part of Barbour's best-selling *Prairie Brides* anthology. Readers can contact Linda at *gnight@brightok.net*.

Scrambled Eggs

by Yvonne Lehman

Dedication

Nancy Mulford
for sharing her Pysanky expertise

Chapter 1

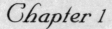

L aura Weston stood at the dairy section in the supermarket, mentally counting as she stacked cartons of eggs on her arm, bracing them against her body.

One.

Two.

Three.

Four.

Five.

And—"Yiiii!" she screeched.

A man came from nowhere, bumping against her, just as she turned to place the eggs into her cart. Instinctively, while using her chin against the top carton for leverage, she let go of the one in her hand and grabbed for the stack. The top one slid off, bounced off the side of the cart, and plopped to the floor.

While holding onto his own carton, the man tried to brace the precariously perched eggs against her chest with his free forearm. The outcome was the top flipping up on the second carton, a mad scramble to catch them before they fell, eggs cracking in the man's hand, and wet slime penetrating Laura's silk blouse, feeling cold and sticky to her body.

Broken, cracked, and rolling eggs covered the area. Literally walking on eggshells, the man tried to move back, stepped into the gooey mess, slipped, and tossed his carton. While trying to hang onto the refrigerated compartment and the cart, he began his impersonation of a Bolshevik dancer. When he grasped the cart, it turned and rolled into Laura, causing her to drop another carton and him to end up on his backside.

Laura's sideways glance revealed people steering around the goop. Others stopped and stared, as if wondering whether to laugh or see if they needed help.

The fallen man came to life and began picking himself up. Despite his face that looked flushed with embarrassment, he grinned. "I never expected to fall for a woman quite so hard."

I wish! came her inadvertent thought, accompanied by a touch of longing. For an instant, she allowed the romantic fanciful notion that this extraordinarily handsome man was deliberately at her feet. The next instant she reverted to being her old realistic self. A plain woman like her, with mousy-brown hair and eyes to match didn't attract men like this.

The glint of gold in his dark brown eyes, dancing merrily, proved her point. Of course, he was joking. At least he had a sense of humor about sitting in a pool of eggs. The flush of warmth she felt rising to her face was instantly replaced by the feeling of sticky goo chilling her midsection. A glance revealed a yellow and white streak down her navy blue skirt.

"I'm sorry," he said.

So was she. Even with egg smeared all over him, he was gorgeous.

Feeling self-conscious at his now-repentant look, and their being watched by a growing crowd, she smiled faintly. "It was an accident."

"Caused by my clumsiness," he admitted, managing to rise to his feet. He made a semblance of wiping the back of his jeans. With an unintelligible exclamation, he held out his hand, revealing a sticky mess dripping from his fingers. Then he spread his hand toward his audience and charmed them with lifted eyebrows, long dark lashes, and a beautiful smile over straight white teeth.

His audience laughed good-naturedly at his performance. If he wasn't, he could be an actor with his charm and good looks. Feeling quite forgotten and glad to no longer be the object of such embarrassing attention, Laura stood admiring this man who could laugh about such an unpleasant situation.

Just then, a scowling man hurried up to them. He wore a white apron and held a roll of paper towels. "I'm the manager," he said. "Are you all right?" He looked from the egg-dripping man to Laura and back again, as if he feared a lawsuit might be on his hands.

"I'm fine," Laura said quietly as the man who had fallen avowed, "Nothing's hurt except my dignity."

The crowd began to disperse as the manager made a

path of paper towels over some of the goop. "I believe you'll be okay if you just step back a little, miss," he said. "And sir, if you can just walk on these towels and step out this way, I'll get somebody to clean this up."

"This was my fault," the egg-coated man said. "I'll pay for the eggs."

The manager lifted his hand. "No. Don't worry about it. You only need to pay for what you buy."

"Thanks," the handsome man said, taking the offered paper towel and wiping his hands. He then stepped carefully along the towels and turned to Laura, who had stepped back and moved the cart toward her. He apologized again. "Here, can I help you put eggs in the cart?"

Forgetting her self-consciousness, she looked up at him and laughed. "Not in this one. It has something dripping from it."

"Oh," he said, grimacing at the sight. "I'll get one of those hand baskets. Will that hold whatever you're planning to buy?"

"Yes. I'm only buying eggs. I'm not presentable for parading up and down aisles for anything else."

Neither was he, she noticed as he moved away, with a most unbecoming wet spot clear across the bottom of his jeans and a couple of streaks down the legs.

"Here, I will get the eggs for you," he said upon returning.

"I'm closer," she said. "Just stand still."

Making sure to walk on a clear spot or on the towels, she counted out six cartons, handed them to the man, who carefully placed them into the basket. Well, perhaps he'd learned something—these weren't hard-boiled!

"That's it," she said after the sixth carton, then reached for the basket.

He shook his head. "The least I can do is carry the basket to the checkout counter and pay for them."

"That's really not necessary," she said, but since he didn't give her the basket, she walked along with him.

"Looks like you're planning to feed an army with eggs," he said and laughed.

"Nope. I'll have these used up within a week, and may need more."

He balked. "Sounds to me like you're trying to commit slow suicide. Do you realize how much cholesterol is in just one egg yolk?"

Laura glanced up into his questioning eyes and couldn't help but grin. "I know how much slimy goo is in one egg."

"Sorry," he said again, for a moment looking like a little repentant boy.

"Actually," she said, "I'm going to decorate them."

"Decorate them?" His brow furrowed slightly and he looked as if he were uncertain whether she had all her faculties. "You do know Easter was a month ago?"

"No!" she said playfully, as if her brain were as dull as her outward appearance. She stopped in her tracks. "Maybe we could just take these outside and play ball with them."

"Hey," he said then, "that really would be a cool game for kids."

"A sticky one," she returned, feeling like her blouse had become part of her skin.

He put the basket on the narrow ledge beside the checkout counter. The clerk rang them up, pretending not to keep glancing at Laura's blouse and skirt. "Egg," Laura said. "We had an accident back there."

"Looks like it," the clerk said, grinning. She said the amount and Laura looked over at the man. He stood, shaking his head with his eyes closed and holding out two one-dollar bills and some change. He moaned and opened his eyes. "You won't believe this. I left my wallet in the glove compartment—"

He was right. She didn't believe him! That easy camaraderie she'd felt now vanished. She reminded herself that you couldn't judge an egg by its shell. The insides could be fresh, fertile enough to grow into an entirely different form, or even rotten. An uneasiness swept over her. Had his bumping into her really been an accident? Was this some kind of sinister game?

She reached into her skirt pocket and took out the ten-dollar bill she'd brought with her and handed it to the clerk, along with a look of chagrin. The clerk just smiled, took the money, gave her change, and bagged the eggs. All the while, the man was making some idiotic excuse about only having come in for a carton of eggs for his mother. His dad had handed him two dollars. He'd left his wallet in his car.

Laura felt like running outside, but with fragile goods, she had to be careful. He trod along, sideways, right beside her, offering to carry her eggs.

"No," she said, wondering if she should scream. Perhaps she shouldn't even leave the store until he had gone. The sun shone brightly on this warm spring day. It was not yet 5:00 P.M. What a perfect setup for an unsuspecting victim of a demented mind.

"I know it sounds far-fetched," he said, and she nodded. "But it's true. I'll just run out to my car and get my wallet."

When he jogged away, in crusty breeches, she hurried to her car. Thankfully, it was closer than his. She had a remote for her aunt's car that she drove and quickly pushed the "unlock" button. By the time the man returned, she was in the driver's seat with the door locked and the key in the ignition.

He came up to the window, waving a ten-dollar bill at her.

She prayed no one was watching. She shook her head and turned the key.

He yelled. "Give me your name and address, and I'll make this up to you."

She didn't even bother to look at him then. If he pulled out a gun to try and force her to open the door, she didn't want to know about it.

He banged on the window. "At least your phone number!"

She backed out of the parking space, determined if he jumped in front of her, she'd run him down. He must have sensed her determination. With a defeated look on his face, he still held out a ten-dollar bill in front of him.

She changed from reverse to drive, then seeing that he wasn't attempting to jump into the car, she touched her cheek, then pointed at him.

Her last glimpse at him revealed him standing there looking thwarted, with his finger on his cheek.

❧

Andrew Franklin had egg on his face.

He'd just met an intriguing woman who drew him like a magnet. He couldn't imagine any other woman he knew who would be so good-natured about him splattering egg all over her clothes. She hadn't been angry for even one second. She'd just looked at him with concern and sympathy for his predicament. She hadn't laughed at him, nor had she accused him of being clumsy.

But, she'd left him standing alone in a supermarket parking lot, feeling crust on his cheek and flaking off a streak of yellow. If he'd known she was going to disappear like Cinderella at midnight, he would have checked out her license number so he could ask a policeman buddy of his to find out who she was. However, he didn't think of it soon enough, and she zoomed out of there too fast for him to catch the number.

He couldn't blame her. If something like this happened to his sisters, he would warn them to get away from such a guy in a hurry. He must look like some kind of idiot to her, or worse.

Then he realized he hadn't bought the carton of eggs he'd gone in for. He went back into the store, stepped carefully around the "Caution! Wet Floor" sign and the worker mopping. After getting his eggs and walking away, Andrew looked over his shoulder at the worker who was eyeing his jeans and identifying him as the culprit who'd been a part of that mess.

Swallowing what little pride he had left, Andrew went to the checkout clerk who already knew about the predicament and paid for his eggs. "Would you happen to know that—um, egg girl who was just in here?"

The clerk looked at him for a moment, reminding him of how the egg girl had looked at him, like he might be some kind of pervert. "I don't know her name." She put the eggs in a plastic bag.

Andrew nodded. "I guess you wouldn't tell me even if you knew."

She handed him his eggs. "Sure, I would. Aren't you Andy Franklin?" He nodded again. "You probably don't remember, but my church's youth group went with yours down to Sliding Rock a few years ago. I went."

Andy snapped his fingers and tilted his head as if to say, "How could I have forgotten?" But he said, "Well, how are you doing these days?"

"Oh, great. I'm planning to go to AB-Tech next fall. I have to work some Sundays, so I don't always get to go to church." She looked apologetic, as if he might give her a lecture. "That's why I don't know her name, but she sings in the choir at my church."

She? The egg girl? "Your church?"

"Yeah. The one a couple of blocks over from yours. Has a prayer garden at the side."

Andrew knew the church. As a matter of fact, he

knew all the area churches. His dad was pastor of the big one on the corner.

On his way home, Andy told himself to forget the egg incident. He had enough on his mind without worrying about a few broken eggs. Still, he kept seeing the eggs scrambled down the front of that woman's clothes and on the floor and feeling the crust on his cheek. He kept seeing her skepticism of him.

He thought of the checkout clerk knowing him. He was a man, but he was also "the preacher's kid." Such "kids" had a stereotypical reputation of not coming up to expected standards. Even though he couldn't remember all the youth of the area, a lot of them would remember him as one who helped out with the youth group.

Not only was his own reputation at stake, but his actions were a reflection on his parents, too.

He really needed to put this straight.

Conscience! What a worrisome thing.

Sunday morning, after hearing his mom question his going to another church and listening to the birds at the feeder chirping a different tune, Andrew walked into the small church a few blocks from where his dad would be preaching. He sat near the back so he could see everyone who came in from all directions. At six foot one, he was taller than most and would be too conspicuous sitting up front. He didn't want to make another spectacle of himself.

Several people greeted and welcomed him. The organist began to play. Pastor Willis, who'd been at Andrew's home on occasion, entered from a side door, ascended the few steps to the dais and sat in a high-backed chair.

Then the choir filed into the choir loft behind the pastor. There she was. On the front row, third from the left. Her medium-length brown hair fell forward along the sides of her face as she sat, then when she lifted her head, it hung in soft waves to her shoulders. He tried not to laugh, thinking of having touched girls' hair that felt stiff, like it was held in place with dried egg. He liked the natural wholesome look of this young woman's warm brown eyes and pleasant smile. He couldn't say one of her features was more appealing than another. Everything just fit together. . .perfectly.

The choir director, who had come onto the dais at some point, lifted his arms, and the choir stood. They began to sing. Andrew realized the young lady's lips were the same color as the peach collar over the cream-colored choir robe. He warned himself to keep his mind on the musical message.

After the introductory song of praise, followed by the pastor's prayer, Andrew thought the young woman looked straight at him. She didn't look again. Maybe it would have been best if he'd just chalked that egg bit up as an accident and forgotten it. But the more he thought of it, the more he wanted to change her last impression of him—which hadn't been favorable. He'd gone this far, so he'd just see it through.

As soon as the service ended, Andrew found out the location of the choir room and made his way to a side door and down a hallway. He saw her then, inside the room, talking to a couple of women. She'd already taken off her robe and looked like spring in a flowered dress. He stepped inside a doorway across from the choir room so others could go on down the hallway. Her voice sounded musical even as she was saying in a concerned tone, "Yes, I'll pray about that." Next, she spoke to someone else, laughed lightly, then said, "See ya." She looked happy.

His heartbeat accelerated when she walked toward him. At the same time his breath seemed to stop. He was able to say one word: "Hi."

When he stepped out in front of her, she stopped cold and gasped. Her hand slapped her chest, covering the heart-shaped locket on a thin gold chain around her neck.

"No eggs. Honest." He gave her his best smile that showcased teeth that had long ago been straightened by braces.

"What are you doing here?" The brightness vanished from her eyes at the same time the smile left her face. He'd never had anyone respond to him so negatively.

Judging by her furtive glance around and the trace of suspicion in her question, he figured he'd better play it cool, lest she scream for help. "I wanted to prove to you I'm not some kind of reprobate. I offered to pay for your eggs, and that's what I came to do."

"I told you that was not necessary," she returned shortly and started walking fast down the hallway, opposite the way he'd just come.

"I have to clear my conscience," he said, hurrying after her.

"How did you know where to find me?" She glanced over her shoulder.

By that time, she'd reached a side foyer next to a partition with a glassed-in office beyond. She must have felt safer there. She stopped and faced him then, waiting for his answer.

"A little bird—" he started, but thought she wasn't in a joking mood. He tried again. "The checkout clerk at the supermarket." He grimaced, adding, "That was before the manager came up and chased me away by throwing eggs at me."

She stared. Then she laughed. It was a small laugh, but still a laugh. "I'd like to have seen that."

"I'll just bet you would," he said. She sort of ducked her head and her cheeks colored slightly. Still, he saw the beginning of a grin, so he ventured further. "I honestly wish you could forgive me."

"Really," she said, "I do forgive you. If it would make you feel better, just put some money in the collection plate."

He'd already done that, but his offering hadn't been egg money. "Please. Let me pay your dry-cleaning bill."

That becoming blush colored her cheeks again. "It's not necessary."

He didn't think it would look too good for him to stand there and try to force her to take money. Maybe he should take her out to lunch. Before he could ask, she smiled. "Thanks for your offer. I need to go now. I have to take my aunt home."

He couldn't remember ever having made such an unfavorable impression on a girl that she was so eager to get away from him. Then he realized he didn't even know her name. He hadn't even introduced himself. As far as she knew, he might be a guy just trying to pick her up. That thought brought a smile. Maybe he was.

Then good fortune smiled on him. The youth director was walking toward them. "Hey, Don."

⚜

As Don neared, Laura saw the look of recognition on his face. Smiling, he caught the arm of—Laura's thought stopped. She didn't even know this man's name. She'd thought of him as "that handsome man." And he was. He'd looked great in jeans and T-shirt, but today he was all shiny clean and dressed in a navy blue suit and maroon silk tie.

"Andy," Don said, "good to see you, man. What are you doing here?"

Andy! So that is his name.

"Don," Andy replied, "would you do me a favor and introduce us?" He pointed from himself to Laura. "Tell her I'm okay."

Don took his hand away from Andy's arm and scowled. "We're in a church, Andy, and I don't think it's the proper place to tell a lie."

"Don, I'm serious."

"Just a minute." Don steered Laura aside and whispered near her ear, "He's the greatest." Then he introduced them. "Andy Franklin, may I present Miss Laura Weston. Laura, meet Andy Franklin. He's a preacher's boy. I'm sure that presents some kind of picture in your mind concerning his character."

Don grinned mischievously while Andy's face clouded. "Thanks for the favor, buddy."

"Anytime," Don said, then slapped Andy on the arm. "Frankly, Laura, he and I have gone on several youth trips together, and I was able to keep him in line fairly well."

Laura watched the good-natured bantering with interest. She'd heard a person only kidded people they liked. She figured these two liked each other. Andy was a preacher's son, and he'd gone on youth trips. Maybe he was as good as he looked.

"Now, what did you say you're doing here?" Don asked.

"Repaying a debt," he said. Andy whipped up his suit coat and pulled a wallet from his back pants pocket. With several bills clearly visible to Laura, he pulled out a ten. "Put this in the collection plate for me, will you?"

"If you're repaying debts, maybe I should put this in my pocket," Don said. He looked at Laura and winked. "Just kidding." He took the money, lifted his hand, and said, "See you guys," and headed toward the glassed-in office.

At that moment, Aunt Vi walked up. She was a young-looking fifty-three-year-old, six years older than Laura's mom. Laura recognized the gleam in her eyes as she glanced from Laura to Andy and back again.

"Hello," she said in her friendly manner, smiling at Andy. "I don't believe I've seen you around here. Are you visiting?"

"Aunt Vi, this is Andy Franklin," Laura said. "My aunt, Vivien Hensley."

"Glad to meet you, Mrs. Hensley." Andy took Aunt Vi's extended hand.

"Franklin?" Aunt Vi mused. "Would you by any chance be related to John and Martha Franklin?"

"My parents."

Aunt Vi nodded. "I've heard your dad preach and have been in many missionary meetings with your mom." She glanced at Laura. "Did you two just meet?"

His dark eyes sparked with the mischief that sounded in his voice. "She and I ran into each other at the grocery store the other night."

Aunt Vi's blue eyes widened. So did her mouth. "You're the egg man?"

" 'Fraid so, ma'am," he admitted with a grin.

"Oh, what I'd give to have seen that. I laughed 'til I cried when Laura told me about it." She laughed then—heartily. "I've never seen a man with egg on his—"

"Aunt Vi!" Laura interrupted, fearing she might say something embarrassing.

Aunt Vi gave her an innocent look, finishing her sentence with the word "jeans."

"She declined my offer to pay her dry-cleaning bill," Andy told Aunt Vi, "so how about you two ladies let me treat you to lunch?"

"Oh, how nice," Aunt Vi was saying, overpowering Laura's mumbled refusal. "But you two don't want me tagging along. I'll just be on my way."

"No, Aunt Vi," Laura protested as her aunt stepped toward the door, "please go with us."

"Well, if you're sure," she said, looking at Andy, who looked pleased as the proverbial cat who ate the canary.

"We're sure," Laura said, deciding that rather than

try to explain to Aunt Vi why she wouldn't go to lunch with Andy, it would be best to do it and get it over with. Apparently, he really was a decent guy and wanted to make up for the egg fiasco.

He held the door open for them. She and Aunt Vi walked past him and out into the sunny spring day. Laura saw no point in this, except to salvage his feelings if he were really sorry. She couldn't imagine what else it might be. This outgoing, handsome, charming man couldn't possibly be personally interested in plain, dull Laura Weston.

❧

Laura insisted Aunt Vi ride in front, then she got in back while Andy drove them to the steak house. They were part of a long line of churchgoers easing along the maze to give their order. Several people knew Andy, and they spoke to him. Aunt Vi and a couple of women greeted each other and mentioned the weather. The menu was steak, chicken, or buffet/salad bar. Like most of the diners, Andy, Aunt Vi, and Laura opted for the buffet/salad bar.

"Where would you like to sit?" Andy asked when they had their trays, drinks, silverware, and dishes. When Laura didn't speak up, Aunt Vi suggested the side room, the upper part of which was windows and the lower half paneling. After filling their plates, Aunt Vi and Laura sat on one side of the table. Andy sat opposite them.

"Let's say grace," Aunt Vi said. While she prayed, Laura wondered how she'd get through this meal, feeling so awkward about it. She shouldn't have wondered.

As soon as Aunt Vi said, "Amen," she began to ask questions. Andy became more interesting with each answer. He received his bachelor's degree from an area university, had worked as an EMT at various levels, then trained to become a paramedic. He now worked twenty-four-hour shifts, 7:30 A.M. to 7:30 A.M., every three days.

"How can you stay awake that long?" Laura asked.

"We can sleep if there's no emergency. But if there is," he said cheerfully, "the siren keeps us awake."

Laura completely forgot her own shyness and found herself greatly interested as he told stories of having delivered a baby, giving CPR to a heart-attack victim, and administering a pain-relieving drug to a teenager with a crushed leg. She smiled at the empathy in his eyes when he said, "Life is fragile, and suffering knows no boundaries. It affects the rich and poor, good or bad, and it's my job to preserve their lives, regardless of race, creed, or color."

"You sound like you love your job," Aunt Vi said.

He nodded. "I don't like to see the suffering—particularly when it happens to little children. But I feel privileged to have a part in helping relieve some of that suffering."

"I pray for workers like you," Aunt Vi said. "I realized the importance of quick action when my late husband had his heart attack. Had it not been for the quick action of an EMT, he wouldn't have made it to the hospital, and we wouldn't have been able to prepare for what was to come a few years later." She took a deep breath, blinked away the moisture, and smiled sadly. "He died just a little over a year ago. That's when my precious niece accepted my plea to come and stay with me for awhile."

Then it was Laura's turn to share a little of her life. She'd transferred from North Carolina State in Raleigh to UNC at Asheville. This was her senior year, and her major was English. She'd been more than eager to accept Aunt Vi's invitation.

Laura could confidently say to Andy, "It was time for me to move out of my parents' home and let them enjoy their later years."

"Darlin'," Aunt Vi said in a reprimanding tone. "You make them sound like they're ready to be put out to pasture. My goodness, your mother is my baby sister, and I'm not ready for the rocking chair yet."

"I didn't mean it that way," Laura said as Andy grinned. "It's just time for me to be more independent and let them have their time together."

Aunt Vi patted her arm like she understood. Laura moved her food around a little with her fork. It was Uncle Jim's death that had made her realize how precious this time could be for her parents. Aunt Vi had felt all alone, so Laura was more than glad to live with her during this transition time. Although there were times that Aunt Vi's eyes clouded and she spoke of missing Uncle Jim so much, she was coping admirably.

Laura felt she was coping well, too. She'd never been an extrovert and had gone through a rough period of self-recrimination after her steady boyfriend dropped her for a prettier, more popular girl right before the prom during her junior year in high school. Laura had felt even more plain after that, but she'd moved on and now counted herself fortunate. Still, this was no time to be thinking of a former boyfriend.

"So your dad's a preacher?" Laura asked, wanting to move into a more positive topic.

"Yes, and I still live with Mom and Dad. Since my two sisters married and moved away, they turned the downstairs into an apartment for me. And like you said," he added, gesturing toward Laura, "I probably should have moved out long ago. But they say they don't mind. I needed to stay with them when I was in college instead of paying dorm fees. Now, it's just convenient, and I can put aside a little nest egg for. . .whatever."

Suddenly his dark eyes glinted with humor. "Let's hope this kind of egg is more secure than those in the supermarket."

Laura and Aunt Vi joined his easy laughter. Still embarrassed by that egg fiasco, however, Laura felt her face grow warm. She looked down, wondering if his "nest egg" was equivalent to a woman's "hope chest." Saving for that big day—called a wedding? Since guys didn't wear engagement rings, one couldn't tell by looking at their fingers.

He mentioned his sisters, nephews, and niece. Laura mentioned her brother, a dentist, ten years older than she, married with one child, living in Greensboro. She rarely saw them, except on holidays. She felt like she'd been in school forever.

"Are you planning to teach, Laura?" Andy asked.

"I'm not sure yet what I will do," she replied, realizing that was as vague as his "whatever." "I have three more weeks of school, which includes final exams. After that, I'll be teaching egg-decorating classes."

He gave a short laugh. "So that was on the level? I thought you were kidding."

"Oh, it's no joking matter," Aunt Vi said. "It's something your mother might like to have Laura come and teach to the women at your church, Andy."

Andy chuckled. "My mom probably got enough of dyed eggs when I was a youngster," he said and launched into a story about spilling the red dye all over the kitchen floor.

"Andy Franklin," Vi said, pointing her fork at him, "I'm not talking about child's play here. You haven't seen egg decorating until you've been to one of Laura's classes."

"Aunt Vi," Laura spoke up, "you're the expert. I'm the novice, remember?"

❧

Vi patted her arm. "I've taught you the process, yes; but with your natural creativity, you'll far surpass me in design."

"You're biased, Aunt Vi," Laura said, lowering her gaze in that modest way of hers.

Vi understood the skepticism in Andy's voice when he asked, "You teach this in churches, you say?" He looked from Laura to Vi.

Vi deliberately poked a forkful of beef and rice in her mouth, forcing Laura to reply to his question.

"Churches are most responsive," Laura explained, "because a religious testimony is involved along with the decorating. I do have a class already set at a local college, though."

"Which one?" Andy asked.

"Mountain College," Laura said.

Vi settled back, smiling inwardly as the two conversed about themselves, the area, and how egg decorating could tie in with one's testimony.

"I help out with the youth at my church sometimes," Andy said. "I wouldn't dare turn them loose with raw eggs." He and Laura laughed together, and Vi knew they were thinking of the store episode. He added, "I can see how the egg could tie in with a devotional. We're always looking for interesting ways to illustrate a biblical teaching, especially at Easter time."

"Well, there's one way to find out," Vi challenged. "Go to one of Laura's classes."

Aware of the quick glances from both Laura and Andy, Vi wondered if she were pushing the envelope a mite. She smiled her sweetest and tried to put on an innocent look. Truthfully, it was time Laura got over that former boyfriend of hers and found a nice young man to go out with. Laura was the sweetest young woman in the world and had been a friend and confidant during Vi's time of grief. That precious girl had sacrificed a lot for her. Vi would do her best to see her niece had the kind of life she deserved.

"Well, this has been a very nice lunch," Vi said. "Andy, you'll have to come eat with us one of these days."

"Thanks, I'd love to," Andy said, holding her gaze long enough to give Vi the impression he meant that. Vi would love to see Laura relating to someone like Andy Franklin. He struck her as being a good egg.

Chapter 3

Since spring rains had come, Laura thought the students might not. After all, this was not a required course, but a minicourse, one of several adult classes the college offered after the regular semester ended. She'd taken her last exam in American Lit only yesterday. Now, she was ready to think through her next step in life. That is, if she passed all her exams. *Strange,* she thought, *how uptight everyone becomes about final exams.* She'd never failed one in her life, yet the thought of failure was ever present when those tests were laid in front of her and all she had to work with was a pencil with an eraser, the time clock, and whatever knowledge was stored in her brain.

Her greater fear, however, was that she might fail God's exam. What steps did she need to take and what lessons must she learn before she knew what He had in mind for her? She wanted His will in her life but wasn't sure if her desires were the same as His. This summer would be a test for that.

As she turned onto the road leading to the campus

of Mountain Christian College, a trace of regret washed over her. She hadn't considered a Christian college when she'd started at State. Although she had saved a little money by working summers, she knew the cost would be out of her parents' range. Aunt Vi had offered to pay for Laura's continued education after she came to live with her, but since it was Laura's senior year, she felt it best not to transfer from a public to private school and not to take advantage of Aunt Vi's generosity by attending a more expensive school.

Irony is. . . , she thought, as if answering an exam question, *incongruity between the natural result of an event and the expected result.* Who would have expected this? She couldn't come here as a student, but was now coming as a teacher.

Laura reveled in that nonsensical thought as she peered out beyond the swipes of the windshield wipers at the impressive medieval-looking gray stone structures and vacant parking lots. Only a few cars were parked near the administration building. Most of those probably belonged to professors grading final exams.

A moment later, Laura reverted to being her usual realistic self. She would need six to eight years more of higher education to even consider teaching curriculum at a place like this. She'd certainly need a more impressive background than "Egg Decorating."

Laura would be teaching for one full day only. No students would be required to take this course, nor would one in a thousand want to take it. Her pupils would be mainly middle-aged and older women with plenty of time and money on their hands. *If no one comes out in this downpour,* she thought, *we won't have a class.*

She sat for a moment after parking on a side street next to the library. Her classroom was located beneath it. Getting inside in a steady downpour with raw eggs and invaluable decorated ones was the trick. She didn't want another fiasco like the one in the supermarket.

No! she warned herself. *Do not think about that. Exactly what you predicted—happened. You told yourself that Andy Franklin couldn't be interested in you.*

Three weeks had passed and he hadn't returned to the church. There'd been no reason to think he would. Not allowing her to forget, Aunt Vi often laughed about the incident and kept mentioning "that nice young man who took us to lunch." Aunt Vi continued to mention his qualities and ask if he'd show up at church again. He hadn't.

That was that. Laura just wished she hadn't gone out to lunch with him and learned to like him. What was the point? If that salved his conscience, which it apparently had, then so be it. At least it had left him with the impression she wasn't holding a grudge against him. After all, it was only eggs.

Thinking of eggs, she couldn't sit there until the rain stopped. That could take days. She forced her way out of the car, opened the trunk and stacked the box of plastic-covered fragile decorated eggs on top of the raw ones. She set them on the soggy concrete step, closed the trunk, slid the keys in the pocket of her raincoat, then ducked her head and carefully made her way along the walkway to the door, hoping someone had thought to unlock it. From somewhere, she heard a car door slam.

She set her box down again, ready to try the door.

"May I?" someone asked, reaching out at the same time she did, and their hands collided.

Laura looked up quickly into a handsome rain-streaked face with raindrops falling on his curly head. *Andrew Franklin!* Their gazes collided until he said, "I'll get your boxes."

The memory of the soggy cardboard bottom struck a discordant note in her mind. "Just hold the door, please." She walked past him with the boxes and into the entry. He hurried in to open the heavy glass door to the spacious classroom.

He switched on the light as she set the boxes on the long table against the wall of glass windows. She turned and headed for the door again.

"Where are you going?" he asked.

"To get the other boxes from the trunk."

"I'll do that," he said.

Deciding not to pretend to be a duck, she reached into her pocket, pulled out her keys, and placed them in his hand. Her fingertips touched the palm of his hand. Their eyes collided again. Strangely, she felt it all the way into her heart. That was silly. She was silly. She hadn't felt this giddy since she was in the first grade and the boy she thought didn't even know her gave her a valentine with an elephant on the front, holding a heart. Inside, it said, "You're my big moment, baby."

Heart collision? she thought, watching him stride

down the walkway past the windows. No, she was just slightly breathless due to the surprise of his being there, nervous about the class, scared that a lot of people would show up, and afraid they wouldn't. These were just natural, everyday concerns, like taking exams or something.

Reminding herself to keep her mind on the issue at hand, she removed the raincoat and hat, looking around for a place to put them, then spied a board with several hooks on the far wall. Her hair was dry above her ears. The rest hung in damp ringlets. The legs of her slacks, from midcalf down, felt cold and damp against her skin. Then, seeing Andy at the glass door, she smiled.

She opened the door for him. "Set those on the table by the other boxes." After he did, he began shucking out of his blue waterproof jacket. Water droplets dripped from his dark hair, down his face, and onto his red-and-white striped knit shirt. His smiley lips were moist; his damp cheeks were slightly flushed beneath his smooth tan skin. Even his long, curved eyelashes and arched eyebrows were wet.

Realizing she was staring, she quipped, "You're all wet."

His beautiful brown eyes narrowed. "First, I have egg on my face. Now, I'm all wet. Is that any way to greet a guy?"

"Well, I'm sort of in the same boat," she said with a short laugh.

"Save that boat," he said, grinning. "We may need it."

She couldn't stand forever just staring at him, breathing erratically. On second thought, perhaps she could.

After all, he was a paramedic. He could give her artificial respiration. That thought made things worse. Quickly, she asked, "What are you doing here, anyway?"

"Coming to class," he said, as if that were obvious. She supposed it was. But why?

"I've been trying to get to you for weeks. I had to work one weekend, and I had to fill in for a friend on another." Looking around, he spied the hooks and walked over to hang up his jacket.

She smiled when he bent over and, with his fingers in his hair, shook his head like a dog would shake his wet body. As he walked toward her again, Laura glanced at the wall clock. "The class doesn't start until nine o'clock."

He followed her glance. "It's eight-thirty now. I came straight from work. I had a couple of runs last night, but I think I can keep from nodding off." With a mischievous gleam in his eyes, he added, "That depends on how interesting the teacher makes the class."

"I'll give it my best shot," she promised. "Anyway, Aunt Vi is coming. She can take over if I get too boring."

He rubbed his hands together. "Okay, what can I do to help?"

"You can set the tables," she said.

"Oh, so I *will* get breakfast," he exclaimed, his eyes dancing.

"Only if you cook it over a candle," she quipped, finding it surprisingly easy to banter with him. She reminded herself not to take him personally, however. He apparently was a paying student, looking for devotional ideas that he'd mentioned when they'd had lunch together. More seriously, she added, "You might get hungry before lunchtime."

He grinned. "I did pick up something and ate it in the car."

Laura thought he must eat on the go all the time. He needed someone to cook for him.

He rubbed his hands together, as if eager to get started. "So, what can I do?"

Laura glanced toward the windows, wondering when Aunt Vi and Ethel Stepp would arrive. Mrs. Stepp had taken the course from Laura at church. Having decided to decorate eggs for a Christmas tree, she wanted to take the course again. She offered to bring Aunt Vi, since Laura had to arrive early to set up the tables.

Laura needed to learn to set up without Aunt Vi but was pleased that Andy was there to help. "I appreciate your offer," she said, returning Andy's smile. "You can put those three long tables into a T shape in the center of the room."

"Yes, ma'am," he said as he gave her a salute and set to work.

Laura decided to look in the bathroom for paper towels. Being successful, she returned to see a white-haired man helping Andy move the tables.

The man said he was Jim. He didn't believe in being late to anything.

"I'm glad," she said. "I could use some help this morning." After she wiped down the white plastic table coverings, she gave them to the men to spread out on the tables. "We'll also need at least twenty-five chairs."

She showed them how to set a place. In front of the chair, they were to put the instruction and information sheets. Individual-sized packs of white tissue belonged on the left. On the right, she placed a sharpened pencil, a toothpick, a rubber band, and a *kitska* for wax. Above the papers, she set a short, fat candle on a cardboard coaster and a small box of matches. She asked them to place only one setting in the middle of the long top of the "T." That's where she'd put her notes and stand to teach.

Laura busied herself with spreading a covering on the table in front of the window. She put the sticky-backed name tags and black magic markers at one end. On the rest of the table, she set out the cartons of raw white eggs, dry dyes, empty pint-sized jars, jars of liquid dye, spoons, large boxes of tissues, and a water pitcher. Then, taking a carton of eggs, she set an egg that she'd cleaned with vinegar beside each candle.

Laura breathed a sigh of relief when Aunt Vi and Ethel Stepp walked in. She did not feel confident to handle all this on her own just yet. Her confidence increased when Aunt Vi said everything looked just perfect to her. Then she began helping Andy and Jim set the tables.

Aunt Vi took a step back and exclaimed, "Everything looks just wonderful." As if on cue, women began to come in groups of three, four, and five, as if they'd been poured out from the sky. Within minutes, the room was filled with excited chatter as they filled out name tags. Exclamations of awe filled the room when Laura set the glass bowl of decorated eggs near her notes.

With a warning of, "Remember they're fragile," she glanced at the clock. Almost time to begin. She didn't have to ask them to sit. Everyone seemed eager. Andy sat at the stem of the "T" where it connected to the center, near where she stood. Jim sat beside him. They all looked at her expectantly.

Laura read off the names of those who had pre-registered. One woman was missing. The names of two had not been called: one woman and Andy.

"When I called about it," Andy said, "I was told I could register during the lunch break."

Laura nodded. "The steps in the entryway lead up to the library. You can register and pay your fees there." He smiled and winked, as if he already knew that. Laura warned herself not to place too much significance on Andy's attention to her. She was by no means the only person there affected by his charm and outgoing personality. Everyone seemed to like him. She liked him too, but she had to guard her heart against anything more than friendship at the present time.

She took in a deep breath and reminded herself to do as Aunt Vi had instructed. *Be Christ-conscious, not self-conscious.* So she looked down the stem of the "T" and began.

"I want to be honest with you in case you can tell I'm nervous," Laura said. "This is only the second time I've taught this class in this area. Last weekend, I taught it at my church. I taught it once at a church in Raleigh. Other than that, I've only done it for friends or family at Easter or Christmas. I began to learn the process from my Aunt Vi when I was eight years old." She introduced Aunt Vi to the group.

Laura then unrolled a soft cloth and took out a crudely decorated egg from the bowl. "This is the first one I ever made. It's fourteen years old." Laura explained that she'd done the simplest kind of drawing and the easiest to decorate. On a deep blue egg, she painted a green wreath with a red bow on one side. On the other half was a yellow star with smaller yellow dots above a triangle representing a stable.

She passed it around so they could see that even a child could make the eggs. Neither she nor her aunt would teach the process to children because of the danger with using lighted candles and hot wax. "If I could make that on my first try at eight years old, just imagine what you can do."

She heard the usual groans, denials, and doubts. Then she passed around one made by her grandmother. The expected "ooohs" and "ahhhs" sounded. "It's over forty years old. We have some in the family much older and more valuable." Then she told the story of an architect who had taken a course from her grandmother. "He is so precise with his measurements and designs that he now sells each egg for thousands of dollars."

Laura could tell the interest had piqued. She then went into the background and meanings behind this kind of egg decorating. "This is an art form called 'Pysanky,' pronounced 'pie-*san*-kee.' The word 'Pysanky' means 'to write.' The process is sort of like writing on the egg with wax, and I'll show you how to do that in a little while. This is a Ukranian form of decorating that dates back to pre-Christian times. Late in the tenth century, the form took on religious significance. For instance, the triangle that used to symbolize fire, air, and water now represents God the Father, Son, and Holy Spirit."

Not wanting to bore them with too much history, Laura referred them to the information on the papers before them. "If you'll look at your papers, you'll read that certain colors have meaning." She read them:

"White=purity

"Yellow=spirituality

"Green=rebirth of nature in spring

"Blue=sky, air, and good health

"Orange=power, ambition, and attractiveness

"Purple=faith and trust

"Pink=success

"Red=happiness and love

"Black=the darkest time before dawn, and it's also called the Color of Remembrance since Christ died for all of us.

"So," she said, "look over the information, the symbols, and possible designs. You can decide to decorate yours freestyle as I did my first one, or in geometric designs like those on your handouts, or you can make up your own design. I'm going to suggest you do a very simple design for practice. Now, if some of you want to go ahead and tackle a more complex design, then go right ahead. The basics are the same."

Laura could feel the group's interest. Jim said he

was an artist and had painted wooden eggs, but he was intrigued by this process. He wanted to know how this process would work on wooden eggs.

"Aunt Vi would be the one to ask about that," Laura replied, and Aunt Vi smiled at Jim when he looked questioningly at her.

Laura tried not to look directly at Andy too often, but she felt his intense gaze on her as if he, too, were quite interested. All the women appeared eager to get started. Some had even picked up their eggs, looking at them as if already seeing a design begin to form. She could tell them more of the symbolism and history in the afternoon segment of the class.

"Okay," she said, demonstrating as she talked, "for a basic design, you first make a faint X on top of the egg and at the bottom. Then put your rubber band around it, letting it lie in the center of each X."

"How do you know that's the exact top and bottom?" one woman asked.

"Usually you can judge by looking. But if you want to be more precise, then measure with a piece of string or thread. If one side is longer than the other, then move your rubber band over to make the sides even."

"These feel awfully light," another woman said. "Are they hard-boiled?"

"No, they're raw," Laura said. "I should have said that at the beginning." She glanced at Andy, who nodded and laid his down, giving her a mischievous grin.

"These are not cooked. With this kind of dye on them, they're not to be eaten. Besides, can you imagine what the inside would be like in just a few days?"

"Phew," said several, imagining.

"After we dye these, we'll blow out the insides."

Andy asked, "Why don't you do that first, then dye them?"

"If you had only the shell," she explained, "the egg would float instead of settling down into the dye. Also, the shell would be more likely to crack if the insides were gone."

"Won't they crack real easy after we make them?" someone else asked.

Laura smiled. They were all thinking and asking questions. That was a good sign. Maybe she was doing all right, after all. "After you dye them, you can put as many coats of clear varnish on them as you like. Each coat strengthens the shell."

When there seemed to be no more questions, she continued the process. "Now hold the egg, with the rubber band around it close to your waist to keep it steady. Then trace a light pencil line along the rubber band, working toward your waist. After you've finished that, you've divided the egg into two parts. Next, you repeat the process going around the center of the egg, which will divide the egg shell into four equal parts."

Laura instructed them individually in the next step, which was to lightly draw the design each had chosen, or to follow her example of drawing in a simple symbol on each quarter of the egg. She had them use the *kitska* by putting wax into it, then heating the tip over the candle. The hot wax was then put over the lines they had drawn with the pencil, and inside the symbols. After that, they dipped them in a light-colored dye. Then wax was applied inside the symbols and the egg dipped in a darker-colored dye. When finished, the wax would be melted by holding it over the lighted candle and wiping it away. The finished egg then had white lines dividing it into four sections, light-colored symbols on a dark background. All of that could later be varnished.

The morning passed quickly and before she knew it, someone asked if it were time for their lunch break. A few had brought their lunch, as had Laura. Some planned to go downtown a couple of miles away; others were going home. Jim and Andy left together.

Some ate quickly and went right back to their eggs. Almost everyone had returned before one o'clock. Andy had covered his egg with a tissue, so she didn't know how it looked. She hoped he wasn't ashamed of it. Some people just had no artistic ability. That's why she showed her first effort, the one she could simply call "freestyle."

He had been conscientious, though, since with twenty-six people present, she didn't have time to give anyone very much attention. He seemed to enjoy working along, occasionally letting Jim take a peek at it, from below the table. Jim would smile and nod.

By about 1:30, when most of them had started on their second egg, having more confidence in working with complex designs, Laura told them more about the symbolism and history. She surprised herself with how well everything had gone. Aunt Vi hadn't had to step in at all, except to help some of the women with dye, simply because Laura couldn't get around to them all at one time.

At 3:30, after helping several women with dye, Laura returned to the head of the table to let the group know they had only half an hour left to work on their eggs. Andy laid his head on the table, with his gaze fastened on her. The next time she looked, his eyes were closed.

After four o'clock, the rain had stopped, the pleased class members had gone after helping clean up, and Andy continued to sleep. "Was I that boring?" Laura asked Aunt Vi, who was helping pack away the dyes.

"You were just wonderful, honey," Aunt Vi assured her.

Jim, who'd stayed to help, chuckled. "He told me he hasn't had much sleep lately."

"Give me your keys, honey, and I can take these to the car while you wake that boy up so we can get the table covering." Aunt Vi and Jim took boxes out while Ethel held open the doors for them.

Laura hated to wake Andy. His lips were slightly parted, and he seemed to be in a deep sleep. Why had he come for this instead of staying home and going to bed? Was he that desperate for a devotional? She couldn't just leave him here. After all, he hadn't paid for the course. That thought inspired her to shake his arm. "Andy," she called. "Andrew Franklin." She shook him harder. "Andy!"

His eyebrows lifted, but it took awhile before the eyelids followed suit. They popped open. He stared as if startled, then blinked. Then, as if he'd never been asleep, he sat up straight. "Is it over?" he asked.

She couldn't help but laugh. He looked so funny and so cute at the same time. "Yes, it's time to go," she said.

He shook his head slightly as if shaking the sleep away. "Well, I guess I get a failing grade for falling asleep in class, and I don't even have an apple with which to bribe the teacher." He grinned and laid aside the tissue covering his egg.

"Peace offering?" he asked, handing his egg to her.

Chapter 4

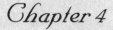

Martha Franklin stood in the kitchen of the brick ranch-style parsonage, dipping chicken in egg mixture, then rolling it in the spicy dry ingredients and laying it in the baking dish. *Where is Andy?* Of course, her twenty-eight-year-old son didn't have to report to her about his comings and goings. Just like she didn't have to cook supper for him, either. But when he wasn't working, she always cooked enough supper for herself, her husband, John, and Andy.

If Andy wasn't going to be home, he always let her know. This morning, he'd grinned and said, "I'm going to decorate some eggs, Mom." Why had he made up such a ridiculous story and grinned so mischievously when he could simply have said nothing? She washed her hands and was putting the dish in the oven when Andy walked in.

"Hi, Mom," he said, pulling out a chair at the small kitchen table where they ate when they didn't have company. Martha straightened, smoothed back her short, gray-sprinkled brown hair, and observed the strange look on her son's face. His next words nearly floored her. "Mom, I want you to be the first to know: I'm finally thinking about the possibility of settling down."

Martha gasped. She stepped over and hugged Andy. "Oh, honey. I'm so pleased. So that's where you were today. Talking to Meg. I heard that she'd come home for a visit."

"Meg? This has nothing to do with Meg."

"What?" Had she heard him right? She pulled out a chair and sat, facing him. He and Meg had dated off and on for over a year. They had differences of opinion when Meg decided she wanted a career in interior design. She was looking into a school in New York. Andy just hadn't been himself after that.

"Well, Andy, you said—"

"I didn't say anything about Meg," he blurted. "That's in the past." She watched his eyes brighten, despite the redness indicating he needed sleep. He reached over and grasped her hands. "I have prayed for the right woman for so long. And, Mom, she's here. I wasn't expecting it, but it was like God knocked me over in bringing her to me. I literally fell for her. Remember the day I came home with egg all over me?"

She remembered. They'd laughed until he'd asked if she could get the egg off his jeans. But what did that have to do with anything? She shook her head, not understanding.

"I suspected it then, Mom. The Sunday I went to a different church, I took her out to lunch. The feeling was even stronger. Then today, when I watched her decorating eggs, I knew. Mom, this woman has something special. She's the most beautiful. . .interesting person I've ever met."

Martha couldn't seem to keep her mouth closed. Had Andy lost his mind? Or was he just so much in denial about Meg that he had invented this? "Andy," she said, moving her hand from under his and patting him gently. "You don't mean this. You're fooling with me, now, aren't you?"

"No, Mom," he said emphatically. He turned his hands over. "Look at the dye on my hands. I've been decorating an egg."

"Now, honey. You may be fooling with me, or you may be fooling yourself, but I know you're in love with Meg. If you think you've gotten over her this quickly and fallen for someone else so soon, it's just not so."

"It is," he insisted. "When you meet her, you'll know. I want you to invite her to have dinner with us tomorrow after church. She's trying to get churches interesting in holding classes on egg decorating. This should interest you and my sisters. Let's invite the whole family so they can meet her."

"Oh, Andy. This is such short notice."

"You cook—they'll come."

"Well," she said and sighed. He gave her that look of his that simply melted her heart. He'd always been able to wrap females around his finger, including his own mother. And too, he was probably looking for some kind of diversion from his broken heart. She would do all she could to help, but she had to speak the truth in love. "All right, Andy. I may have to send you to the store later. But for your sake, and the sake of this girl, I have to tell you. Be careful. You're on the rebound."

"Oh, Mom," he moaned. "That's ridiculous. I've heard those things, too, and even said a few of them to some of the youth at church. Love is supposed to be blind. You can't eat: you can't sleep. Well, all that is nonsense. My feelings for her are as clear as—"

Martha watched him as he glanced out the window at the overcast sky, and he changed what he was about to say. He began again. "As clear as a blue sky. I'm so hungry I could eat that raw chicken you put into the oven. I'm going to take a nap. Would you call me when supper's ready?"

"Yes, dear." She didn't know what else to say. She'd have John talk to him later. Andy stood and stretched his arms over his head. "Have you told this girl that you think you're serious about her?"

"No, no. She wouldn't believe it any more than you do. She's wary of me. I'm going to need some help getting her to even like me."

A sound borne of irony escaped Martha's throat. That statement confirmed Andy was deluding himself. There wasn't a girl between nine and ninety who wouldn't fall for Andrew Franklin. Could he have made this up, pretending he was over Meg? "What's this girl's name, Andy?"

His arms came down. After a thoughtful instant, he said "Laura" as if it had just dawned on him.

Staring, she waited for the rest. It didn't come. All

that came was an "Um." She seriously doubted the girl's name was Laura Um. He glanced away and blinked a couple of times with a blank look on his face. His shoulders moved in a slight shrug, before he strode from the room, saying, "I have to make a phone call. Don't forget to wake me."

Someone needed to wake him up to reality. Martha continued to sit, dazed at what was happening to her son. Andy said he was in love, and he didn't even know this girl's last name. She knew the breakup with Meg had hit him hard, but she had not suspected that an intelligent, exceptional boy like Andy could go so far off the deep end.

❧

"Oh, Aunt Vi, that's wonderful. I'm so glad you and Jim are going out for lunch together," Laura gushed after Vi hung up the phone.

"This is nothing personal, Laura," Vi told her niece. She'd told herself the same thing, and yet found herself looking in the mirror a few times more than necessary and even asked Laura if her earrings matched her suit.

That's when Laura had said she looked perfect and behaved as if this lunch was more than business. Vi reminded her niece, and herself, that this was strictly business. "Jim teaches an occasional continuing education class in arts and crafts at one of the junior colleges. He thinks a good class might be a combination of decorating eggs, real and wooden. After lunch, I'm going to look at his eggs."

"That's a great idea, Aunt Vi."

Vi nodded. It was good to have Laura's approval. She'd always counted on her husband's advice, but he was gone now. That was hard to face, but the Lord was making opportunities for her to reach out to others. She'd learned Jim lost his wife six years ago. They both understood the need to talk to someone else and share memories. She'd spent many years as a happily married woman. Now, her happiness would be in watching Laura find and settle down with the man God had for her.

Turning her thoughts toward Laura, she smiled. "Now, something personal is Andy Franklin's inviting you home to meet his family."

"Oh, Aunt Vi, don't say that," Laura reprimanded. "He just thinks his mom will be more receptive to having an egg-decorating class at her church if I talk to her at home instead of just mentioning it hurriedly after a worship service. Andy fell asleep during the class, and he's trying to make up for it."

"Now, Laura," Vi said, "don't tell me that young man is only interested in eggs. I mean, he gave you his egg." Andy had divided his egg into four equal parts. On each quarter was a big red heart against a yellow background. It was beautiful in its simplicity and symbolism. "I think he's trying to tell you something."

Vi saw the color suffuse Laura's face. She'd come to recognize Laura's insecurity. Vi knew being overly sensitive, which spurred self-consciousness, was a part of the creative personality. She'd tried to tell Laura that, but it didn't take away the feelings she had of not quite being or doing well enough. That had probably come from having an older brother who excelled in every area.

"Laura, I really like Andy. He's not only about the best-looking young man I've ever seen, but he's a dedicated Christian in a job of helping people, a charmer, to be sure, has a wonderful sense of humor, is full of energy—"

"Aunt Vi!" Laura stopped her. "I can't let myself get serious about anyone." She laughed self-consciously. "I don't even know what God wants me to do with the rest of my life."

Vi admired her niece, who wanted God's will in her life above all else. "We'll just keep praying about that, honey. God will let you know when His timing is right."

❧

"Do I look all right?" Laura asked her aunt before leaving for church. "I want to look conservative, but not like a dud."

"Oh, honey, you couldn't look like a dud if you tried. You look lovely. That's a sweet little spring suit. Now the skirt's a little short for my taste, but very conservative compared with what they're wearing now— even to church. And you look good in green."

Yeah, Laura was thinking. *Andy could say, "Hey, you look great. You blend in so well with the bushes."* Other women could wear blue or green and enhance their eyes, but what in the world enhanced light brown? She wasn't about to dab color on her eyelids and look like a dyed egg.

Having received Aunt Vi's approval, which she would have gotten had she dressed in a pillowcase, Laura returned to her room for a last look in the mirror. There was nothing more she could do. She felt more nervous about going to Andy's home for lunch than she had been teaching that class, but she couldn't turn down the opportunity. If she held a class at the biggest church in the area, then smaller churches would want the same. She picked up her Bible, purse, and small basket containing two eggs.

During the church service, Laura forced herself not to look at Andy too often. He sat near the back like he'd done the first time she'd seen him there. After the service, he met her outside the choir room and drove her to his parents' nice brick home. "Oh, my. How many people will be here today?" she asked, when Andy pulled up behind several cars parked in the double-car driveway.

"Just family," he said. "My parents and sisters."

They were all so friendly and nice, Laura immediately felt at home. She could readily see Andy got his stature and good looks from both parents. Pastor John was an older version of Andy, except he wore eyeglasses and had some gray in his thinner dark hair. Martha Franklin was attractive and trim, exactly what Laura expected a wife of an important man of the community to look like. The sisters, Denise and Joanie, seemed extremely glad to meet her. Their husbands were polite and shook her hand. The five children ranged in age from eight months to seven years. Except for the baby, they were running through the rooms, chasing each other.

"Could I hold her, please?" Laura asked. "I haven't held a baby in years. Not since my brother's children were little."

"With pleasure," Joanie replied. "She's heavy."

"Oh, she's just precious." Laura sat in a chair with the baby on her lap, facing her. She sang a little song while the baby watched her lips, then laughed and tried to get her mouth. Everybody gathered around to watch, except the children chasing each other.

About the time Mrs. Franklin said she would put dinner on the table, the baby decided she need a change and Joanie took her. Laura offered to help with dinner.

"No, you're our guest," Mrs. Franklin said. "All I have to do is take some things out of the warmer and heat other dishes up in the microwave."

After they were seated and Pastor John, as he wanted to be called, gave thanks, they all began to ask each other personal questions. She learned that Joanie and her family lived nearby and went to Pastor John's church. Denise lived an hour's drive away, and her family came this morning just to meet her. That was incredible. Denise must really have a penchant for egg decorating. Both sisters and Andy had gone to the same university from which Laura just finished her senior year.

After the formalities, the fun began. The discussions became a battle between mother and daughters. Andy was the object of discussion, Pastor John was an impartial referee paying more attention to his plate than the conversation, and a verbal battle ensued between mother and daughters.

The sisters said Laura needed to know what she was getting into, associating with Andy. They accused him of being lazy and self-centered. His mother sang his praises, telling that he graduated from college with a 4.0, worked at saving people's lives, and helped out with the youth on his days off.

To Laura, he sounded more like his mother's description, but she liked the bantering that went on between him and his sisters. She got the impression they might be a tad jealous. In fact, they agreed that he was their mother's favorite because he was a boy and the baby.

His mother just pursed her lips and shook her head, but didn't deny it.

Andy rebutted, "Well, who was it that could get anything they wanted out of Dad, when I couldn't?"

"Somebody had to take up for us," Joanie said while Denise added, "He's still Mama's little boy, living at home."

"Now, Denise. He has his own rooms, and he's saving his money. Anyway, it would be ridiculous to pay for an apartment when he's never there."

"He's taking advantage of you," Joanie said.

"He's being sensible. Besides, he does things around here."

His dad decided to get into it. "He cut the grass once last summer." He laughed like it didn't really matter.

"He keeps the couch warm," Denise said and hit Andy on the arm with her fist, causing Andy to blanch and drop the mashed potatoes off his fork.

"You guys are just jealous because you were in too

big a hurry to get away from home," he accused.

That started a whole new debate. While the sisters argued, Andy just kept eating and looking smug. Laura thought he was the cutest thing she'd ever seen. She liked the playful interplay. She hadn't had that with her older brother, who behaved like the stereotypical older brother, looking after her.

She was amazed they could feed their children and keep up that kind of debating. It had all started by Joanie saying that Laura needed to know what Andy was really like. She didn't know why they thought she needed to know, but she didn't mind knowing. He was truly wonderful.

Andy encouraged Laura to show her eggs while they ate the cream-cheese-frosted carrot cake his mom had made for dessert. Laura showed one that was free-style and one with an intricate design. Pastor John said, "Very nice," and the other husbands nodded. The sisters were delighted and said they wanted to learn how to decorate eggs. Andy's mom seemed genuinely pleasantly surprised, examining the eggs carefully. "These don't look like your ordinary Easter eggs," she said and smiled.

"They look more like Faberge," Denise said, impressed.

"Well, since you all like them," Andy said, "why don't you set up a class and let Laura teach this at your church?"

Both sisters agreed it was a great idea.

When Andy stared at his mom, she said, "That's

something to think about. It's a possibilty."

Andy winked at Laura as if it were a cinch. Laura wasn't sure. His mom didn't pursue it further. She began to clear the table. Laura stood and touched her hand. "Let me do this, Mrs. Franklin. You cooked. I saw that dishwasher in the kitchen and I know how to operate one."

"No, no. This won't take long."

"You're going to make us look bad," Joanie warned.

Laura laughed. "You have little ones to watch. Really, I want to do this."

Denise said they had to get back in time for church that evening. Joanie and her family prepared to leave, too. The baby had to take a nap.

"Now that school's out, I'm available for baby-sitting," Laura told her.

"Oh, great. I might take you up on that. She really took to you. I guess Andy has your phone number."

"I do," he said.

"It's also in the phone book under my aunt's name. Vivien Hensley."

While the grandchildren and grandparents were giving kisses and hugs, Laura began clearing the dining room table. Andy sat in the kitchen.

"Aren't you going to help?" she asked.

"I don't want to mislead you, Laura. The truth is, I don't do dishes. In case of emergency, I have and would again. That's when there's no dishes left to eat out of and you can't hold the food in your hands. I do a lot of gross things in my line of work, but dishes are not my thing."

Laura loved his straightforwardness. By not trying to impress her, he greatly impressed her. She returned his smile as he sat and watched her parade back and forth with dirty dishes.

By the time Mrs. Franklin returned, Laura had most of it done. Andy was sitting at the kitchen table. "We'll finish up, Mom. Why don't you and Dad go take your Sunday nap?"

"I know you're trying to get rid of me, Andy, but I will not leave a guest in here to clean up the kitchen." She began to help Laura. After the dining room table was cleaned and all the dishes in the dishwasher, Mrs. Franklin expressed her pleasure and gratitude to Laura for coming to dinner.

After Mrs. Franklin left the room, Laura was surprised that Andy asked her to sit at the table. She thought he'd take her straight home. She sat across from him. "I would take you downstairs to see my room," he said, "but Mom and Dad don't like the idea of my taking just one gal downstairs unless she's a friend I've known forever."

Laura nodded. She understood. They hadn't known each other long enough to be friends. Still, he was being very nice and helpful to her. He took a deep breath, then began. "You heard how my sisters talked today."

"Oh, I knew they were kidding you. I think it's just great you guys can do that."

"Well, yes, they are kidding, but they can get

incredibly honest. They will eventually tell you everything I've ever done and every girl I've dated, so I want to beat them to the punch."

Laura didn't know what to make of that. When were they going to tell her? During an egg-decorating class? Why would it matter to him? Maybe because he was a sensitive guy and wanted people to think the best of him. That was probably it. Look how he'd tried to make up for bumping into her at the supermarket and then falling asleep in her class. He was a super guy.

"There's one girl in particular they harp about. Her name's Meg. They expected me to marry her. I told them Meg had other plans, and they got the idea I was jilted. They asked if I had other plans, and I said no. Now, they've all got the idea I'm heartbroken. I can't convince them I meant that I had no plans—not 'other' plans."

Laura nodded. Maybe he needed someone in whom to confide. "How long did you and she go together?"

"Um, about a year and a half."

Laura nodded and cleared her throat. "Well, I can see why they might think it was serious."

"It wasn't. We modeled together. We liked going out and at one point it got kind of serious, but we both realized we were trying to push that relationship. When you start getting a little age on you, you begin to consider settling for less than the best. Now, I'm so glad I didn't."

Laura thought that might be the explanation of the

egg. He'd painted it to express his love for Meg. Then giving it away would be a symbol of letting go.

For a moment, she wondered if she should tell him what was going on in the back of her mind. Immediately, she thought better of it. She sat still and quiet, in case he needed to talk more. He did, but it was not about his love life, or lack of it. Instead, he asked, "Would you like to ride around and look at churches? And graveyards?"

"Oh, I would!" Laura couldn't imagine spending the afternoon in a more delightful way. She could see the churches where she hoped to teach egg decorating, and she loved to read old tombstones.

The sun began to drop behind the horizon by the time he dropped her off. Aunt Vi came to the door as they walked up the sidewalk. She invited him in and asked if they'd had supper.

"I didn't even think about," Andy said with an apologetic look at Laura.

"Neither did I," she replied. "Would you like to come in for something?"

"Thanks, but I'm going home and hit the hay. I've had about four hours sleep in the past thirty-six hours."

"Come eat with us Sunday after church," Aunt Vi invited.

"Sorry, I have to work. But," he added, "I'll take a rain check on that."

Laura stood and watched as he strode down the walkway to his car. She waved when he stood at the driver's door, looked at her, and lifted his hand in farewell. She gazed down the empty street after he'd gone. Then she lifted her eyes to the clear night sky. A half moon shown brightly. Stars began to twinkle.

She saw no sign of rain.

Chapter 5

O ne of life's storms struck two days later. Andy called early in the morning to tell Laura that he'd been on a emergency call the night before. To his shock, the patient had been Jim, from her egg class. He'd had severe chest pains and was now in ICU. "Due to ethical considerations, I wouldn't normally reveal this, but Jim asked me to call you," Andy said.

"Oh, yes. I'll want to go and see him. Aunt Vi will, too."

"Let me come by and pick you two up."

Not only did Andy come by, but when they got to ICU and were told Jim couldn't have visitors just yet, Andy sweet-talked the nurse into letting them look in on Jim long enough to let him know they'd visited and would be praying.

"He's so young to have this happen," Vi said. "He's only sixty-four."

"It can happen at any age," Andy reminded her.

Aunt Vi nodded. "You two can go on if you like,"

she said. "I'm going to stay here for awhile. Laura, you could come back for me later. Jim doesn't have any family close by. He has a brother in a nursing home in California. I'll be around to make a call or do whatever is needed."

"Are you sure you're up to this, Aunt Vi?" Laura asked.

Her aunt nodded, blinking back the moisture from her eyes. "I want to do it, Laura. I know a little about grief and fear of what might happen. Maybe I can be of help to Jim or even some others who have to wait around here."

"Let's say a prayer for him, right here," Andy said.

Laura couldn't hold back the wetness that spilled from her eyes when Andy fell to his knees, right there in the hospital waiting room and said a quick prayer for Jim, for all those who would attend him, and for all of Jim's friends and loved ones.

She didn't think she even closed her eyes. She heard the prayer with her ears, but a saying she'd heard somewhere kept buzzing in her mind—*a man is tallest when he's on his knees.*

❧

Over the next few days, Andy was more impressed with Laura than ever. She had called everyone who'd attended the college egg-decorating class, and half of them wanted to take part in what she planned. On Saturday, they met at Vi's and spent the day making eggs for Jim.

These didn't have to be artistic, just a personal message expressing "Get Well" wishes.

"We can also put a symbol of faith on each one," Laura suggested. "That way, it can be a witness to any-one—doctors, nurses, or friends—who comes to visit Jim, and he can tell them what the symbols mean."

Andy hadn't slept much the night before, but he wanted to be a part of that unique project. He'd never been so impressed with anyone as he was with Laura's creative way of witnessing about her faith. Each time he was near her, he became more convinced that she was the one he wanted by his side. . .always.

❧

"Giddie-up. Giddie-up. Giddie-up."

"Whoa, horsey!" Laura yelled and reached for four-year-old Timmy just as Andy turned the corner from the carpeted hallway onto the tiled kitchen floor. The little one was about to slip off. Andy-Horse whoaed and Laura straightened the little one, eager to gallop.

"Ouch!" Andy exclaimed. "Good thing that he's not wearing spurs."

They laughed as Andy continued playing horse, even for baby Celeste while Laura walked along beside them, holding her on.

After Celeste had her bottle, fell asleep, and was in her crib, Timmy sat down to watch his last video for the night, an animated Old Testament story of Moses. He ate apple slices and peanut butter that Andy had fixed for him.

Laura made sure everything was cleaned up and put away, and she washed the baby's bottle while Andy read Timmy a bedtime story, then listened to the little boy's prayers. Laura was sitting on the couch when Andy came in, carrying a pillow. He propped it in the corner opposite her and leaned his head back.

"You'd make a great dad," she said.

"Only if there was a great mom around." He laughed lightly. "I'm good in case of emergency, but I'd need someone like you around for preventive measures, so there'd be no dire emergency."

She smiled. *Not me*, she reminded herself when her heart had leapt. *Just someone "like" me.* "I love children," she said.

"I can tell." That beautiful smile of his melted her heart.

Still smiling, he closed his eyes. She realized he had gotten off work that morning after having worked a twenty-four-hour shift. When he came over to Joanie's, he'd told her that. He tried not to sleep very much during the day so he could get a good night's sleep.

Joanie had called her on Monday, asking if she could baby-sit on Friday night. She and her husband wanted to go out for dinner and a movie. Laura was eager to sit with the children. Right before Joanie left, she said, "Andy probably told you he'd come over and help."

Andy hadn't told her, but she'd been more than pleased when he came. Already, several times, they had gone together to the hospital to see Jim, then to Jim's home after he was released. He hadn't required surgery, but would need to be on medication for awhile and lower his cholesterol.

Every time Laura saw Andy, she was even more impressed with his good qualities. She doubted that many men would volunteer to baby-sit their sister's children. She could understand that parents might want to go out occasionally, but she could also understand how a man and woman could enjoy spending their lives together, at home with their wonderful children, just being a family.

After checking on Celeste and Timmy, both of whom were asleep, she turned the lights off except for a table lamp and returned to her corner of the couch. She didn't want to turn on the TV and disturb Andy. Anyway, she doubted there'd be a program as interesting as watching his parted lips twitch slightly and his chest rise with easy breathing.

She felt like she could watch him sleep 'til kingdom come. She had to settle for watching him 'til Joanie and her husband returned.

❦

Andy hadn't told Laura yet that he loved her and intended to make her his wife. He figured she was getting the idea. He wasn't taking her out to dinners or movies, but he was involving her in his life. The second week after they baby-sat together, he again went to her church, then they ate what she helped cook at Aunt Vi's. The three of them had gone to visit Jim that day.

The following week, she sat beside him in his dad's church, and they worshipped together. Andy wanted that to happen for the rest of their lives. When he looked over at her and smiled, he thought she must surely be able to read his mind and know how he felt. The two of them went to the steak house with his parents for lunch.

The two of them baby-sat again for Joanie in June. Laura taught several egg-decorating classes for women's groups and several area churches. He drove her down to Denise's house when she was going to teach the egg class at Denise's church. Andy spent the day keeping Denise's three children. Then Andy and Laura stayed for supper.

By the time the Fourth of July rolled around, she was with him or in his thoughts all the time. She was in his life and in his dreams. Neither spoke of love. He didn't think it necessary. It was too obvious. No one says, "I think I need air to breathe or water to survive." It's just an accepted fact of life.

They went together to his parents' house for a cook-out. All the family was there. His sisters loved her. Their children vied for her attention. She was part of the family, but he feared that if he took her in his arms, he might never let her go. This was not a trial-dating period. He knew, without a doubt, he wanted this woman for his wife. He would try to be patient. He still needed to prove to his mom that he was not on the rebound from Meg.

✦

Martha Franklin felt ashamed of herself for giving Andy the impression she had anything against Laura. When she saw Andy and Laura together, she felt it was obvious that girl would be willing to follow him to the ends of the earth; but Martha felt if Meg snapped her fingers, Andy would go running. Somebody was bound to get hurt if this continued, and it would probably be Laura.

She felt even worse after bringing the possibility of an egg-decorating class before the Women's Missionary Society. To her surprise, they enthusiastically endorsed the possibility. Martha was not keen on the idea, but being the pastor's wife and program chairman of the society, she had to attend. In fact, she was in charge of setting it up and introducing the teacher.

"Laura," she could honestly say upon entering the fellowship hall, "this is lovely, the way you have place settings at the table. I would have come sooner had I known you went to such details."

"Oh, you've done enough, Mrs. Franklin. It's so kind of you to ask me here. You and your family are the most wonderful people I could know."

"Thank you, dear," she said, feeling far from wonderful. She was grateful for the distraction of women coming into the room. By nine o'clock, over fifty women attended, more than came to some of their special programs.

Martha wondered if she had underestimated Laura when she told of her reasons for holding the classes. "Those of you in church know the Gospel," Laura told them, "but I'm hoping to teach this to groups who are not Christians. It's a way for me to explain the meaning behind the designs and symbols."

Martha was impressed with the history of the art form being handed down within a family for generations. She listened intently as Laura explained that

Pysanky had been part of the Ukraine for centuries. It had been associated with spring. The peasants believed that magical power was embodied in an egg. They decorated the eggs in the spring to celebrate the warming of the sun as it brought new vigor to life.

"In 988," Laura said, "the Ukraine accepted Christianity. It was then the eggs took on deep religious meaning, representing the joy that Christ brings into our lives." She explained the symbols that were once pagan were now religious.

"The sieve or net look," Laura explained, "suggests the religious 'fishing for men.' The triangles are symbols for the God the Father, the Son, and the Holy Spirit."

Martha could very well conceive of her explanations being a witness to her faith. The cross or the butterfly represented the resurrection of Jesus. The fish was the ancient symbol for Christ. Ladders suggested prayer. X's with a line though them was for the crown of thorns. The grapevine symbolized the blood of Christ. A leaf suggested new life.

There were so many more, and Martha could readily see how one could effectively witness to her faith while teaching others an art form at the same time. Yes, Andy had been right. She should not have trivialized what this girl was doing. Tears came into her eyes as Laura related the legends involving Mary, the mother of Jesus.

"One such legend tells that Mary gave eggs to the soldiers at the cross of Jesus," Laura told them. "The dots on the eggs represent her tears. Another legend was that Mary took an apron full of eggs to try and bribe Pilate into releasing Jesus before He was crucified. Her teardrops made permanent marks on the eggs. When Pilate refused her plea, she let go of the apron and the Pysanky eggs rolled over the ground into many parts of the world, spreading Christianity wherever they went."

Martha found herself caught up in the history, legends, and art form. For her first design, she chose free-style of various symbols after having divided her egg into quarters. Using the *kitska* and wax, she covered everything that was to remain white. Then she placed her egg in yellow dye for five minutes. After patting it dry with a tissue, she waxed everything that was to remain yellow. She continued that process until her egg of many colors was finished.

Carefully, holding the egg over the candle flame, she melted the wax and gently wiped away the liquid. The thought of blowing the insides out of the egg made her nervous. "I'm afraid I'll crack it," she wailed.

Laura encouraged her. "Just make a small hole in one end with this hat pin," she said, "and make one just a little larger at the other end."

Although cringing, Martha did it. Several of her friends applauded when the shell didn't crack. "How hard should I blow?"

The group laughed with relief when Laura held up a bulb syringe and said that's what she should use to blow the insides out of the egg into a bowl. Everyone crowded around to watch.

"We won't have time to varnish today," Laura said. "But you can do that at home."

Martha was so pleased with her egg, she decided upon a more complex design for the second one of the day. Carefully, she went through the entire process, taking over two hours. She had an egg that Laura told her, in private, was the best any student of hers had produced on only her second try.

She was proud of it. She'd chosen a continuous line around the egg, representing eternity. She chose to design an eight-pointed star, the ancient symbol for Christ, on each half of the egg. Each point came near the dividing line. Between the points and the line, she painted small circles, representing Mary's tears. In the small spaces remaining, she drew and dyed various kinds of flowers, representing love.

Four o'clock came before Martha realized it was time to quit. She finished the dyeing process but hadn't melted off the wax nor blown out the inside of the egg. Laura said, now that they knew how, they could finish at home. She had given them written instructions of all she had taught them.

On the way home, Martha stopped by the hardware store and picked up a small can of clear varnish. She proudly showed her eggs to John that evening and to Andy when he came home from work the following morning. She could honestly tell Andy that she admired Laura's artistry, teaching ability, and commitment to the Lord.

His "I told you so" look and arm around her

shoulder as he pulled her close kept her from saying she still did not think that meant he and Laura were meant for each other.

Chapter 6

By the end of July, Laura knew the past three months had been the most wonderful and most difficult of her life. She loved Andy Franklin with all her being, but right from the beginning, or at least during that first lunch, she couldn't imagine that anyone would not love him. He was everything and more than any woman could want in a man.

And yet, she had to accept her feelings were not mutual. She was grateful that she apparently fulfilled in him some kind of need in his life. Maybe it was for a friend in which to confide. In the past two weeks in particular, while they sat in Aunt Vi's porch swing, watching the stars come out, he told her everything about his life, what he'd done right and what he'd done wrong.

She told him about herself, too, which was dull compared with his many glamorous girlfriends and his job as a paramedic. She had asked God to make clear what direction her life should take. Andy's help in introducing her to his family, resulting in their churches inviting her to teach her egg class seemed like God was speaking directly about her future. Strange, how something could be so wonderful and sad at the same time.

Her future was decided, and her relationship with Andy was defined. They were friends. Someday, she would look back upon this summer without all that emotional upheaval that surrounded her now, in his presence. Soon, she would share her future plans with him.

She did not expect that sharing to come so soon, nor in the way it came. After supper on a Tuesday, she and Andy sat in the swing. He began to outline the past few months from his point of view.

"Laura, we've known each other for several months now. You've met my family and have seen me in many family situations. I've seen you at church, here at Aunt Vi's, at my family outings, and in your egg class. I know how you relate to people, and you know that about me. We've shared our pasts as honestly as we know how. I think we've covered just about everything important. Except one thing." His face was shadowed by the departing sun.

"Except one?"

He turned in the swing, his body, as well as his face, in her direction. "The future," he said.

Laura smiled and looked down at her hands in her lap. She nodded. "I've been thinking I should share that with you."

"Oh, Laura. You can't imagine how relieved I am to hear you say that. I've been afraid to say anything, thinking it was too soon or you didn't feel the same."

Laura stared at him. What did he mean? What had she said to elicit that response from him?

The next thing she knew, he stood. With the lift of his hand on hers, he brought her up to stand in front of him. His arms came around her and his lips met hers. Knowing this had to be a dream, she did not protest. She thought she had kissed before—but no. This was a real kiss. This was no puppy love, no experimenting with how it felt to be kissed. This was a part of her whole being, involving her heart and soul.

Before she had finished, Andy moved her away, far enough to speak. "I'm in love with you, Laura. I want us to get married. As soon as possible. I see no need to prolong the misery of living without you. Laura, to me you're like an oasis, and I'm a perishing man in the desert. My life is going to be desolate unless I can drink at that fountain. Will you marry me?"

The interminable silence hung between them as the sun gave up its spot in the sky and sunk below the horizon. Dusk settled. Andy waited for her to compose herself. When she finally looked up at him, her face was wet with tears. "I need to pray about it."

She couldn't believe she had the strength to say that.

His shadowed face looked as if he, neither, could believe it. "You don't love me?"

"Yes, I love you," she said. Her knees felt so weak, she sat back in the swing. Andy continued to stand, as if turned to stone. "But I believe God has confirmed He has something else in mind for my life. Oh, I want to marry you. But I can't. Can you understand that?"

He looked for all the world like a shell, in which all the insides had been blown away. Finally, he moved. Turning his back, he walked to the banister and held it for awhile. When he faced her again, he spoke, in a subdued tone.

"You asked if I understand," he said quietly. "My answer is yes and no. If God isn't first in a relationship, it's doomed for failure. He has to be first in everything, but I've been so sure you're the woman for me. It seems so right. Why would I feel such a great love for you and want to spend the rest of my life with you if it isn't God's will? I'm a Christian. You're a Christian. What does God have for you that would exclude me? Is there someone else you haven't told me about?"

"No, Andy. There's no one else. I just believe God is leading me in a different direction."

"Can we discuss it?"

Laura shook her head. "Not until I'm sure."

With pain in his eyes and in his voice, he said sadly, "If it were anything else, I would fight for you, try to win you over. But I won't try and interfere with God's will for you."

He turned and walked away.

Laura knew this was the hardest test God could have given her. How could she give up the most wonderful man she'd ever known?

That man had brought her hope and help and fulfillment and love. Maybe God wanted her to experience those things so she could tell others that God had a purpose and plan for them, even if they lose what seems most important in life. God is Creator and Sustainer. He must be first. It was possible for a person to have God and the love of their life. Laura would like to have that, but it seemed God was telling her to go in a different direction.

With tears in her eyes and an ache in her heart, accompanied by a strange calm deep within, she watched Andy go.

❧

Martha had just finished cleaning the kitchen and mopping the tile floor when she heard the back door open and someone come into the foyer. Who could that be? Andy had gone to see Laura, so she didn't expect him back so soon. Her quick glance revealed Andy standing in the doorway, staring across the mopped floor as if it were a river too wide to cross.

She laughed lightly. "Come on through, Andy. I still have the mop in my hand."

He didn't go through but stepped inside and sat at the kitchen table. He stared for a moment at his clasped hands in front of him. Had he broken up with Laura? Had he realized he was on the rebound from Meg? Something was bothering him. She carefully walked over and touched his hands. "What's wrong, Son?"

He looked up with a somber expression in his eyes. "I asked Laura to marry me, Mom."

"Well, what did she say?" Martha asked, as if she wouldn't know.

Andy didn't answer immediately. He looked down again, and his shoulders slumped. Had she failed her son by not being supportive? She'd told him all along he was on the rebound, but if he was making a mistake, it was her duty as a mother and a Christian to stand by him and help however she could.

After all, she thought, *I'm not the one who has to live with Laura.*

That thought brought such unexpected images in her mind that she had to do something to escape them. Wanting him to know she didn't want to spoil this time for him, she murmured with as much enthusiasm as she could muster, "Well, congratulations, Andy."

He still didn't respond. Instead, he walked over to the countertop and fingered a decorated egg that still had wax on it. Pasting on a smile, she walked over to him. Why did he have such a stark look on his face?

Then, in a choked voice, he told her, "She turned me down, Mom."

Impossible! Not just because he was her son, but Andrew Franklin had everything going for him—looks, personality, character, intelligence, and a heart for the Lord. That girl would never in a million years have an opportunity like this again. Something was wrong with a girl like that who would turn Andy down. Now, Meg might do it for a career. But. . .Laura? The egg dyer?

"Why?" she finally asked. Andy's mouth didn't seem able to get any words out. He shook his head and hurried from the kitchen, leaving the egg on the countertop.

As if in slow motion, Martha watched the egg roll

to the edge and plop onto the white tile. Accompanying the greenish-yellow ooze was an almost unbearable stench. She'd forgotten to blow out the insides. Her egg was rotten. Martha felt her stomach tie in knots. She put her hands on it and sat in a chair at the table.

John came to the doorway. "Whew! I thought we had a skunk in here."

"No," she said. "Just two rotten eggs, and one of them is named Martha."

John cleaned up the mess with paper towels, mopped the spot, and turned on the ceiling fan so the stench could float out through the open windows. Then he sat down at the table and reached for Martha's hand. "You can make another egg. Laura won't fault you for breaking that one. She's a sweet young woman. A real diamond among the coal." Caressing her hand, he added softly, "The way those two look at each other reminds me of us when we were going together. Your big eyes shining with love just took my breath away."

"Oh, John," she wailed, looking over at him with eyes swimming.

"Now watch out," he teased, "you're looking at me that way."

She shifted her gaze to the table and shook her head. "I've had the wrong attitude, John. I think maybe I've just been jealous of another woman taking my son away from me."

"Oh, I'm sure it's deeper than that, Martha. Remember how my blood boiled every time the girls went out on a date? And then when they wanted to get married, I almost lost my religion."

She smiled through her tears and nodded. She hoped she wasn't as bad as she looked to herself right now. Regardless, it was over. She needed to think about Andy right now. "He asked her to marry him, John—and she turned him down."

"Well, Martha, we've always prayed that the Lord will lead our children to the mate He has for them. Let's have faith that He will do that. Andy's probably in no mood to talk tonight. I'll talk to him in the morning. Let's pray about this." He laid his hands, palms up, on the table, and Martha put hers in his and closed her eyes.

After John's prayer of asking God to give Andy the strength and wisdom to deal with the situation appropriately, Martha felt him squeeze her hands. "Now we just leave it up to the Lord," he said. She nodded, but knew he was much more adept at doing that than she. There were still matters of the heart she had to get straight with the Lord.

Even as John was leaving the kitchen, Martha was struggling with that thought she'd had earlier. *I don't have to live with Laura.* It seemed her mind opened up and a vision of reality came in. Suppose, just suppose, heaven forbid, that something happened to John, and she had to give up the parsonage and go live with one of her children. Andy didn't have a home, so she couldn't go there.

She loved her daughters dearly but had to admit she and they were strongly opinionated and often disagreed on many issues, including how to raise their children. In their homes, she would have to keep her opinions to herself, lest she upset everyone and be shipped off to a nursing home. She would simply have to hold her tongue and grow old as full-time baby-sitter, chief cook, and bottle washer.

Laura always helped with the cooking and cleaning up. She didn't ask, but after that first Sunday, she'd just come in and set the table and helped in other ways. Laura had left her home and friends to come stay with an aunt who lost her husband. How many young people would do that?

She loved her daughters and sons-in-law dearly. Now, thinking of Laura as a daughter-in-law, she realized she could live with someone like Laura. The young woman had a gentle nature, a loving spirit, and a strong desire to witness for the Lord. Yes, if she had to live with someone, she would like it to be someone like Laura.

But Martha was not the one in question here. It was Andy.

Yet, what had she wanted for her son? Someone like Meg, beautiful and effervescent, long and lean, with fingernails to match. Someone who complimented Andy's extraordinary good looks.

With a moan, Martha lay her head on the table. Some people were like hard-boiled eggs. Some were soft-centered. Some looked good on the outside but were rotten inside. Martha wished that cleaning up one's insides were as simple as taking a bulb syringe and rinsing out an egg with clear water.

Chapter 7

W hy?
Why had Laura turned him down? How
could God let that happen? Her rejection
hit him hard. He'd never had a girl tell him no about
anything. In fact, he'd gotten the impression they sort of
clamored after him. Not just single ones either. Contrary
to what his mother thought, he hadn't wanted to marry
Meg. She was a great girl and they'd had fun, but it
hadn't disturbed him at all that she was going in a different direction with her career. She simply didn't have
the kind of inner beauty that radiated from Laura.

For days he poured himself into his work, and on
his off days he helped the youth director with his many
summer activities with young people. He tried not to
think, just get through the days until the disappointment and hurt would ease.

His wounded pride healed first, but he didn't think
his heart ever would. He even got over blaming God.
The fault lay with Andrew Franklin. He had to face
facts. He was not good enough for Laura. There was

something about him she couldn't accept.

As the days and weeks of July turned into August, Andy could no longer escape what he'd pushed aside for a long time. He hadn't asked God's opinion about his life's mate. Oh, he knew she should be a Christian woman and committed to the Lord. He thought it was his own responsibility to use his intelligence, common sense, observations, and feelings. He'd expected a woman to come along someday and hit him like a ton of bricks, but he hadn't expected her to come along and make his life as precarious as slipping and sliding on broken eggs.

Doing what he'd done for weeks, he sat on his couch after supper, thinking the same old thoughts, feeling the same old despair. What was he to do now? What could he do? Where could he go?

Where could I go but to the Lord? came to mind. That was one thing about being a preacher's son. He couldn't escape the words of hymns and verses of the Bible.

Couldn't I?

Knowing that thought to be untrue, he decided it was time to get on his knees and be honest with himself and with God. Kneeling by the couch, he recalled that he'd told Laura that God must be first in a life. He believed that. God had always been a part of his life. He'd known what he was doing when at age six he'd accepted Jesus into his heart and life as his personal Savior. He hadn't always lived an exemplary life, but he'd always felt the chastisement of the Holy Spirit when that happened, and he had grown closer to God through the years. He wanted to serve God with his life and his work and be a witness for Him.

With reservations.

Yes, with reservations. It wasn't easy to tell the Lord He could have all of you. Well, he could tell Him. But to mean it was another thing. *What is best in life? What I want? Or what God wants for me?*

Andy knew the answer. It wasn't easy to accept. "God," he prayed then, "lead me to put You first, not myself. Lead me to put Laura's well-being ahead of what I want. Maybe I would be a hindrance to her."

His prayer changed then. Instead of focusing on himself, he truly wanted what was best for Laura. "Lord, lead her into a definite assurance of Your will. And God, lead me to put You first. If my life is not what You want, if I am not committed enough to be a part of Laura's life, then forgive me. Make of her what You put her on earth to be. God, show me how to serve You better. I give this to You. You give peace, Lord. I need it now."

Rising from his knees, Andy felt a sadness, a loss, a dying of hope and expectation, but he felt a strange kind of peace, too. He wanted Laura for himself, but more than that, he wanted her to have a life that was committed to God. God could give her a much fuller life than Andy Franklin ever could. Even in his heartache, Andy knew that God could give Andy Franklin a more fulfilled life than anything or anyone on earth.

He sat on his couch. "God, give me that fulfilled life. My job is helping people. I've felt that is Your will for me. It's what I've enjoyed and wanted. I'm open now to what You've been trying to tell me for a long time."

Andy sat for several minutes, so long his heartbeat slowed, his mind drifted, his eyes closed, and peacefully, he drifted off to sleep.

⁂

Laura had been tempted to say "No" when Andy said he'd like to come over and share something with her; but in her silence, he'd said he wasn't going to try to pressure her and that his life had taken a different direction.

She didn't know whether to feel good or bad about that. Perhaps it was best he could move on so quickly, so easily. For her, she would remember him forever. The easiest thing in the world would be to fall into his arms, agree to marry him, and ignore the will of God for her life, but she knew that was not where fulfillment lay. There would always be a gnawing misery deep inside her. When the choice became Andy or God, she had to choose God.

Then, too, Aunt Vi and Jim becoming friends seemed to be another indication from God that it was time for Laura to move on. But now that Andy implied he had moved on, perhaps that was a sign that such a marriage between them was not made in heaven. She sat on the porch swing, waiting. When he drove up, her heart ached for Andy, whom she loved so dearly but could not have.

She was glad he didn't sit beside her, but backed up against the banister, holding on with both hands. "I needed to let you know this, Laura," he began. "I believe God brought us together for a reason." He held up his hand to stop the words she started to say.

"No, let me finish. I'm not saying He wants us to marry. Apparently He doesn't. But my relationship to you has brought me into a deeper commitment with the Lord. I've ignored His voice for a long time, but during that time He has been preparing me just the same. He's prepared me for medical missions with my paramedic training and experiences. He's calling me to the mission field, perhaps to places like Honduras, where there is such devastation and need. So, I just wanted to thank you for being such a committed person and breaking my heart, which was necessary to make me listen to God."

"Andy," she choked out. Her hands came up to her fluttering heart. "Oh."

"Laura," he called, rushing to her "what's wrong? Did I say the wrong thing?"

"I don't know, Andy. Oh, this scares the daylights out of me."

"Do you need some water?"

Laura fanned herself with her hand. "No. I'm just so. . .shocked."

"What? That I'm going to the mission field?" She heard his self-conscious laugh. "Don't you know God can make a silk purse even out of a sow's ear?"

"No, you don't understand. Andy, that's why I could not marry you. For a long time I've wanted to serve God by witnessing about Him through my egg decorating. This summer, with your help and encouragement, I realize that's a possibility. I can influence women with wealth and position. I can also teach children about the Christian symbolism by letting them color drawings of the eggs."

"I'm glad," he said. "That's a powerful witness."

She nodded, wondering how he would react to her next statement. But as soon as she said it, she knew. What she didn't know was whether that was the sunshine or the moonlight on his face and in his eyes, when she said the next sentence. "And, Andy," she told him, "the reason I thought you and I weren't meant for each other is that. . .God has called me to greater needs on the mission field."

✍

Martha did not feel like a mother-in-law. She honestly felt like she was gaining another daughter and was proud of that. The blinders had fallen from her eyes, and she even had to remind herself not to take over completely with the wedding plans. Aunt Vi did a rather thorough job in that area, too. But she was so thrilled when Laura decided to be married at Martha's church. Of course, John would officiate.

The wedding took place during the third week of October, when the hills were alive with leaves brilliantly displaying their colors of red, orange, green, gold, and egg-yolk yellow. The bridesmaids wore emerald, a nice contrast with all the surrounding brilliant colors of the hills and bouquets.

Martha didn't know if she'd ever seen a more beautiful woman in white advancing down the aisle while the traditional wedding march was played on the piano.

She had never seen a woman walk down a runway with the kind of beauty and love radiating from this woman. God could not have chosen a more fitting match for her son. God knew she couldn't have chosen wisely for him. She'd never seen her son so content and pleased with his life.

At the reception, Andy made the announcement to the guests of his and Laura's commitment to missions. Then he lifted his punch glass and made a toast. "To my dad who felt he needed to pray for me without ceasing."

The guests chuckled, kindly, at that. "And to the two most wonderful women in the world. My mother who has guided me throughout the years, and my wife who has vowed to stand beside me as we serve the Lord together."

Martha thanked God that she had learned some valuable lessons. Andy was right about one thing. She had taught him what true beauty is and that is what emanates from a heart committed to the Lord. Laura was pretty, and her inner beauty shone like a candle in the dark. Martha had needed some work on her little light. She thanked God that He was in the lamp-polishing business.

✽❧

Barbados was beautiful this time of year. But Laura knew that anyplace, even on a remote mission field somewhere, would be all right with Andy by her side. The morning after the wedding night, he asked for breakfast to be sent to their room.

"Just sit and take it easy," he said. "We will have

seventy years of pampering one another. I want to start off first because you are so precious to me."

He just kept smiling while she sat at the little table next to the window, watching morning break over the swaying palms and white-tipped ocean waves.

Soon, breakfast was wheeled in on a cart and a silver tray placed in the center of the table. After the waiter left and Andy said the blessing, he explained his purposes. Very seriously, he said, "Don't expect this all the time, but I think this is a fitting way to symbolize how we met and the perfect way to start our marriage.

He lifted the lid. Laura gasped and stared. Then they both laughed as they lifted their forks and dug into the platter of. . .scrambled eggs.

YVONNE LEHMAN

As an award-winning novelist from Black Mountain in the heart of North Carolina's Smoky Mountains, Yvonne has written several novels for Barbour Publishing's **Heartsong Presents** line. Her titles include *Mountain Man,* which won a National Reader's Choice Award sponsored by a chapter of Romance Writers of America, *Call of the Mountain, Whiter Than Snow,* and *Catch of a Lifetime.* Yvonne has published more than two dozen novels, including books in the Bethany House "White Dove" series for young adults. In addition to being an inspirational romance writer, she is also the founder of the Blue Ridge Christian Writers' Conference. She and her husband are the parents of four grown children and grandparents to several dear children.

Test of Time

by Pamela Kaye Tracy

Dedication

*To the faculty, staff, and students of York
Christian College during the '79–'81 school years.
Friendships made in the presence of
Christ are everlasting.*

*"Do not judge, and you will not be judged.
Do not condemn, and you will not be condemned.
Forgive, and you will be forgiven."*
LUKE 6:37

Chapter 1

Peach. And mint green. She'd chosen the colors because they made her think of sherbet, cool and summery. The peach-colored wall did feel cool to Rebecca Payne's cheek, but there was nothing summery about the empty room now. Her bottom lip trembled, but she bit down to stop that foolish impulse. It was just a room, an empty room, nothing more. Reba forced herself to step away. Inanimate walls offered no comfort. Still, for the last three years, this room had been the hub of Reba's home. Hers and Ray's.

"Mommy, don't cry. You said Daddy's in heaven."

Yes, Reba had told Ray's five-year-old daughter that. Believe it? She wasn't sure, but no way was Reba going to allow Hannah to be hurt by any of this. It had been six months since Ray's death. Reba was mourning a home; Hannah was mourning her father. There were two Rays, and Reba didn't know which one to mourn. She loved the one who had sat in the peach-colored room, with his feet on the coffee table, stroking his daughter's hair while Hannah told him about sticking her face in the grass, pretending it was water, and seeing how long she could hold her breath. The other Ray was the man who had put a lien on the house—had it ever really been a home to him?—without her knowledge. That Ray had also borrowed against a life insurance policy before it matured. He'd owned three credit cards she wasn't aware of, although her name was on the plastic, and now she owed money she never knew had been spent.

What kind of wife was she? Her husband had a gambling problem, and she hadn't a clue.

"Mommy, are we leaving yet? Bark wants to go." Hannah stood, forlorn, in the empty hallway with her shirt half tucked in, and the dog's leash clutched tightly in her fist.

Reba took one last look around. "I'm just making sure we didn't leave anything."

"Like what? All the rooms are empty. We sold everything." Hannah's bottom lip trembled, but she didn't have the maturity to use her top teeth as a clasp. "Even my bed."

I'd lament a princess bed, too, if I were five. Sometimes Reba wondered if she'd ever been five. At that age, she'd already been in second grade, her father calling her profoundly gifted. At home, she'd shared a room with her sisters who all wanted a private room. None of them wanted to share with a little girl who still wet the bed. Reba gathered Hannah into her arms and walked out the front door for the last time.

Hannah wiggled to the ground. "Let's go."

The station wagon started on the second try. Bark, the chihuahua with nerves of steel, yapped angrily at the house disappearing from his view. Was he telling it not to follow or barking his disappointment at its failure to remain a home?

"Where are we going again?" Hannah's long blond hair needed washing. Her stubby fingers left a streak of dirt that smudged the map of New Mexico, the state they were leaving.

Reba gripped the steering wheel. As soon as they arrived at their new home and got a few paychecks behind them, she'd work on Hannah: Shine her daughter up; take her for a haircut; buy her new clothes— clothes that would do a future kindergartner proud. Hannah glared fiercely at the map, trying to mimic her father. Since the child couldn't read, the map was nothing but a prop for a little girl who needed to feel important, loved.

"We're going to Iowa. Creed, Iowa. Say it," Reba urged.

"Creed, Iwa."

"Close enough." Pulling out on the interstate, Reba set the cruise control and pointed the car in the direction of a place she'd planned never to return to. Her undergraduate days were memories best forgotten. This was not a full circle she'd ever imagined completing. She was going back to help a dear friend in a bind. The regular English teacher at Shiloh Christian College left on emergency leave just one week before classes began.

Reba had an advanced degree in English and needed a job. Most of all, she needed to get away from Albuquerque, New Mexico, and the pall of a life that hadn't really been hers.

When Hannah wasn't looking, Reba slipped off the wedding ring Ray had placed on her finger and dropped it in her purse. She'd worn it through the funeral, through the burial, and during the meal she'd shared with Ray's parents last night. They, and Hannah, needed to see the ring; Reba didn't.

❧

A college freshman sat opposite Mason Clark. Mason squinted. Was this really his college roommate's brother? Mason could see no resemblance between this pierced, wacky-haired teenager and Mason's one-time valedictorian suite-mate.

"So, like, what I want to do is transfer from the morning class into a different afternoon class."

Mason fought the urge to tell the young man about proper campus attire. School didn't officially start until Monday. James—who insisted he be called Jag—was checking in early and calling on his big brother's best friend.

"Why?"

"Well, like, I hear this Mrs. Robards is, like, really strict and hard. I want a different English teacher. I, um, well, English is not my favorite subject."

Jag leaned forward. That's when Mason saw the tattoo peek out from under the T-shirt sleeve. Praying hands? Was that covered in the student handbook?

A tattoo? Unbelievable. Mason had met Barry's parents. They were conservative types from Blair, Nebraska. They'd frowned at Barry wearing his baseball cap backward.

"You sure you're Barry's brother?" Mason asked.

"Yep, I got a picture to prove it."

The smile did it. Mason could see a hint of his old roommate's smirk in that slight uplift of the lips. Mason wanted to bury his head in his hands. His superiors thought he could relate to this generation; he was only twenty-seven, and at one time he thought maybe he'd be able to. But he'd never been as daring as them. The closest he'd come to rebellion was one night—best forgotten —just two weeks before his college graduation, and that had been an accident.

Jag's record didn't read like the felony report Mason expected. According to the references, James Aaron Gilroy was an "A" student who worked summers at a camp for the mentally challenged and nights at a video store. His ASAP and SAT scores showed he was more than ready for college. English should be no problem for this kid. Under the heading "high school activities" Jag had included both football and chess club.

"So, the only reason you want to transfer is because you're afraid of having Mrs. Robards as a teacher?"

"I'm not afraid!"

"Okay, you hope to avoid having Mrs. Robards as a teacher?"

"That's better."

"Mrs. Robards no longer teaches here. I'm not sure

who is taking her place. You'll have a different teacher."

"That's cool." Jag visibly relaxed. Sitting back in the stiff, wooden chair, he studied Mason's office with interest.

"Ah, Mr. Clark. I couldn't help but overhear." Cindy, the history department's work-study student paused at the door. She sent Jag a look that was clearly an invitation to chat later. "The new lady is moving into her office. I think her name is Mrs. Payne."

"Wow," said Jag. "Maybe I should check her out. See if she looks easy."

The word choice was not the best, but Mason knew what the kid meant. What Jag wanted was to transfer into Mr. Hillman's English class, and not because Jag had problems with his mother tongue. Jack Hillman was in charge of the school newspaper and often dismissed class early in order to get back to putting out the latest edition of the *Shiloh Reporter*. He was also a notoriously easy grader, which was why that particular English class was full. Jag's transfer couldn't happen.

Jag was out of his seat and down the hall, following Cindy, in seconds. Mason frowned as he walked behind the girl. There was only one empty office down this hall. It had been Mrs. Robards's. After she left, it had been allotted to him. Two days ago, he'd rolled fresh, white paint on those office walls. If not for the paint fumes, *he* would have moved in this morning.

Cindy stood at the door to that office. Jag balanced on tiptoes and stared in. The look on the kid's face said he'd found the English teacher of his dreams!

Great, thought Mason. *The English teacher of Jag's dreams has taken residence in my new office.* Well, even if it made him an ogre, he'd let the new woman know her mistake before she had too much moved in.

"Excuse me." Mason sidestepped Jag's feet and got his first look at. . .

"Rebecca Harper," he whispered, loud.

"It's Payne now," she said, turning around. Reddish-brown hair caught the sunlight. Her head tilted in the inquisitive angle he remembered so well. The pug nose—he'd once dreamed about kissing that nose—was as cute as ever.

Reba still had the ability to make him tongue-tied with simply a look. *Yep,* thought Mason, relinquishing his new office and any hope of having a coherent conversation.

She'd come close to ruining his life—well, maybe he was exaggerating a little—just two weeks before he graduated from college. Worse, he could tell by the look in her eyes, she didn't remember him.

Chapter 2

J ag immediately entered the small office and took the hammer out of Reba's hand.

"I'm Jag. I'll hang the curtain for you, ma'am."

"I'll help," Cindy offered.

Reba surrendered the hammer but didn't move. "This office isn't big enough for four people."

"I'm in your nine A.M. English class." Jag pushed aside the chair Reba had been about to stand on. Sticking two nails in his mouth, he held up the white curtain rod and aligned the end with the pencil lines Reba had marked.

Cindy shrugged and scooted out into the hall to watch.

"What are you doing here?" Mason asked. Not that he wanted to have a conversation in front of Jag, but waiting was impossible.

"I'm going to teach English. I didn't catch your name."

My name; she wants to know my name. "Mason." He meant to sound annoyed, but did he intend to sound angry? "Mason Clark. I know you're going to teach English, but why here?"

"This is where I received the job offer, Ma—" Recognition dawned in her eyes.

Mason watched as her fingers went together, a tight resemblance of praying hands, then fidgeting hands, finally nervous hands. She didn't really remember him, did she? What she remembered was his name.

"You two know each other?" Jag had the rod attached and was reaching for the curtain.

"Yes," said Reba.

"Not really," said Mason.

"Not really," echoed Reba.

"Yes," said Mason.

Jag looked at them both and summed it up. "Cool." He stuffed the curtain in Reba's hand, gave a two-fingered salute, and exited.

"I didn't know you taught here." Reba sat the curtain down on her desk.

"Would that have stopped you from coming?"

"No."

"But people might find out—"

"Mason, that night was over six years ago. I don't think it's currently a hot topic for dinner conversation."

"I remember."

She stepped around her desk and looked in his eyes. "I'll bet you do remember. You always worried about the wrong things, Mason. Let it go."

"But what if—"

"If you worry about it, people will notice, and then it

will come up. If you let go, no one will think about it."

"My job is to offer guidance. I'd hate for the students to find out that I've been advising them against doing things I, myself, have done."

Picking up the curtain, she jabbed the first hook in the fold. "Mason, the only one who ever believed you were perfect was you."

❧

The elementary school was catty-corner from Clark Hall, and Hannah had found the playground. From the second-story window, Reba watched the five-year old swing as high as she could. Opening the window, Reba called an unnecessary, "Be careful."

Hannah waved while Bark jumped at her feet. His red leash, which should have been in Hannah's hand, trailed behind him like the tail of an erratic kite. The boy from earlier, Jag, looked up from the bench he was sitting on. Iowa cottonwoods shaded the small playground. The few freshmen who had shown up early for orientation milled around the grounds. This boy, the tall one who could put up a curtain without standing on tiptoe, pointed at Hannah and then at Reba, his nonverbal communication asking the question, "Does she belong to you?" Reba nodded, momentarily worrying about Stranger Danger, and then berating herself for suspecting everyone. Surely, a scant thirty-six hours out of New Mexico, she could move about freely.

"I'll watch her," the boy called.

Reba hesitated.

"I'm in your nine A.M. English class." He shouted

the words as if they were the magic combination for permission. And, they were. This was Creed, Iowa, after all. Reba smiled, waved, and turned around to face her office. Her very empty office.

She didn't own any outdated English textbooks to make the office look academic and her shelves impressive. She hadn't taught before, so no one had given her the crafty wooden apples or brightly colored certificates scripted with "Teachers Have Class" or "To Teach Is to Touch a Mind." She didn't even own an electric pencil sharpener.

The only things Reba could add to the office were a handful of diplomas and a picture of Hannah.

"Rebecca, do you have a moment?"

He was back. Mason Clark. Funny how she'd almost failed to recognize him from all those years ago. He had changed. Gone was the skinny, too-tall-for-his-feet nerd. There were muscles where skin and bone used to be. Short, wavy, brown hair complemented chocolate eyes. Reba suspected his dirty blue backpack had been replaced by a leather briefcase. Two years ahead of her in school, he'd been so devoted to the straight and narrow that he never looked right or left.

"Come in, Mason."

He glanced at the reams of computer paper stacked on the one student chair, then stepped to the window and leaned back against the radiator. Taking note of the empty bookcase and unadorned walls, he remarked, "Kinda bare in here."

"My contract is only for a year. Dean Steward

thinks Mrs. Robards will come back. I'd best not get my hopes up."

He crossed his arms and frowned. Now that was a look she remembered. Almost everything else had changed. A perfect crease ran down each leg of his tan Dockers. He'd been a button-down cambric shirt kind of guy as a student, now he was a golf shirt kind of guy. Mason had always tried to project success. Now it looked as if he'd refined that talent. Reba refused to be impressed. She reached for her soda and tried to look nonchalant.

"I didn't know you'd kept in touch with Roger Howard." Mason didn't move.

She'd forgotten how direct he could be. "He's my husband's. . .my late. . . He was Ray's uncle."

"Ray?"

"My husband. He died. Six months ago." Reba mentally added, *three hours, two minutes;* it had been straight up noon.

"I'm sorry." Mason's face lost its defensive look. He'd always been perfect for leading the devotionals. Sincerity became an art form when attached to Mason Clark. "It must have been sudden."

Yes, bullets were sudden. That was true. "Mason, you're not in here to talk about the last few years of my life. What do you want?"

"You always were to the point."

"And you were always trying to make sure the point was safe before you sharpened it."

"Reba, you didn't know me that well."

"I wrote for the school paper, Mr. Class President. Remember? I had to make your successes interesting." Reba went to the window and watched Hannah and Jag for a few moments, but the determined look on Mason's face distracted her. She'd seen that look often, from him. Back during their school days, he'd always made time for her interviews but acted busy. Like she was interrupting his valuable schedule. He didn't look busy now.

"I know you think the past is swept under the carpet, but I'm not so sure. Some of our students are precariously balanced between two worlds. I have to deal with them every day. It's in their best interest to have a role model they can rely on."

One thing for sure, Mason Clark was still a headache.

"Tell you what," Reba reached down, picked up her purse, and slung it over her shoulder, "you don't need to worry about the past. I won't even tell anyone that I know you. It will be like we're meeting for the first time."

"That's not quite honest."

"What do you want?"

"I want to keep it low-key."

"You got it."

"Reba, I don't think you understand."

"No, I do understand. I just don't care."

Mason left, shaking his head and muttering tersely. Reba stared at the barren bookcase shelves. Maybe she could pretend Mason wasn't around to chip away at a past that was already set in cement.

He'd always had luck on his side. The very building

was named after his family. Clark Hall. It sounded like a name for a television weatherman. She remembered Shiloh's Family Days and the masses of Clarks who flocked to the campus to support Mason, picnic, get their picture taken for the school paper, and laugh. Oh, they'd donated plenty of money, too. She'd written their story two years in a row. The Clarks who needed multiple pews in the Shiloh Chapel.

Reba had usually sat with about four others who did not have family attending. She'd tried not to mind that only she and the foreign exchange students were alone.

She locked the office door behind her. The sun shone through the windows of Clark Hall's second story and accented dust particles that swirled toward the high ceiling's track lighting. All the offices had closed doors, except the one at the end. Mason's, no doubt. He probably put as much time into his job as he had school.

Shaking her head, she chuckled at a distant memory. Every senior class president had a goal. They all wanted to contribute something from their graduating class, something that would be remembered by future crops of students. Mason wanted to update the college's front sign. Instead of the ancient, imposing looking, wooden-roofed board, Mason wanted a glossy, plexiglass sign. He'd gotten it, too.

She'd had to write three articles about that sign. Mason had dedicated almost half a year to raising the money. The sign had fallen over during a tornado watch not even a year later. The remaining pieces—those that hadn't blown away—were too numerous to reconstruct.

Reba wondered if Mason knew what real worries were. Did he have to worry about anything serious? Did he understand what it felt like to budget for his next meal? Had he ever coasted down a busy street concerned about his car's brakes? Could he imagine the trials a single parent faced—especially a single parent who didn't know who had killed her husband, because they hadn't been caught?

Chapter 3

The first Monday of school was always disorganized. Mason directed two lost freshman out of his History 101 class and into the Spanish room next door.

The yellowing window shade at the back of the room had a jagged tear. The sun managed to shine through in just a way to blind him. He left the security of the podium and started walking between the aisles. "Read the syllabus. It is law. Notice how tardies affect your final grade."

The door opened. Jag walked in. Mason felt sure that some of the students were mentally deducting a point from Jag's final grade. Those students would probably even verify the points with Jag at the end of the semester. Most students didn't look as if they cared. They probably didn't believe Mason. A few did exactly what he wanted them to, which was read the syllabus.

"I want you to especially note the attendance policy. Three absences and you're dropped."

Jag hadn't even taken a seat. His hand shot in the air,

and he asked, "What about sports-excused absences?"

"Coach Martin will give me the names and dates. If you read the syllabus you'll notice I wrote that. Also, your homework is due the next time you attend class."

"All of it?" Jag asked.

"All of it."

Mason walked around while the students read his syllabus. His first-hour class rubbed sleep from their eyes while they mused over homework and six upcoming tests. His text for this class started with Christopher Columbus.

After more than half the class penned their names on the syllabus's signature sheet, Mason had them open their textbooks to page seven and called on Jag to read the chapter's introduction. Picking up the roll, Mason tried to put names to faces. There were three names he couldn't pronounce, and four people hadn't bothered to show up. It was an unfounded rumor that instructors did nothing on the first day, as those students who hadn't bothered to purchase the textbook were finding out.

Jag read until the end of the section. Mason chose two more students, then assigned six questions before dismissal. Two more classes went exactly the same.

Mason ate lunch in the cafeteria, then headed over to his office. Unless he missed his guess, there'd be some students waiting. Since there wasn't an opening for a full-time counselor, Mason taught but was allotted a few students to guide. His degree was in Social Sciences, and his minor in History had not been obtained with teaching in mind. He wanted to be a full-time counselor. He wanted to help students figure out they weren't alone; Christ walked with them, and they all could shape their own destinies. His dream was tarnishing. What they hadn't told him in college was that youth had its own language, and there was no way to decipher the code. Worse, he suspected he'd missed out on his own generation's jargon.

The waiting room was full. A few students started to stand when he entered, but Linda Simms, the secretary, shooed them back. "Give him a moment."

"All for me?" He raised an eyebrow. Mason worked with the students whose last names began with G–M. Most of them had registered over the summer. Their schedules should be fairly accurate. Usually the changes didn't come until day three.

He helped the first student with a job-related transfer, then helped a second student who felt overburdened and wanted to change his schedule. When a third student asked about changing English teachers, Mason caught on. Mrs. Robards transition from sixtyish lady with beehive, to twentyish lady with sparkling eyes had not gone unnoticed by the male population of Shiloh Christian College.

Taking a breath, he stuffed the transfer cards back into his desk and opened his office door to announce, "If you're hoping to transfer into Mrs. Payne's English classes, they're full."

The waiting room emptied. Linda shook her head. "Now why didn't I think of that?"

"Have you met Rebecca Ha—Payne?"

"No, but I hear she'll be coaching the softball team, so I expect I'll get to know her real soon."

The powers-that-be had all kinds of things planned for Rebecca Payne. Mason wondered if Reba was ready to coach softball, sponsor a sorority, and help with the yearbook. Somehow, he doubted it. There was an air of sadness about her that hadn't been there before. Oh sure, she was mourning a husband, but something else had gone missing from her personality. Just what, Mason couldn't put his finger on. "I'm going to step out for a moment." Mason left Linda alphabetizing freshman files and restocking drop/add slips.

Fall in Iowa was a beautiful collage of oranges, browns, reds, and greens. The wind whipped through Mason's hair as he strolled down the curving sidewalk toward Clark Hall. His office, and Reba's, occupied the second floor. The first floor was devoted to classes. The hallway smelled like chalk, perfume, and dust. Reba's class was at the end. Peering in, he saw her standing by the chalkboard. She'd written her name in neat curls of letters.

The students were reading a piece of paper, probably her syllabus. A few of the guys alternated their attention between the paper and the woman.

Mason watched as Reba walked to the board and wrote, "No Payne, No Gain." Next to that, she wrote, "Know Payne, Know Gain."

Now this was the Reba he remembered. Her blue jean skirt brushed against perfectly shaped knees. Her white shirt, covered with a crocheted vest, accented a slender form that looked too young to be in front of a classroom. He'd thought that this morning when they'd introduced her in chapel. Her hair was shorter than before, barely touching her shoulders, but with a natural curl that bounced when she spoke. She was still animated. He'd loved those interviews when she worked on the paper. She'd balanced a notebook on her lap and kept her pencil stuck above her ear. She never took a single note. Reba couldn't, because she talked with her hands. Every word came with a gesture, yet she never misquoted him or left out an important detail.

Mason needed to get back to the office. He had plenty of things to do. Transferring more students into her classes was not one of them, though with every fiber of his being, Mason knew had he needed an English credit, he'd be first in line trying to enroll.

Chapter 4

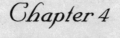

The day-care center was two blocks north of SCC. Reba parked her car and hurried in, surprised at how much she had missed spending the day with Hannah.

Hannah had been two when Reba and Ray got married. From that time on, Reba had embraced motherhood and relished seeing the world through Hannah's eyes.

The letter A was at the top of the color page. Hannah haphazardly crayoned blue and orange onto what was supposed to be an apple. Reba signed the time card and braced herself to receive forty-five pounds of happy child.

"Do I start kindergarten tomorrow?"

"No, Monday, but we're headed there now."

"Good. Marky's going to be in my class."

"Marky?" Reba looked around.

"His mother already picked him up. He has a cat, too."

"We're not getting a cat."

"Okay, but if we had a cat, we wouldn't ever have mice. That's what Marky said."

Shiloh Christian Academy was on the same plot of land as the college—a plus in Reba's mind. It had daycare, too, although Reba was hoping not to have to use it. Air-conditioning escaped out the doors as they went in. A secretary greeted them with a smile and a sheaf of papers to fill out. Reba handed over copies of Hannah's birth certificate and medical records.

The kindergarten teacher met them in her room. The Christian school tested all incoming students, but Reba wasn't worried. Hannah was bright, already knew her letters, most of the single sounds, and how to write her name. While Hannah pointed out colors on a chart, Reba explored the school. Ray would have loved this place with its hallway self-esteem posters and trophy case of spelling bee ribbons and Bible Bowl awards.

"Mrs. Payne?" The kindergarten teacher called down the hall. *What was the woman's name again?* Reba wondered. Luckily the sign outside the class proclaimed, WELCOME TO MRS. HENRY'S KINDERGARTEN CLASS.

Hannah stood at the chalkboard drawing circles while Mrs. Henry handed Reba a supply list and said, "She did fine."

Reba skimmed the inventory and realized from now until the next paycheck, McDonalds was out. "Hannah, the bathroom is right down the hall. I want you to go there and wash your hands after."

Skipping between the desks, Hannah paused at one and said, "I'll sit here. Marky is way across the room."

That important announcement accomplished, Hannah bounced out of the room.

"You have some questions?" Mrs. Henry sat on Marky's desk.

"No, not really. I wanted to let you know that Hannah's father died a few months ago. I'm not sure she understands he isn't coming back. She's usually happy, but every once in awhile. . . Well, every once in awhile." Reba stopped. How could she put into words something she sensed as a mother. "She's wet her pants a few times, and that's unusual. Um, she stares into space a lot more now. I made sure the office had my home phone, my office, and my pager. Don't hesitate to call if you notice anything unusual or if she needs me for anything."

Mrs. Henry nodded, her face somber. "How did he die?"

How did he die? It made sense that someone would ask that question. Reba had known it would happen, expected it, but she didn't want to answer.

The words came out a croak. "He was in an accident."

"Ready, Mama?" Hannah stood at the doorway, already alert to the fact that Reba was talking about Ray. Hannah's head tilted to the side inquisitively. Ray had that habit, too, always looking like there was something more to be said.

Taking Hannah's hand, Reba left the kindergarten room as fast as dignity would allow and before the teacher could ask any more questions. Grief was such a tangible sorrow and not one Reba was willing to touch with a stranger.

"Are we going to the store? I want a pink shirt."

"This school has a dress code, honey. Looks like you'll be wearing lots of blue and white."

"Dress code?"

"It means all the students wear the same outfit."

"No cartoons?"

"No cartoons, but we'll get you a special headband. Okay?"

A few minutes later, Reba realized she'd be washing clothes every night. She picked out one navy blue jumper and white collared shirt. They'd also be eating lots of peanut butter. The school supply aisle was not the bargain it advertised. Hannah didn't want plain yellow pencils; she wanted cartoon character ones. They cost a dollar more. The smallest bottle of glue looked pitiful traveling down the conveyor belt towards checkout. And, although Reba hadn't touched a single designer folder or school box, there they were, traveling merrily toward her checkbook.

"Hannah Lynn Payne!" Reba plucked mouse-eared erasers out of the cashier's hand. "We don't need these."

When the amount glowed from the register, Reba knew even if she turned her purse upside down and unloaded every spare chunk of change from the black hole, she'd not have enough. It was only a matter of cents, but sales tax obviously differed from New Mexico to Iowa. Reba had no clue what to put back. She'd been as frugal as possible. Not the uniform. She could use pencils from her office, but. . .

"Everything okay?"

At first, Reba thought the checkout lady was asking the question, but the male voice didn't jive with the blond perm or red lipstick.

Mason Clark stood behind her. He held an electric pencil sharpener box in one hand and an open wallet in the other. "Do you need some money?"

"No."

The cashier repeated the amount.

"Reba, let me help."

"We bought too much," Reba insisted, grabbing the pack of eraser tops. The deduction didn't change the decimal, nor did it effect the ten's place.

Who turned off the air-conditioning? Reba wondered, wiping perspiration from her brow. If she'd been wearing a sweater, she'd have shed it by now.

When the plastic ruler and watercolors left the conveyor belt, Hannah's mouth opened. "Mama!"

"This is stupid." Mason handed the cashier a fifty and growled, "If you don't charge me for all her belongings, I'll talk to your manager."

The cashier hit the sale key.

"Maybe I'll go to the manager," Reba sputtered. "I told you we didn't need any money."

"The manager is my cousin, Phil. He's a senior at Shiloh. You won't have him in class." Mason took the bag containing his pencil sharpener and guided Reba out of the way so the next customer could be taken care of.

Hannah had the plastic bag with their purchases. It was bigger than she was. The child had given up so much. Reba didn't want to take anything else away.

"Fine. Thank you. On payday I'll return the money."

"Payday? That's going to be more than three weeks for you. Do you need a loan?"

Reba rolled her eyes. "No, everything is fine."

"Didn't your husband provide for you before. . . ?" Mason's gaze traveled downward. "Who is this?"

"My daughter, Hannah."

"Daughter?"

"I'm in school. Want to see my new blue dress?" Hannah started to rip the bag, but Reba took it.

"Mason, it's going to be hard acting like we barely know each other if you insist on paying for school supplies. Thanks for helping. I do appreciate it. I don't like it, but I do appreciate it. We need to go now. I haven't fed Hannah yet."

"McDonald's," Hannah suggested.

"Spaghetti from our stove top," Reba amended.

"But you said—" Hannah began.

"I said we'd see. That doesn't mean yes." Taking Hannah firmly by the hand, Reba started for the door.

"I like spaghetti," Mason said.

"Come over," Hannah invited. "I'll show you the neat doghouse we builded in our backyard. Bark likes it."

The exit was just a few feet away, so close. Hannah always warmed up to strangers. So had Ray. The invitation had more to do with snazzy pencils than common sense, but what five-year-old had sense? Reba looked at the exit longingly before arguing, "Mason, this is ten-minute spaghetti, nothing special."

"I was going home to a microwave dinner. Spaghetti

sounds plenty special. Besides, you can call it payback for the school supplies."

"Fine." Reba sent Mason a tight smile and exited the store. She didn't want anyone to know she was broke. Now Mason would know when he saw her house. . .and what was not in it.

❧

Stupid, stupid, Mason told himself as he headed for his Cherokee. He needed to avoid Reba, not dine with her. And she had a kid! This Ray character, who didn't think to provide for his wife, must have been been dishwater blond, because Hannah didn't look much like Reba. The kid was cute. Mason's nieces and nephews were cute, too, and they especially looked cute once he peeled their sticky hands off his jeep's door handles, or should they come to his house, away from his books. The kids all loved him.

Barely a week went by when a niece or nephew didn't call to see if they could spend the night with him. At Christmas, Mason was the only adult to receive coloring books and yo-yos in his stocking. He was the only Clark over twenty-one to have every action figure from the latest space movies. Half of it, he knew, was his brothers and sisters letting him know that it was his turn to produce grandchildren. The other half was some invisible force that drew kids to him.

Reba turned into the driveway of the house straight across from Clark Hall. That made sense. The Webbs were missionaries in India. It was the perfect house for Reba to rent.

Hannah jumped out of the passenger side and ran to the end of the driveway to point to where he should park, which was right behind Reba, the only place to park. Hannah obviously took after her mother: bossy.

Reba went into the house without a backward glance. Clearly, she didn't want him here. The sensible thing to do would be to suddenly remember a conflict of schedule. Instead, he opened the door, stepped outside, and let Hannah grab his hand and drag him around to the back.

"This is Bark. He's a chiwowwow."

What the dog was, was a poofed-up sausage of a canine with twigs for legs. Bark took an immediate dislike to Mason. Growling, the beast bared his teeth and made attacking bull movements.

"Bark!" Reba called from the kitchen window.

Bark shut his mouth, gave Mason a dirty look, and strutted to his doghouse.

"What is that?" To Mason's eye, it looked like the dog lived in a short, wooden teepee with many doors.

"That's his doghouse. Isn't it beyooootiful? Me and Mommy made it this morning. And we didn't use a hammer."

No kidding. Before he had time to format a comment about the doghouse that badly needed to be condemned or the pink ribbon stuck on the dog's head and inching its way toward the dog's chin, Hannah was dragging Mason over to a tree. "I'm going to build a treehouse." Next, she sat on the awkward swing. The seat was so off balance that Hannah had to hold herself in place. "We hung this up, too. Mama's afraid of hives so she hurried. I like climbing to the top of trees; I'm not afraid of hives. I wanted to help. Mama says I'm too little, but I like hammers. They are my favorite thing, except when they smash my finger instead of the nail. Once I smashed Mama's finger instead of the nail, but we got the bookcase together, except it leans. Do you think the books will fall out?"

He opened his mouth to answer.

Hannah lowered her voice and confided, "Mama comes out here and swings when I'm not looking."

Mason looked back at the house and through the kitchen window where he could see Reba preparing the spaghetti.

"And this is where we go if there's a torndo." Hannah pointed to the cellar. "I've never been in a torndo. Mama says it's when the wind blows hard. I saw *The Wizard of Oz*, so I hope one happens. Have you ever been in a torndo?" This time she waited for an answer.

"When I was in college, a tornado came through this area. It didn't really strike here, but it blew a lot of things down."

"Houses?" Hannah said hopefully.

"No."

"People in rocking chairs?"

"No."

"Dogs?" Hannah glanced at Bark and looked indecisive.

"Signs," Mason told her. "Cheap signs."

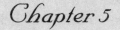

Chapter 5

The serious softball players were angry that this was their first practice. A few didn't care. Five of the players complained about having to practice at all. While observing and encouraging their warm-up exercises, Reba tried to tie names to the histories she'd studied over the weekend.

Reba had gone over all their stats and knew both she and they were at a serious disadvantage. Even though this was only intramurals, the first game was Saturday. Plus, these girls would be hers when softball season started. Many of them were already hers, on the volleyball team. Shiloh wasn't known for its women's athletics. Reba wasn't known for losing.

Cindy, the English department's student aide, smiled encouragingly. Too bad Cindy could catch but not throw. Reba started putting the girls to positions.

"Tiffany." The first name came out strong, but Reba choked on the last name. Her third baseman's last name was. . .but surely, Clark was a popular name. They couldn't all be related to Mason.

Redheaded, a gum chewer, and sassy, Tiffany Clark

wore tight shorts and makeup that begged comment. Reba would guess the girl majored in complaining and had a bright future.

Reba snapped her own gum and crooked a finger. "My notes say that you only played half season last year. Want to tell me why?"

Reba's notes also said why.

"The coach and I had a difference of opinion."

"Yes?"

Tiffany had the grace to shift her glance downward, but the gumption to state, "She said she was the coach, and I said she wasn't."

The girls were waiting for the next move.

"Are we gonna have that problem this year?" Reba asked.

"I don't know. I guess that depends on whether you coach or just sit there and tell us what to do."

"Just so you know," Reba said, "it will not take me half a season to bench you."

"Just so you know," Tiffany responded, this time looking Reba in the eye, "I'm good."

Reba smiled. "Let's see how good." Putting the girls into places, Reba stepped up to bat. Cindy was fighting tears over being placed in right field. Tiffany snapped gum and—"Hi, Uncle Mason!"

The ball Reba meant to line to third limped to the pitcher.

Except for passing Mason in the hall and noticing him at chapel every morning, Reba had managed to avoid the man.

He had charmed Hannah, and almost every night

for the last two weeks she'd asked when he was coming back over. Reba and Bark weren't won that easily.

Mason had turned the spaghetti dinner into a big deal. He taught Hannah to coil the noodles around her fork. He made a happy face with the meatballs. He took up too much space in the kitchen, and he wore the wrong aftershave.

He wore jeans today. A light blue T-shirt accented how much his shoulders had spread in comparison to his lean body.

Tiffany snapped a bubble. Reba turned just in time to witness an exaggerated rolling of the eyes. This time, Reba's bat sent the ball screaming to third, where Tiffany didn't even have time to move to catch it.

Before the girl could comment, the catcher tossed Reba another ball, and she spun one between Tiffany's legs.

Two complainers shut up. They turned the bills of their baseball caps around, squatted, and yelled, "Aaa, batter, batter."

Two hours later, the only one who left practice unhappy was Cindy. Mason had opened his briefcase, graded papers, talked on his cell phone, and watched Reba the whole time. When practice ended, he walked with Tiffany to his car, and they drove off. *Yeah, right, like he was here for his niece.* Reba knew better. Still, it was much too soon to enjoy the attention of a single man—especially a single man who made bumping into her a hobby while claiming that they needed to avoid each other and the past.

She had enough to worry about without Mason

adding to it. There were times when she still turned in the night, expecting to hear Ray snoring. Occasionally, she caught the scent of his aftershave at the grocery store. Hannah still ran through the front door yelling, "Mom, Da—"

Reba was putting the last bat away when she glanced at her watch. Six-fifteen.

Six-fifteen!

Day-care at Hannah's school ended at six. Every fifteen minutes tardy was an additional five dollars. Racing across the baseball field, she managed a record two-minute sprint.

"I was the only one, Mommy." Hannah's scolding surpassed the day-care teacher's disapproving look.

"I'm sorry, honey. I was helping the softball players and time got away from me."

The uniform Reba had put on Hannah this morning looked like it had seen combat. There was a tear in the sleeve. A ketchup drip made a path from collar to hem. One sock stretched toward Hannah's knee; the other hid in her shoe. Dirt had found a magnet. "Marky never goes to day-care. His mother picks him up right at three. I want to be picked up at three."

"I will pick you up at three on Mondays and Wednesdays."

Hannah's sigh said, not good enough. Reba rubbed between her daughter's shoulder blades and took a breath. It was truly a beautiful day. She'd finally mastered all her students' names, softball practice turned out better than she'd hoped possible, Hannah missed being with her mommy, and Mason had come to practice.

No! Reba stopped in her tracks, so suddenly that Hannah stumbled.

"What, Mommy?"

"Nothing, baby; I was just thinking."

Thinking things best left alone, Reba told herself. From every angle, Mason Clark looked to be a nice guy, but Reba had been fooled before. This time, she had Hannah to think about.

❧

Over a hundred college students attended Shiloh Church. Mason figured another hundred trekked across town to Community Church, just to be different, and he knew at least another hundred didn't bother to attend on Wednesday nights. Of course, he figured that same hundred didn't come on Sundays either.

Mason taught a class on faith and works. Most of his students were the kind who were willing to get their hands dirty in order to make society a better place. He had future social workers, counselors, and lawyers, plus a few soon-to-be ministers. He also had a handful of females who'd placed him on their wish list. Dating a student was not something Mason intended to do.

Mason struggled to vary what his group did. School had been in session for a month. Their first service project had been sewing dolls for the small hospital that Creed shared with neighboring Trinity, Iowa. The tiny cloth dolls were used to demonstrate to children just where the surgery would take place. A doll used to explain a tonsillectomy would have an X drawn on its throat. The students gathered in the hospital's small cafeteria, pushed tables together, and stitched for two hours. Cindy and two other girls managed five dolls each. Mason had struggled through two. The rest of the young men had produced snowmanlike monstrosities that were sure to cause soon-to-be young owners to either howl with laughter or scream with fright.

Mason tried to organize at least one outing a month. He'd been wondering what to do next. Seeing Reba's house spearheaded an idea, though he knew she'd hate it. That's why he'd proposed doing it this Saturday. The girls' volleyball team had an away game. As assistant coach, Reba needed to attend. Mason's class would have at least a three-hour window in which to work. The Webbs had been gone four years. The first renter had not been kind to the old house.

There were sixteen in his class. Half of those nodded that they could be there.

Jag grumbled, "I have to take pictures of the volleyball match for the paper."

"You could miss it once," Cindy said. "Someone else could take pictures."

"No, I'm working, too. Mrs. Payne is taking Hannah along and hired me to watch her."

Mason looked from Cindy to Jag. They were dating, already—too soon, in Mason's opinion. Cindy's blond hair was swept into a ponytail, and she wore a dress. Jag's jeans were torn. His T-shirt advertised a rock group, a Christian rock group, but still not a T-shirt to wear to church.

What was Reba thinking, hiring Jag to baby-sit? Hannah was much too impressionable. It had to be money. Cindy probably charged more an hour than

Jag. That had to be it.

The class agreed on the time; Mason dismissed them, erased the chalkboard, and stepped out into the hallway. He hadn't seen Reba in church. Maybe she attended Community. Of course, back in college, she'd been one of the hundred that hadn't attended services regularly. Had that changed? Most of his friends got even more serious about church once they had children. His older brother, Richard, had.

Mason chuckled as he entered the foyer. Groups of people milled around, talking, planning, hugging. He didn't see Tiffany, and he'd promised to drive her to the store. Tiffany was a handful, and so much like Richard that Mason sometimes wanted to throttle her. The whole family had prayed. Tiffany hated church, refused to attend after she turned sixteen, and seemed to be drifting into the wrong crowd. Always one to be on the go, as a senior in high school, Tiffany had attended Encounter in Abilene, Texas, only because it got her out of town. The weekend rally among Christian youth was a turning point. Mason could only imagine what words, songs, prayers, got through to the girl, but she came back with a new perspective.

Had that happened to Reba? Had she found peace with God after being expelled from Shiloh? There had to be some difference for Roger Howard, a noted Bible professor, to recommend her for employment. The man had pull, but the fact that she was a relative wouldn't earn her even a last-minute position. Her IQ would be in her favor, but her age would not. Mason wondered when Roger, who was on a mission trip in Africa, would return. Reba needed family.

She'd been a sophomore, just like Tiffany was now, when she got kicked out of Shiloh. That was six years ago. Hannah was in kindergarten. The little girl had mentioned that fact no less than ten times during supper. Kindergarten meant at least five years old. Reba became a mother about a year after leaving Shiloh. How had she wound up with Professor Howard's nephew? Mason had to admire her, though. She'd still managed to finish school and get an advanced degree. She was a smart one. That's how he'd first met her. He was a junior, and she a lowly freshman. Only seven students had signed up for Latin: five religion majors, Mason, and Rebecca Harper.

His first thought when she walked into the classroom, pushing the envelope on the dress code—much like his niece and Jag—was that she might be all of twelve years old. Then, she'd proceeded to rearrange the grading curve so that five prospective pastors and Mason had to form a killer study group and make the library a second home. He hadn't taken Latin second semester. He'd next met up with her the following year as class president. She worked on the school paper. She no longer looked twelve, yet she still appeared fragile to him. Mason Clark, youngest son of Wayne and Betty Clark, suddenly didn't think the world centered on him. He knew the world centered on her, and that he wanted to be in that sunshine.

"Hey, Uncle Mason, you coming?" Tiffany yanked on his arm. "You feeling okay?"

One of the deacons was locking the doors. "Yep;

I'm thinking about our service project this Saturday."

"I think it's cool that you're going to work on Mrs. Payne's house. It's a dump and could be so pretty. I like her dog."

"You like Bark?"

If Mason knew one thing about Tiffany, it was that she never stood still. So, when she stopped, grinned, and got a funny look in her eye, he knew he was in for something. "What?"

"How do you know her dog's name is Bark?"

"She has the office down from mine."

"Really—what's my dog's name?"

"You have a dog?"

"Only for the past ten years."

"Tiffany, so what if I know her dog's name?"

"Oh, Uncle Mason, this is cool. She's good. We have the best workouts. You know, I did wonder why you came to my softball practice. I mean, you never did before."

"I was giving you a ride to the movies."

"Yeah, but you got there two hours early. One of the girls said she saw you and Mrs. Payne at Wal-Mart together. I can't believe you didn't tell me!"

"Tiffany, there's nothing to tell." Mason forced himself not to predict, *yet*.

Chapter 6

The volleyball team lost, but Reba had high hopes. They were only a month into their season. Both Cindy and Tiffany had acted distracted. The referee had been less than consistent. Volleyball was not Reba's game. She'd been a so-so player. At five foot three, she'd never managed the maneuvers necessary to do more than set the ball.

Reba ushered her group of students into the station wagon. Hannah sat in the middle, between Reba and Tiffany. Cindy and Jag were in the backseat.

"Pizza?" Tiffany suggested.

"Ice cream," Cindy countered.

"I need to get back to the dorm," Jag said.

Reba wondered if the young man was savvy enough to realize that neither pizza nor ice cream were in her budget yet.

The wind blew leaves across the neighborhood as she pulled onto her street. The rev of an overexuberant lawn mower warred with the noise of a friendly football game across the way. Reba thought that was one of the great things about her house. There was always something to see. She and Hannah often sat on the porch swing for hours and watched the college students play, study, and court.

As she pulled into the driveway, Reba noticed full bags stacked by the huge cottonwood in her front yard. The ankle-deep leaves were all gone. Closer scrutiny revealed there was no longer a hole in her screen door, and the porch swing looked suspiciously cleaner? Darker? Painted!

Tiffany's grin spoke volumes. Jag and Cindy had Cheshire smiles. From the backyard came a young man Reba didn't know. What looked to be pieces from Bark's doghouse were in his arms.

Count to ten, Reba told herself. After the wagon stopped, somehow Hannah managed to get from the middle to outside before Tiffany. Bark came around the corner. First he jumped on the strange young man's leg to be petted. Then, he ran to Hannah and jumped on her. He quickly circled to sniff Reba's shoe, and once assuring himself that his family was all right, he raced to the backyard and barked his Number Three Special Killer Guard Dog impersonation.

"It's Mason," Reba muttered.

"Yep," Tiffany agreed.

Unlocking the front door, Reba was greeted by the mess she'd left this morning. At least Mason hadn't had the audacity to enter her house. She quickly went to the back door.

The porch rails had been fixed. Hannah's swing now

hung equally balanced. Bark's new doghouse had one door. Everything looked great, including the man pushing the lawn mower. This was quite possibly the first time she'd seen Mason in shorts.

"Mason Clark, come here!"

He kept pushing the mower and pointed to his ears to let her know he couldn't hear.

Cindy helped Hannah into her swing. Laughter joined mower until Reba put her hands over her ears.

Jag was in the kitchen. "Mason ordered pizza. Do you have paper plates or can I borrow your wagon to go to the store?"

"We have napkins. That will work." Looking out the side window, Reba saw the rest of Mason's crew. They were cutting down the bush that had melded with the fence in a great tangle of limbs and chain links before dying. No way could she gripe at Mason in front of all these students who had given up part of their Saturday for her.

One of the students looked up and waved. "Hi, Mrs. Payne. You have a great dog."

Reba nodded. So far the only person Bark hadn't welcomed into his domain was Mason.

What did Bark know that Reba didn't?

❦

It was all Mason could do to keep his eyes closed while Jag said grace. Mason wanted to watch Reba. The students' easy laughter helped somewhat, but it took Reba until the second piece of pizza before she relaxed. Although Mason knew she was irritated at him, it was worth it to see her laugh and joke with his Bible school class.

After the final piece of pizza disappeared, most of the students headed for the dorms. Reba did the few dishes and watched out the kitchen window as Cindy and Jag took Hannah to the swing. Mason stuffed the pizza boxes into the trash.

"I'll do that later." Reba folded the dish towel over the faucet and sat at the table, one leg curled under the other, and sipped her soda while watching Hannah in the backyard. "You probably have other things to do."

Mason honestly couldn't think of anyplace he'd rather be. "No, let me. This is easy."

"I can't believe you did all this. The kids from your Bible class are great."

"I had most of them last year, too. There are only two new ones. Jag, and a girl who's on your softball team."

"Mason, this is too much. Please don't surprise me again."

"Why not?"

"Didn't you tell me, that first day in my office, that you didn't want people to tie us together?"

"I've rethought that. You surprised me. I expected to find a Mrs. Robards impersonator, and instead I found a piece of my past who still could leave me speechless."

"Speechless! You? Never."

"You mean to tell me you didn't know?"

"Know what?"

"I always felt tongue-tied around you. When we went to school here, all I wanted to do was take you out."

She'd been swirling her soda glass, clinking the ice first on one side then the other. The glass stilled; Reba let go and folded her hands. "I didn't know. Why didn't you tell—no, I can figure that out. I was so confused all those years ago. Do you know how old I am, Mason?"

"I know you're a lot younger than I. That's one of the reasons I never asked you out. Class presidents manage to be privy to lots of interesting tidbits. You had the highest IQ in the school, yet you never joined the Honor Society or represented Shiloh at any of the conferences."

Reba looked out the window, that faraway look back on her face. "This place was my first taste of freedom. I started sight-reading at three. I don't even remember how I learned. Freaked my parents out. I had a sister in second grade who needed remedial tutoring. It used to annoy her when I tried to tell her the right answers.

"When they took me to kindergarten, the school arranged for testing. Suddenly I was in a program for gifted children, not just a program but a whole different school. A van came and picked me up every morning and brought me back in the late afternoon.

"My whole elementary experience was put under a microscope. They kept bar graphs of everything. I can still hear the questions: How much sleep did I need? Was my milk allergy related to my intelligence? How many ear infections did I have? And how high was my tolerance to pain?

"As for academics, I learned a lot, but was always the youngest in my class. I never felt like I belonged. Yet, as my parents kept telling me, 'What an opportunity.' You know, all I ever wanted was to change places with my sisters. Believe me, my elementary school experience was all the Honor Society I wanted. A high IQ doesn't mean friendship and fun."

"And I always wanted things to come easy," Mason admitted. He tied the top of the trash bag and took it to the back door. He helped himself to another soda and sat at the table. "My two older brothers were straight A students. So were my three sisters. The first time I brought home my report card and my family found out I was average, they thought it was because I was the baby. They blamed themselves and by second grade I had a tutor. I think, at that time, I was the only Clark who didn't touch things and have them turn to gold. I had to work twice as hard at everything."

"Mason, why aren't you married?"

A cool breeze swayed the curtains of the window above the sink. Reba had lined the ledge with flowers. An embroidered sampler exclaimed, "Kiss the Cook." Mason knew somewhere there was probably a similar stitching urging, "Hug the Chef." His mother had the same decorations in her kitchen. "After I left Shiloh, I went to the University of Lincoln for my postgraduate work. I dated, even got engaged, but never found exactly what or whom I was looking for. Tell me about . . .Ray?"

"I met Ray because of Roger Howard. Mr. Howard was my Bible teacher when I was here. He liked me. Said my answers to his Bible tests weren't rote. He stuck up for me, you know."

Mason knew. Roger had quoted Scripture about forgiveness and cited examples of other students who had made similar mistakes and yet not been expelled. Not that Mason had been in attendance at the impromptu school board meeting that late Saturday night. He'd just had family on the school board, family who was sure there'd been a mistake about Mason's involvement.

Mason had stuck up for her, too, but he'd bet she didn't know that. He'd demanded that he be expelled, along with her. He'd threatened to call the Shiloh newspaper and report discrimination. Sunday morning, instead of going to church, he'd headed to Reba's dorm, determined to sit down with her and mastermind a plan—a plan to what, he hadn't known—but it hadn't mattered. She wasn't there. By Monday, she hadn't just left the school, she'd left Iowa. And Mason had always felt slightly guilty that he'd graduated two weeks later when she'd lost all her credits.

"I knew that." Mason wanted to take her hand, tell her he was sorry, but now was not the time. "Mr. Howard's quite a man. I had him for Bible, too. I've always respected him."

"I went to live with his sister."

"What about your family?"

Reba choked back a laugh. "They were so mad. Here I was, with opportunities beyond belief. As Mom said on the phone that night, 'We've spent so much time on you.' I was the first Harper to go to college. I'll bet you didn't know that. When Mr. Howard offered to get me into another school, they were thrilled. Guess how old I was when all that happened, Mason?"

He shook his head.

"Sixteen."

And she'd looked twelve, he remembered.

"My parents thought by sending me to a Christian college, I'd be safe. Me, I no longer cared, but when I got here I loved it. It was the first time I didn't have to fit in some predetermined mold. Even better, my sisters weren't telling their boyfriends that I was weird. I could take whatever class I wanted, sorta, and make friends, but everyone was. . ." She didn't meet his eyes, instead staring at her glass.

"Was?"

"So different. Mature. They knew things I didn't. Things you couldn't read about in books."

"How old was Ray?"

"Nine years older than I. Thirty when he died. He was the son of the family I was staying with. Mr. Howard's nephew."

"You married pretty fast."

She started twirling the soda again. "No, I didn't."

"Well, Hannah's five. It's only been six years since I last saw you."

"Oh." The glass slid toward the edge of the table. Reba stopped it and took a breath. "Ray already had Hannah when we married, but in all the ways that count, she is my daughter."

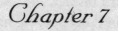

Chapter 7

R eba wrote PLEASE DOUBLE-SPACE across the top of a freshman English composition. *Five down, forty to go.* Gray, heavy clouds hung low in the sky. They hovered, close, seeming to eavesdrop on the music Reba's radio played. October already, and there'd be snow soon. Hannah could hardly wait. Reba checked her watch. She had fifteen minutes before day-care ended.

Footsteps sounded outside, hesitating at the door. Reba waited, trying not to anticipate. She and Mason had formed a tentative friendship. He hadn't pressed for more information after the night he'd helped fix up her house, and Reba hadn't finished analyzing exactly why she'd opened up to him. Had she felt free to discuss her past because Mason Clark had participated in one of its turning points? He might well be the only person who could understand what she'd gone through. Had the wall gone tumbling because he genuinely seemed to want to know about her?

Truthfully, she was amazed he'd stuck around long

enough for a friendship to form. What a riot to find out he'd had a crush on her. He'd seemed so removed from everything she'd been doing back then.

"You need anything else, Mrs. Payne?" Cindy stepped into the office.

"No, I'm fine. You go."

"Jag's baby-sitting for you tonight. Can I come over?"

"Not tonight." Reba wanted to say yes. She had to respect that Cindy bothered to ask. That spoke volumes about what kind of girl she was. And Jag was a find. Not only could he make Reba laugh, but he knew exactly when to interrupt conversations. He'd picked exactly the right time to barge into the kitchen for a soda that Saturday—before she'd told Mason too much.

Never in her wildest imagination had Reba thought to hire a male baby-sitter. Linda Simms, the department secretary, recommended a handful of girls, but Jag came with Cindy. Within a few minutes, Reba knew who Hannah felt more comfortable with. His references were impeccable. He had three younger sisters to prove experience, and his school records were carbon copies of Reba's own. No wonder the hair stuck straight up and his arm was tattooed; he was making a statement, telling the world not to assume.

Maybe if she'd had more of his self-assurance, she'd have had an easier time. Jag's parents had allowed him to go to a regular school after elementary, plus they'd kept him in an age-appropriate grade.

She put the rest of the essays into a folder, locked the office, and walked to Hannah's school.

"Hey, Mama, guess what?" Hannah left the kinder-garten line and skipped toward Reba. The safety patrol student hurried to keep up. Hannah shoved a handful of papers in Reba's hands and hugged a bunny-shaped backpack. "Next Thursday is Open House, and Mrs. Henry wants you to send brownies."

"Are you sure?"

"Yup; she said that it would be nice for mommies to bring brownies and be on time. Didn't I give you that note last week?"

"Thursday? Oh, Hannah, I've got a volleyball game."

The backpack hit the ground, and Hannah dragged it for a few feet before saying, "But you'll come here first?"

Searching the papers in her hand, Reba found the notice. Seven. The game started at 4:30, and she was in charge because the head coach had a doctor's appoint-ment. Reba bit her lip. At the earliest, it would end at seven. . .but it was a half-hour drive away. "I'll see what I can do, Hannah. I promise."

Times like this, she really missed Ray. With two parents, at least one could surely schedule important events such as Open House.

"We're working on 'G' today. I colored Gary the Great Dane who eats grapefruit. I really wanted to color Gloria the gorilla who eats gumdrops, but Marky grabbed that one first."

Hannah skipped ahead. She looked both ways and waited for Reba to catch up before they crossed the street. Heading for the backyard, she kept her promise to feed Bark each afternoon. For some reason, Hannah had the idea that taking good care of Bark was a habit that would earn her a cat.

Reba opened the door, turned the television on for noise, and went into the kitchen. Two hours until Wednesday night services. Reba had been slow finding a place to worship. The church on campus was convenient, but going there with her own students left her open for attending church as a teacher more than as a fellow Christian. When worshipping, Reba wanted to make friends, deepen her walk, and be a part of a family. Mason spent a lot of time rehashing homework assignments after the closing prayer. Maybe if she didn't have Hannah, she'd be more open to that kind of accessibility, but she wanted Hannah to understand that you went to church for worship, not to interface about school schedules.

Still, Mason and Tiffany acted like her attendance at their congregation was like a gift. Reba found it hard not to look forward to such a welcome. Hannah had switched allegiance from Mason to Tiffany and liked the college girls who taught the kindergarten class.

Opening the kitchen window, already knowing the answer, Reba hollered, "What church do you want to go to tonight? Community?"

"No," Hannah shot back, "our church, across the street. I like that one. I can hear Bark barking when we stand outside."

Well, that was certainly an important consideration when deciding on a church home. Shiloh didn't have volleyball practice on Wednesday, and the Christian elementary school didn't assign homework, so Wednesday was actually a pretty easy day. Reba stirred macaroni and cheese into a dinner, kept one eye on the backyard, and read her curriculum book for tomorrow's lesson. Mason said teaching got easier. She believed that. Right now she had to do every assignment the students did, trying to predict where questions would arrive. Already she'd discovered textbooks weren't perfect. She'd had to go back and change grades after her first test because of comma splices.

She was deep in the world of "commas of address" when the phone rang.

"Hi, Thelma." Reba settled down on a kitchen chair. Ray's mom was a talker. During their half-hour conversation, Reba agreed to return to Albuquerque for Thanksgiving. Hannah needed to spend time with her grandparents, and Reba missed them, too.

Ray's parents were the best thing that had happened to Reba. What an amazing awakening to suddenly live in a home where the family sat down to dinner together, discussed daily events, thanked the Father for all His blessings, and enjoyed board games more than television.

Living with the Paynes had also been eye-opening about how carefully some families had to budget money. Reba's family made and spent money in the same breath. Darrel Payne, a minister, had budgeted God first and everything else after. That first year living with the Paynes had done more to prepare Reba for life than all the fancy preparatory schools.

After agreeing to let Thelma and Darrel pay for half the plane fare, Reba put Hannah on the phone for a quick Granny hello.

By the time Hannah hung up the phone, Reba had set supper on the table, but her appetite was gone. They were going back to Albuquerque. November would have been Ray's birthday. It made sense that Thelma and Darrel Payne wanted family close. What would it be like to sit across from Thelma and Darrel and face Ray's empty chair? Also, Reba never felt comfortable knowing that the men who shot and killed Ray hadn't been caught.

✌

The service project for October was going door-to-door in the neighborhood and passing out fliers inviting people to church. Mason didn't canvas. Instead, he paced the sidewalk, trying to keep all the students in sight. His older brother Richard remembered taking sodas and munchies from strangers. Mason didn't trust that much. He put two males and one female per group. They handed out a handwritten invitation to attend services, a business card with the address and phone number of the church, and a one-page Bible study. If anyone expressed interest in the Bible study, the students were to offer to sit outside, whip out their Bibles, and help explain the paper. They'd spent four weeks going over the Bible study in class, role-playing the questions people who'd never been to church might ask. Mason loved it because it gave opportunity for the students to ask questions they, themselves, might have but were too self-conscious to ask.

The good news was, about every fifth house already belonged to a church family. The bad news was, not even every fifth house was willing to give time to the students. It wasn't by accident that Mason ended the excursion in Reba's neighborhood. He knew she and Hannah spent lots of time on the front porch. Any excuse to be in the neighborhood got him a little closer to gaining her trust. Actually, he figured Bark would be harder to win than Reba, but that was more a physical battle than an emotional one.

Cindy and Jag already cuddled on her porch swing. Tiffany danced across the front yard with Hannah riding on her feet.

"We already ordered pizza," Jag said.

Reba smiled weakly.

The sweet sound of a campus devotional drifted across the lawn.

"Mommy, can I?"

After getting permission, Hannah dragged Tiffany across the street. They were followed by a troop of students. Hannah started young on her college experience.

"She already knows more songs than I do." Reba scooted over so Mason could sit on the porch swing.

He sat down, purposely not hugging the edge and purposely sitting close enough so his hand could accidentally brush against her hair after he rested it across the back. "I have two nephews who can speak Spanish simply because their next-door neighbors speak Spanish. Children are amazing."

"How did your service project go?"

"We managed to hand out twenty information packs. As for how it went, well, we won't know that until we see visitors at services."

"I don't remember anyone ever knocking on our door," Reba remarked.

"Where did you grow up?"

"Arizona."

"Ah, not exactly the Bible Belt. I know you said your parents sent you to a Christian college because they thought it would be safe, but how did they decide on Iowa?"

"Pure happenstance. I was in a program for advanced kids called Vanguard. I'd completed their curriculum. Only a few colleges were open to the idea of letting a sixteen-year-old live in the dorm. One of the Vanguard counselors recommended Shiloh. She'd attended here and loved it. She made a few phone calls. I wound up being part of a study charting how starting college early bodes for younger students. They especially were interested in the differences between small versus large campuses. Needless to say, I'm not part of a success ratio."

"You were straight A."

"I was also racking up demerits at the speed of light."

She stopped, and Mason wondered if her next thought was, *Before I got kicked out.* Someday they needed to broach that subject, get it out of the way, and at least for him, start forgiving.

"Enough of that," Reba said. "Let's talk about you."

"Me? I'm not nearly as interesting as you."

"Just how big is your family?"

"Big enough to still be front-page news. You were the only reporter to poke fun at how many pews my family took up on Visitor's Day in chapel."

"I was amazed."

"You should see us at Christmas. Speaking of which, my mother said you could come to our place for Thanksgiving. It's about a two-hour drive. There are tons of children Hannah's age."

"Thanks, but Hannah and I are flying to New Mexico. Ray's parents really want us to be home for the holiday."

It was unreasonable to be jealous of a dead man, but it seemed no matter what topic Mason and Reba settled on, Ray was a part. Mason preferred Bark as competition.

Chapter 8

It was amazing how quickly Creed, Iowa, had become home. Reba's shoes crunched through snow as she made her way to the front door.

"Mommy, let's call now so Bark can come home! Hurry."

Mason "dog-sat" while Reba and Hannah had enjoyed Thanksgiving in New Mexico.

"Let's just get the suitcases unpacked."

Mason had been true to his word. Reba had been afraid he'd forget to come over and turn on the thermostat, but heat greeted their arrival.

Hannah raced up the stairs, her suitcase bumping behind her.

Two seconds later she was back. "Can I call now?"

"Let's go check your room first?"

"Oh," said Hannah, "did I have to put the clean clothes in my dresser and the dirty clothes in the bathroom?"

"That was the idea."

Hannah raced back upstairs. Reba went around

turning on all the lights. That was another habit she'd developed after Ray was killed. The dark seemed too frightening.

Taking her suitcases to her room, she turned on the light and blinked at the sudden glare. The room was small, the closet smaller yet. In some ways, selling all their furniture had been a blessing. There was no way it would have fit in this house. A crocheted blanket covered the bed. Reba had made it after graduating college. She'd married Ray and set about being a wife.

Funny, she'd thought Ray had been more like his parents. He'd acted like them when he'd moved back home. When they'd gotten their own house, he'd been different. Good, still kind, but not as focused. He'd hated that she was smarter than he, not that he'd admit to it. He'd insisted she stay home and raise Hannah. She'd loved that part; raising Hannah had been a dream. They'd played in the park, watched movies, and learned to roller-skate. It was like getting a piece of her own childhood back, and Reba learned that the greatest thing in life was not getting more letters after her name, but getting chocolate-laced hugs from a little girl who called her Mommy. A little girl who now stood in the doorway.

"Can we call now? Hey, why are you just standing there? Are you sad? I know, you miss Bark. We better hurry."

Mason answered on the second ring, as if he'd been by the phone waiting. He immediately came, bringing

Bark and leftover turkey. He left when the ten-o'clock news came on, and Hannah gleefully remarked that she was staying up so late that maybe she wouldn't need to go to school tomorrow.

❧

The freshmen came back to classes in much better moods. Most had gotten a fix of family and were glad to be back in a place where parental reins were a distant memory. Still, there were a few who openly admitted they did not intend to return a second semester. Others were quiet, already knowing grades would be a problem when it came to who was footing the bill.

Reba stood by the podium at the front of the classroom. She pulled her sweater tighter around her. Usually the heater made the room unbearable, but today the cold seemed to seep through the planks in the floor. She looked around the room. It was hers now. She'd put cheerful posters over the dents in the walls. She'd had the students make bright-colored collages along with their essays. "Okay, Cindy, why don't you give the class an opinion about gas prices?"

"Fredrick's Gas Station downtown has the highest prices I've ever seen."

Reba nodded. "Jag, give us a factual statement."

"Fredrick's charges $1.52 a gallon for unleaded."

Cindy glowed. Jag could have given any kind of a response, but the fact that he chose to add to hers showed their togetherness.

Later, walking to her office, Reba tried to remember feeling any interest in the college boys while at

Shiloh. No, she'd spent most of her time dating a townie. She'd never forget him. Glenn Fields was the reason she'd gotten kicked out of Shiloh.

Opening her office door, she stepped inside, laid her book bag on the floor, and crossed to the window. Cindy and Jag were making snow angels. Winter break was in three short weeks, and the two would be separated for almost a month.

Reba checked her calendar. Volleyball season was over, and preparations for the yearbook were in full swing. Jag and about five others diligently took pictures. Cindy helped.

"What are you doing tonight?" Mason stood at the door. His brown-and-white sweater had snowflakes clinging to it.

"Where's your coat?" Reba moved toward him, then paused. Ever since he'd dog-sat Bark, she'd fought the urge to touch his hair, straighten his tie, kiss his check. It was all Bark's fault. Reba and Hannah hadn't even been gone a week, and in that short time, Bark had decided Mason was master.

Now when Mason stopped by, Bark wiggled all over and begged to be picked up. Since Mason lived a mere two blocks away, Hannah loved to walk down to the end of the street—as far as she was allowed to go. If she saw Mason, she'd holler for him to come over. If that didn't work, she let go of Bark's leash, and the dog was off. Reba took to making sure she always cooked for three, just in case.

"Reba? You okay?" Mason hadn't moved.

"Oh, snow days do this to me. I tend to drift. What am I doing tonight? Why?"

"Well, if you were willing to get Jag to watch Hannah, I thought we'd go out. Just the two of us."

He was asking her out on a real date—not just an I'm-a-nice-guy-who-keeps-coming-around-for-no-reason-and-let's-do-something. Reba suddenly wanted to say "yes" although that would mess everything up. The minute she agreed, there'd be more intimate talks. He'd want to know more about her marriage with Ray. Luckily, tonight's dilemma was easy. "It's the Winter Program at Hannah's school. I can't miss it. She still reminds me about missing Open House."

"Okay. I'll go to the Winter Program with you, but how about this weekend? Saturday? Just you and me."

So much for putting off the decision. "Mason, things are good between us. Why chance ruining it?"

"Because we might not ruin it, as you say, but improve it. I'm willing to be honest. I was half in love with you when you were sixteen. I figure the other half arrived the day I saw you in my office and you didn't know who I was."

"I remembered quick enough!"

He stepped into the office, closing the door behind him. Reba's mouth went dry. She sat on the top of the radiator, although she was no longer cold. Mason put his hands on either side of her. She'd noticed his eyes were the color of chocolate, but she hadn't known how deep the swirls of toffee and caramel went. She somehow had missed the invitation there. Oh, she'd known he was interested, but—

"Reba," he said, his voice next to her ear, "I'm going to make sure you never forget me again."

Then, he kissed her.

❧

Families filled the auditorium. Mason looked around, surprised by how many people he recognized. There were a few scattered singles, and Mason was humbled by the fact that had he not joined Reba, she'd be sitting alone at Hannah's Winter Program. He'd taken his three-pew family for granted.

The head of the school board said an opening prayer, the principal gave a short greeting, and the lights dimmed. Children dressed as trees decorated the stage. Who knew trees could sing so well? Reba leaned forward, mesmerized. By following her gaze, he figured out which tree was Hannah. The kindergartners stole the show. If they weren't falling, then they were singing the song a beat after the rest or five decibels louder.

Afterwards the families went to the cafeteria for hot chocolate and dessert.

Hannah, the tree, ran off but quickly returned, leading another tree by a limb. She pushed that tree toward Mason. "This is Marky. He's my best friend. He has a dog *and* a cat."

Mason shook the limb.

"Are you Hannah's daddy?"

Reba froze beside him, a brownie halfway to her mouth. Hannah lost her smile also.

"No," Mason said. "I'm just a friend."

Marky ran off. Hannah gave Mason a confused look, then followed her friend.

"I'm sorry," Mason said, taking Reba's hand. "I was not expecting that question."

"Neither was I."

"What does Hannah know? I mean, you haven't even told me how Ray died."

"Hannah's too young to know. It would just scare her."

"Death is part of living. Surely, she needs to know that."

"Ray didn't die because he was sick. He was murdered."

She started wringing her hands. Mason took one and stroked her fingers. She started to jerk away, but he applied gentle pressure and didn't ask any more questions.

"You don't have to tell me."

"So much for keeping secrets. That is why we came to Creed. I wanted Hannah away from the papers. I didn't want to chance her hearing anything about Ray. I want her to remember the man who played catch with her in the yard. I don't want her knowing that Ray borrowed money from the wrong people, and when he didn't pay it back on time, they killed him."

❧

Mason's apartment looked out over a convenience store and a parking lot. A week had passed since Reba confided in him, and she had avoided him ever since. He hadn't a clue how to approach her. That she avoided him proved she didn't want to talk about it. He honestly didn't think they could leave the incident alone, though. It was out there; they needed to get past it. If Mason was honest with himself, Ray's death wasn't the only issue they needed to face and resolve.

He walked to work. It was easier than driving on ice. Opening the door to Clark Hall, Mason switched on the light, took off his overshoes, and stuck them in a closet, then hurried up the stairs.

"Mr. Clark."

Jag sat in the waiting room. The secretary hadn't arrived.

"How did you get in, Jag?"

"Do you really want to know?"

"Yes."

"I picked the lock. You have a ridiculously easy lock to pick. It didn't even take me a minute."

"Where did you learn to pick locks?"

"Television."

"I'd rather you not do it again, okay?"

Jag hadn't taken his tennis shoes off. Snow clung to them, and a wet circle was spreading on the floor.

Mason hung up his coat and walked to his office. Jag didn't move. His legs were straight out, crossed, and for the first time he avoided Mason's eyes. *Oh, no,* thought Mason, *Cindy.*

"Come in, Jag. Let's get it over with."

Jag picked up a folder from the seat next to him. His jean jacket was unbuttoned, and if Mason wasn't mistaken, he was wearing the same shirt as yesterday.

Mason sat at his desk. Jag took the same seat he'd occupied back in August when he'd wanted to transfer into a different English class. That had been the day Jag met Cindy. That had been the day Mason met Reba, again.

"You know I'm taking pictures for the school newspaper?" Jag spoke to his hands. They writhed as much as Reba's usually did.

"I think that's great. I've seen your work. You're good."

"Yesterday, the editor assigned me to take a picture of you. He wants one of Mrs. Payne, too."

Mason could understand the newspaper wanting Reba's, although if he remembered right, they'd already done the "Meet the New Teacher" article.

Jag put a folder on Mason's desk. "I took this from the editor's desk. I've had it since five yesterday. I could not decide what to do."

Mason took the folder. Opening it, he saw two double-spaced typed pages. This wasn't about Cindy. It was the headline that jumped out at him. ALCOHOL, RESPONSIBILITY, AND FRIENDSHIP: HOW DO THEY MIX?

Chapter 9

The elementary school called at noon. Hannah's temperature was almost one hundred. Reba raced over, signed Hannah out, and came back to Clark Hall. She had two classes and no time to get a substitute.

Cindy ran to Reba's house and brought back some medicine and blankets. Reba put Hannah next to the radiator on the floor. Linda Simms agreed to keep an eye on her, and Reba decided to get her lectures done quickly and assign library time. Anything to keep close to her baby. Her first class went fine. Her two o'clock was a little different. Jag arrived ten minutes late. Instead of taking his usual chair in the front, he headed for the back and then avoided her gaze. When she called on him, he answered the questions but initiated no discussion. By the time she'd hurried through her notes, her own head was pounding.

She barely managed to get her office door open before she heard Hannah's words. "Mommy, I threw up."

Linda Simms mouthed, *It was spit.*

Hannah was getting too big to carry. The sidewalks were slippery, and any other day Mason would be there to offer his help. After getting some broth inside Hannah and turning out the bedroom light, Reba sat at her new, used couch and hit the button on her answering machine. Dean Steward's voice was curt, "Mrs. Payne, could you attend a meeting in my office at three?"

It was stand-up three now. Reba got her directory and called the dean's office to beg off. Five minutes later, she hurried around the living room picking up Hannah's toys and the mass of ungraded papers on the coffee table. Whatever Dean Steward wanted to talk about was so vital that he was coming over.

Peeking out the window, Reba felt her stomach hit the ground. Not only was the dean making his way to her house, but Jack Hillman, the sponsor of Shiloh's school paper, and Mason Clark were trudging along.

Mason brought in kitchen chairs so there'd be enough seats in the living room. Reba poured coffee and waited.

Dean Steward cleared his throat. "This is the first time we've faced a situation like this."

"Like this?" Reba asked.

Mason opened his briefcase, pulled out a folder, then handed her a piece of paper.

Reba read the headline, skimmed the rest, then closed her eyes. Mason had worried about this since her first day. Their names were near the end of the article. "When will this hit the stands?"

"Next Friday," Jack Hillman grunted.

"We would rather the piece not run—" Dean Steward began.

"But most of my journalism students already know. Furthermore, that's what the paper is for: to print information. Sometimes that information is. . ." Jack frowned and gave Reba a compassionate look. "I thought I'd pull the article, but it's not negative. It's mostly informative. I think we can turn this into a good thing. Look at you now, Reba."

Reba decided not to tell him about her doubts or Ray's death. She looked at Mason. Funny, now that the past was about to hit the present, he looked calm.

"Is my job in danger?" Reba asked.

"No," Dean Steward said. "We knew about your past before we hired you, and we also knew about your present. As far as we're concerned, you've presented a wonderful Christian example to our students. We're pleased with your performance. When Roger Howard told us about your work in Albuquerque, the board was unanimous about hiring you. This meeting is mainly to try to formulate a response. Students will have questions."

"Mommy, I threw up!" Hannah called from the top of the stairs.

Before Reba could stand, Mason did. "Gentlemen, Mrs. Payne has a daughter who needs her attention. The last time she and I faced a dean about this matter, she paid the consequences. This time, it's my turn."

❧

Glenn Fields had relocated to Omaha, Nebraska. A few phone calls and Mason had an address. It had been a sleepless night, a prayerful night, a night when Mason desperately wanted to call his own father but decided that, this time, it was all up to him.

During the long drive, he tried to rehearse what he wanted to say. Nothing sounded right, but closure seemed to dictate that without meeting with Glenn, there would still be this area of open wound.

Mason was often guilty of presupposing. He'd expected Glenn to live in a run-down apartment in a part of town best avoided. Instead, Glenn's house was near a golf course where the snow hid the favorite pastime of the neighboring residents.

Children played in the yard. Their snowsuits hid age and weight. The front door opened before Mason could stop the car.

Glenn Fields had been Reba's friend. Mason knew the guy. It was hard not to. Mason had kept up with Reba's activities, and Glenn was one of Reba's activities. Still, if Glenn had passed Mason on the street, Mason wouldn't have recognized him.

The first thing Mason noticed was the absence of a wheelchair, or at least crutches. Glenn held the door open invitingly.

The living room was bigger than Mason's apartment.

After a handshake, Glenn introduced, "This is my wife, Bunny."

Bunny had obviously just gotten off the exercise bike Mason could see in the family room. She looked a lot like Cindy with her swept-back hair and winning smile. "We're glad you stopped by. It will do the two of you good to talk."

Bunny had coffee waiting in the kitchen. Glenn limped slightly as they walked. If Mason hadn't been looking, he wouldn't have noticed it.

"Thanks," Mason said, accepting a steaming mug. "I appreciate your meeting with me."

"I'm curious. Why are you here?"

Mason took a folded piece of paper out of his pocket. "I thought I'd let you look at this."

Glenn read it, then passed it back. "So."

"I owe you an apology," Mason said. "When you—we—were in the accident, I didn't even feel sorry when you lost your leg. I figured you'd asked for it by drinking and driving."

"Tell me something I don't know." Glenn's words could have been harsh, but they weren't. They were curious.

"Did you know Reba is now teaching at Shiloh?"

"Yes."

Mason blinked. "Really."

"She's been here twice. Brought her little girl. The kids play just fine. You see, Reba did feel sorry about my leg. She's kept in touch with me. But, if it will soothe your conscience, that accident wasn't your fault. I harbor no grudges. It was my own stupidity."

"Am I here to soothe my conscience?" Mason took a sip of coffee. It burned, but he forced himself not to flinch. "I guess I am. Look, I've felt guilty since that night. I managed to stay in school; Reba didn't. I walked away from that accident; you didn't. Now, Reba's little girl might find out about this incident because maybe there was something I could have done that night six years ago that I didn't."

"Reba's a lot tougher than you think. She always has been."

Mason nodded. "Well, I've got an idea. It's not perfect. It might not even make things better, but I think it's worthwhile. I wondered if you were interested in helping out."

࿔

Shiloh's chapel period began at eight in the morning. As a student, Reba had paid over eighty dollars in tardy and absence fines her first year. Her second year, she'd doubled that. As a teacher, she hadn't missed or been late even once.

She sensed the looks from some of the students. The paper had been issued that morning. Readership had probably doubled thanks to the story about her and Mason.

Reba looked around, not down. She had been baptized two months before she married Ray. She'd made mistakes, but so had Paul, so had the disciple Peter, so had Dean Steward—she just couldn't name his.

Jag fell into step next to her. "You okay?"

"Fine; quit worrying."

"They made Harry Raymond take your picture when I refused."

"Well, Harry in no way did me the justice you would have."

To Reba's surprise, Linda Simms was sitting with

the teachers. Was she here for support? Good; Reba welcomed it. Slipping in next to Linda, Reba reached for a songbook and waited. Dean Steward led the opening prayer. After the amen, he paused. His posture and facial expression encouraged—no, demanded—that the room quiet down. "We're having a special program this morning."

Mason stepped to the podium. "My name is Mason Clark. Many of you know me as your history teacher. Others know me as a guidance counselor. If you've missed meeting me, maybe you ought to check out the Faith/Works class at Shiloh Church.

"Six years ago, I graduated from Shiloh Christian College. I cannot tell you how many times, I, like you, sat in the audience and listened to speakers. I looked forward to being a speaker myself. And, in my visions, the best thing about being a teacher/counselor at Shiloh, was that I could do it better because *I* was a grand example."

Reba looked about the auditorium. She'd watched Mason stand at that podium many times, but never had he made her shiver.

Mason continued, "This week I've spent a good deal of time in Proverbs. Chapter 11, verse 2 especially hit home. 'When pride comes, then comes disgrace, but with humility comes wisdom.'"

Reba looked about the auditorium. No one was asleep. If the eyes strayed from Mason, they went to her. . .or they watched the man stepping up the center aisle.

Glenn Fields!

For the next half hour, Mason alternated between quoting Scripture and admitting a mistake from his past. A mistake that really hadn't been his. The students listened, because in reality, the world was all around them, and drinking was a national pastime they couldn't ignore.

Before Glenn took over the microphone, he rolled up his pant leg. The artificial limb looked real from a distance, pink up close. Reba closed her eyes. While Glenn spoke, she remembered.

It had been a Friday. Her roommate had gone home for the weekend, and Reba was ready to rock. Glenn Fields was not like anybody she'd met. He'd dropped out of high school. He had a place of his own. He used words she wouldn't say, and he never ran out of things to do.

They'd gone bowling. Reba remembered how scared she had been when he started drinking—though to her shame, it wasn't because of the drinking, but because there were other Shiloh students at the bowling alley who were watching. Even the fear was accompanied by a thrill of daring.

Why did Mason face the students this morning as if he owed them an explanation? He'd been at the bowling alley. He'd watched Glenn drink. When the lights of the bowling alley dimmed and Shiloh's curfew neared, Mason had offered her a ride home.

Reba had no clue whether accepting that ride would have made the outcome different. Mason, ever the good scout, had followed them to Glenn's car and tried to take the car keys.

Glenn answered with his fists. To Reba's surprise, Mason didn't turn his cheek.

She'd been in the passenger seat already. Mason left Glenn and ran to her side of the car. Reba could still see his hands reaching for her as Glenn, furious, slammed himself behind the wheel, jabbed the keys into the ignition, and began to move the car.

Mason ran to his car and started to follow.

Traffic didn't notice the spectacle edging into its midst. Glenn looked in the rearview mirror, saw Mason, and stepped on the gas. He didn't look as he pulled out into the street. Metal met metal and—

"Reba, are you all right?" Linda whispered.

Just as Reba still didn't know how to answer the questions about Ray's death, being asked "Are you all right?" at this moment wasn't one easily addressed.

❧

Her ten-o'clock class didn't have an empty seat. Every student made it on time. Reba opened her teacher's manual and started on adjectives. The students didn't whisper or pass notes. When the class ended, instead of filing out the door, every student made his or her way to the front. Cindy was the first to offer a hug.

Reba remembered her very first day at Shiloh. She'd gotten out of her mother's car and had been hugged by many people she didn't know. It had been a shock. Her family was not one to show physical demonstrations.

When did I stop hugging? Reba wondered. Sure, she

hugged Hannah, and she hugged. . . Who else did she hug?

No one since Ray.

By the time the last young man shook her hand, Reba was ready to sit down. Mason stood at the door of her classroom. With flowers. Glenn Fields was behind him, smiling.

"Don't tell me you two became friends?" Reba's voice croaked as she fought the tears.

"Glenn says we have to."

Shaking her head, Reba took the flowers and asked, "Why?"

"Well," said Mason, "Glenn expects you to visit often now that you're this close. If we should happen, to say, get married, then I'll be around a lot more."

"I'm not ready to talk marriage."

"I know. That's why I brought flowers instead of a ring."

Epilogue

T he last day of school dawned with the sunshine of promise. Reba scanned the church's flower-decked auditorium as she walked down the aisle on her father's arm. She felt a little faint. Instead of a typical chapel program, today Shiloh Christian College hosted a wedding.

Hannah held the flower basket tightly, her knuckles white. Thelma and Darrel Payne sniffled from the front row. Reba's father joined her mother and sisters on the bride's side; as for Mason's side of the church, seven rows of Clarks beamed approval.

Reba felt Mason take her hand. His fingers tightened. Never, in her whole life, had Reba felt so secure, so loved, so safe. Hannah didn't leave; she took Reba's other hand.

God had even taken her fear of Ray's murderers away. Instead of facing the world alone, Reba and Hannah had Mason and at least seven pews full of backup bodyguards. And, there was the Greatest Bodyguard of all overseeing the whole shebang.

The minister started, "We gather in God's presence to unite Rebecca Suzanne and Mason Dean in holy matrimony. . . ."

PAMELA KAYE TRACY

Living in Glendale, Arizona, where by day she teaches first grade at Southwest Christian School and by night she teaches Freshman Reading at Glendale Community College, Pamela had her first novel of inspirational fiction published in 1999 by Barbour Publishing's **Heartsong Presents** line. She has been a cook, waitress, drafter, Kelly girl, insurance filer, and secretary, but through it all, in the back of her mind, she knew she wanted to be a writer. "I believe in happy endings," says Pamela. "My parents lived the white picket fence life." Writing Christian romance gives her the opportunity to let her imagination roam.

A Letter to Our Readers

Dear Readers:

In order that we might better contribute to your reading enjoyment, we would appreciate you taking a few minutes to respond to the following questions. When completed, please return to the following: Fiction Editor, Barbour Publishing, Inc., P.O. Box 719, Uhrichsville, OH 44683.

1. Did you enjoy reading *Lessons of the Heart?*
   - ❑ Very much. I would like to see more books like this.
   - ❑ Moderately—I would have enjoyed it more if _____
   _____
   _____

2. What influenced your decision to purchase this book?
   (Check those that apply.)
   - ❑ Cover
   - ❑ Back cover copy
   - ❑ Title
   - ❑ Price
   - ❑ Friends
   - ❑ Publicity
   - ❑ Other

3. Which story was your favorite?
   - ❑ *Love Lessons*
   - ❑ *Scrambled Eggs*
   - ❑ *Beauty for Ashes*
   - ❑ *Test of Time*

4. Please check your age range:
   - ❑ Under 18
   - ❑ 18–24
   - ❑ 25–34
   - ❑ 35–45
   - ❑ 46–55
   - ❑ Over 55

5. How many hours per week do you read? _____

Name _____

Occupation _____

Address _____

City _____ State _____ Zip _____

If you enjoyed

LESSONS

of the

Heart

then read:

Gift OF LOVE

Gifts are given in love in these four modern romance stories

Practically Christmas
A Most Unwelcome Gift
The Best Christmas Gift
The Gift Shoppe

If you enjoyed

LESSONS
of the
Heart

then read:

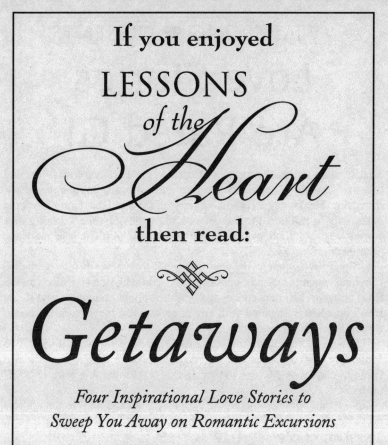

Getaways

*Four Inspirational Love Stories to
Sweep You Away on Romantic Excursions*

Spring in Paris
Wall of Stone
River Runners
Sudden Showers
